KAREN BROWN'S

Italian
Country Inns & Itineraries

KAREN BROWN TITLES

California Country Inns & Itineraries

English Country Bed & Breakfasts

English, Welsh & Scottish Country Hotels & Itineraries

French Country Bed & Breakfasts

French Country Inns & Itineraries

German Country Inns & Itineraries

Irish Country Inns & Itineraries

Italian Country Bed & Breakfasts

Italian Country Inns & Itineraries

Portuguese Country Inns & Pousadas

Spanish Country Inns & Paradors

Swiss Country Inns & Chalets

KAREN BROWN'S

Italian
Country Inns & Itineraries

Written by

CLARE BROWN

Sketches by Barbara Tapp
Cover Painting by Jann Pollard

Travel Press
Karen Brown's Country Inn Series

Travel Press editors: Karen Brown, June Brown, Clare Brown, Nicole Franchini
Susanne Lau Alloway, Iris Sandilands
Technical support: William H. Brown III, Aide-de-camp: William H. Brown
Illustrations: Barbara Tapp; Cover painting: Jann Pollard.
Maps: Brenden Kootsey of Cassell Design.
This books is written in cooperation with Town & Country-Hillsdale Travel, San Mateo, CA 94401

Karen Brown's Guides, P.O. Box 70, San Mateo, CA 94401, tel: 415-342-9117
Distributed USA & Canada: The Globe Pequot Press
P.O. Box 833, Old Saybrook, CT 06475-0833, tel: 203-395-0440
Distributed Europe: Springfield Books Ltd
Norman Rd., Denby Dale, Huddersfield HD8 8TH, W. Yorkshire, England, , tel: (0484) 864 955
A catalog record for this book is available from the British Library

Library of Congress Cataloging-in-Publication Data

Brown, Clare.
    Karen Brown's Italian country inns & itineraries / written by
    Clare Brown ; sketches by Barbara Tapp. Cover art by Jann Pollard.
    [5th ed., updated and rev.]   p.   cm. -- (Karen Brown's country inn series)
    Distributor from cover
        Includes index.
        ISBN 0-930328-48-5 : $14.95
            1. Hotels, taverns, etc. --Italy--Guide-books. 2. Italy-
    -Guidebooks. I. Title. II. title: Italian country inns &
    itineraries. III. title: Italian country inns and itineraries. IV. Series.
    TX907.5.I8B76 1993   92-39207
    647.944501--dc20   CIP

To My Best Friend, Bill
With Love and Gratitude for
Many Miles of Memories

Contents

INTRODUCTION   1–18

ITINERARIES

    Italian Highlights by Train & Boat   19–34

    Romantic Hilltowns of Tuscany & Umbria   35–44

    Mountain & Lake Adventures   45–62

    Rome to Milan via the Italian Riviera   63–72

    Highlights of Southern Italy & Sicily   73–90

HOTEL SECTION

    Hotels Descriptions–Listed Alphabetically by Town   91–236

    Inn Discoveries by Our Readers   237–240

    Reservation Request Letter   241

MAP SECTION

    Key Map   243

    Regional Maps Showing Location of Hotels   244–257

INDEX

    258–270

Introduction

Of all the countries in the world, there is none more magical than Italy: truly a tourist's paradise—a traveller's dream destination. No one could be so blasé, that within Italy's narrow boot there would not be something to tantalize his fancy. For the archaeologist, there are some of the most fascinating and perfectly preserved ancient monuments existing today—just begging to be explored. For the gourmet, there is probably the best food in the world. For the outdoors man, there are towering mountains to conquer and magnificent ski slopes to sample. For the lover of art, the museums are bursting with the genius of Italy's sons such as Michelangelo, Leonardo da Vinci, and Raphael. For the architect, Italy is a school of design—you are surrounded by the ancient buildings whose perfection has inspired the styles of today. For the history buff, Italy is a joy of wonders—her cities are veritable living museums where you are surrounded by the ghosts of Caesar. For the wine connoisseur, Italy produces an unbelievable selection of wine whose quality is unsurpassed. For the adventurer, Italy has intriguing medieval walled villages tucked away in every part of the country. For the beach buff, Italy's lakes and islands hold promise of some of the most elegant resorts in the world. For the religious pilgrim, Italy is the cradle of the Christian faith and home of some to the world's greatest saints. The miracle of Italy is that all these treasures come "packaged" in a gorgeous country of majestic mountains, misty lakes, idyllic islands, wonderful walled villages and gorgeous cities. Plus, the climate is ideal and the people warm and gracious. Italy is truly a perfect destination.

ABOUT THIS GUIDE

This guide is written with two main objectives: to describe the most romantic small hotels throughout Italy and to "tie" these hotels together with itineraries that include enough details so that you can plan your own holiday.

This introduction explains how to use the guide and also touches upon what to expect while travelling. After the introduction comes the main part of the guide which is divided into two sections. The first section outlines itineraries with sightseeing suggestions along the way. The second section of the book includes a comprehensive list of hotels (appearing alphabetically by town). We have personally inspected each place that we recommend and describe its ambiance and merits in our write up which is followed by an illustration and practical information such as address, telephone numbers, rates, etc. None of the places to stay pays to be included so our choices are strictly based on which places we think you would most enjoy. The hotels featured in our guide vary tremendously: some are deluxe, grand hotels fit for a king and very expensive; others are quite simple little cottages tucked away in remote hamlets that are less expensive. We include them all if they have "personality", charm and an antique ambiance. There are a few hotels which are included that do not quite live up to the criterion of "old-world-charm": the reason they have been included is because in their particular area there just were no "perfect" choices, and since you might need a place to stay, we tried to find the very best possibility. The hotel descriptions are followed by fourteen maps which pinpoint the locations of featured places to stay. At the back of the guide we feature "Discoveries from Our Readers." These are hotels and inns that our readers have shared with us, but which we have not yet had the time to personally inspect.

CURRENT–ELECTRICAL

You will need a transformer plus an adapter if you plan to use an American-made electrical appliance in Italy. The voltage is usually 220, but sometimes it varies and is 115 or 125. Check with the manager of the hotel before plugging anything into an electrical outlet. Frequently the larger hotels can loan you a properly adapted electric hairdryer.

DRIVING

DRIVER'S LICENSE: An American or English driver's license is valid if you are in Italy on a holiday. However, if you are renting a car, certain age limits apply. Please check on the age limit policy with the car rental company.

GASOLINE: Gasoline (petrol) is very expensive so plan ahead and budget this cost as part of your trip if you are driving. If you purchase a car in Europe and it is registered in a country other than Italy, you can buy gas discount coupons at the border.

ROADS: The Italian roads are nothing short of spectacular. You will discover some of the finest highways in the world. In fact, the Italians are absolute geniuses when it comes to their engineering feats (which actually is not such a surprising fact when you think what a fantastic road system the Romans built two thousand years ago). Nothing seems to daunt the Italian engineers. You would think the mountains are of clay instead of solid rock, the way the roads tunnel through them. Sometimes a roadway will be seemingly suspended in mid-air, as it bridges a mountain crevasse.

TOLL ROADS: Italy has a network of super expressways that draws the whole country into an easily manageable destination by car. Once you are on the toll roads, the kilometers slip by and you can go quickly from almost any area of Italy to another most efficiently. However, be forewarned: these toll roads are very expensive. It seems that about every half hour a toll station appears and you owe several dollars. But, every cent is well spent when you consider the alternative of creeping along within a maze of trucks and buzzing motorcycles, taking forever to go only a few miles. Use the toll roads for the major distances you need to cover, and then choose the small roads when you wish to meander leisurely through the countryside. The toll roads are mystifying until you learn the system—even then it is confusing because just when you think you have the operation "down pat" you will find it varies slightly. But this is the most common routine: first follow the green expressway signs toward the toll road. Sometimes these signs begin many kilometers from the expressway so be patient and continue the game of "follow-the-sign". Each entrance to the expressway handles traffic going in both directions. As you enter into the toll gate there is usually a red button you push and a card pops out of a slot. After going through the toll station you choose the direction you want to go. Leaving the expressway there will be a toll station where your ticket will be collected and you will pay according to how many miles were travelled.

ROAD SIGNS: Before starting on the road prepare yourself by learning the international driving signs so that you can obey all the rules of the road and avoid the embarrassment of heading the wrong way down a small street or parking in a forbidden area. There are several basic sign shapes. The triangular signs warn that there is danger ahead. The circular signs indicate compulsory rules and information. The square signs give information concerning telephones, parking, camping, etc.

FOOD and DRINK

It is almost impossible to get a bad meal in Italy. Italians themselves love to eat and seem to make dining a social occasion to be with family and friends, so the restaurants are filled not only with tourists, but also with the Italians who dawdle at the tables long after the meal is over, chatting and laughing with perhaps a glass of wine or a last cup of coffee.

You will soon get in the spirit of the game of deciding which kind of restaurant to choose for your next meal—and the selection is immense, all the way from the simple family trattoria where mama is cooking in the kitchen to the most elegant of gourmet restaurants with world renowned chefs. Whichever you choose, you will not be disappointed.

The Italians are artists when it comes to pasta, seen on every menu and prepared in endless, fascinating ways. Delicious green salads are always on the menu. Wine of course is offered with every meal. You rarely see an Italian family eating without their bottle of wine on the table. Unless you are a true wine connoisseur we suggest the regional wines. If you ask your waiter to assist you with the choice, you will flatter him and discover many superb wines. Some of the most popular wines which you will see on the Italian menus are: CHIANTI, a well-known wine produced in the Tuscany area south of Florence; MARSALA, a golden sweet wine from Sicily; SOAVE, a superb light wine produced near Venice; ORVIETO, a semisweet wine from the Umbria area near Assisi and EST EST EST, a beautiful semisweet wine produced near Rome. The story that we heard about the last wine, Est Est Est, is lots of fun and perhaps even true. It seems that many years ago a wealthy nobleman was travelling south, and being a true gourmet both of food and drink, he sent his servant before him to pick out all the best places to eat and drink along the way. When the servant neared Rome he found such a divine wine that all he could relay back to his master was EST EST EST, which students of Latin will remember means Yes Yes Yes. And the wine is definitely still "Yes Yes Yes," as are most that you will enjoy drinking in Italy.

HOTELS–BASIS FOR SELECTION

This guide does not try to appeal to everyone. It is definitely prejudiced: each hotel included is one we have seen and liked. It might be a splendid villa elegantly positioned overlooking one of Italy's romantic lakes or a simple little chalet snuggled high in a mountain meadow. But there is a common denominator—they all have charm. Therefore, if you too prefer to travel spending your nights in romantic old villas, appealing little chalets, dramatic medieval castles, ancient monasteries, converted peasants' cottages and gorgeous palaces, we are kindred souls, you can follow the paths we have suggested and each night will be an adventure.

For some of you, cost will not be a factor if the hotel is outstanding. For others, budget will guide your choices. The appeal of a simple little inn with rustic wooden furniture will beckon some, while the glamour of ornate ballrooms dressed with crystal chandeliers and gilded mirrors will appeal to others. What we have tried to do is to indicate what each hotel has to offer, and describe the setting, so that you can make the choice to suit your own preferences and holiday. We feel if you know what to expect, you will not be disappointed, so we have tried to be candid and honest in our appraisals. Also, some hotels are ideal for children while others are definitely adult oriented. We have indicated these special situations under the hotel descriptions.

HOTELS–COST

The price for a room in Italy has soared. Even simple places to stay seem desperately over-priced. This is due both to inflation and the fact that the dollar is weak in relationship to the lire. However, if you study carefully the rates given in the back of this guide, you can still find a few bargains available and can plan your trip using one of the less expensive hotels as your "hub" from which to venture out each day. Because hotels are so expensive, we have also published *Italian Country Bed & Breakfasts* which makes an ideal companion to this guide. The maps in both are similar, making it easy to choose a place to stay from either book. Not only can you save money by sometimes choosing a bed and breakfast for a night's accommodation, but also enjoy the experience of staying where you have the opportunity to know your host and fellow guests.

HOTELS–CREDIT CARDS

Many small hotels do not accept credit cards. Those hotels that do accept "plastic payment" are indicated in the hotel description section using the following abbreviations: AX–American Express, EC–Eurocard, MC–MasterCard, VS–Visa, or simply–All major.

HOTELS–DECOR

Italian hotels frequently reflect a rather formal, sometimes fussy ambiance. In a few instances (which we note in the hotel descriptions) the hotels are decorated in a more simple, charming country mood, but this is not the norm. When antiques are used, they are very often the fancy, gilded variety.

HOTELS–HOW TO INTERPRET THE RATE

In the hotel reference section in the back of the book each hotel shows a rate that reflects the approximate nightly cost for two persons including tax, service and continental breakfast. There are a few hotels where breakfast and one other meal (either lunch or dinner) are included in the rate and, if so, this too is noted. Please use the rates given only as a general ballpark guide because each hotel has such a wide range of price possibilities that it is impossible to project with complete accurately. Also, each year there is some inflation. However, the lire price quoted will help you anticipate the approximate cost. When you plan your holiday, check the current exchange rate with your bank. Hopefully the dollar will become stronger and travelling in Italy will again become a bargain.

HOTELS–HOW TO ECONOMIZE

For those of you who want to squeeze the most value out of each night's stay, we have several suggestions:

1) Travel off season—spring and fall are usually lovely in Italy and the hotels often have bargain rates.

2) Ask for a room without a private bathroom—many hotels have very nice rooms, usually with a washbasin in the room, but with the bathroom "down the hall".

3) Ask if there is a weekly rate—frequently hotels will offer a price break for guests staying a week or more. If travelling with children, ask if there is a special family suite at a lesser price than separate rooms.

4) Supplement your hotel accommodations with a few nights in a bed and breakfast chosen from *Karen Brown's Italian Country Bed & Breakfasts*. This companion guide features places to stay throughout Italy in private homes, villas and farmhouses that open their doors to paying guests. This book is available in book stores or can be purchased directly from the publisher (order form is at the back of this guide).

5) Ask about rates with meals included—if staying for three days or longer, many hotels offer a special rate including meals: MAP (Modified American Plan) means two meals a day are included, AP (American Plan) means three meals a day are included.

6) Last, but not least, is the most important way to save money. Stay out in the countryside instead of in the cities. We cannot stress enough how much more value you receive when you avoid the cities—especially the tourist centers such as Rome, Florence, Milan and Venice. Of course stay right in the heart of town if you are not watching your budget, but if you are trying to squeeze the greatest value from your lire, choose hotels in the countryside and take side trips to visit the pricey tourist centers.

HOTELS–RESERVATIONS

People frequently ask, "Do I need a hotel reservation?" The answer really depends on how flexible you want to be, how tight your time schedule is, in which season you are travelling, and how disappointed you would be if your first choice is unavailable.

It is not unusual for the major tourist cities to be completely sold out during the peak season of June through September. Be forewarned: hotel space in Rome, Florence, Milan and Venice is really at a premium and unless you don't mind taking your chances on a last-minute cancellation or staying on the outskirts of town, make a reservation. Space in the countryside is a little easier. However, if you have your heart set on some special little inn, you certainly should reserve as soon as your travel dates are firm. Reservations are confining. Most hotels will want a deposit to hold your room and frequently refunds are difficult should you change your plans—especially at the last minute. So it is a double bind: making reservations locks you into a solid framework, but without reservations you might be stuck with accommodations you do not like. During the height of the tourist season, some small hotels will only accept reservations for a minimum of three or more nights. However, do not give up because almost all of the hotels that have this policy will take a last-minute booking for a shorter period of time if you call along the way and there is space. For those who like the security blanket of having each night pre-planned so that once you leave home you do not have to worry about where to rest your head, several options for making reservations are listed below:

TRAVEL AGENT: A travel agent can be of great assistance—particularly if your own time is limited. A knowledgeable agent can handle all of the details of your holiday and "tie" them together for you in a neat package including hotel reservations, airline tickets, boat tickets, train reservations, ferry schedules, theater tickets, etc. For your airline tickets there will be no service fee, but most travel agencies make a charge for their other services. The best advice is to talk with your local agent. Be frank about how much you want to spend and ask exactly what he or she can do for you and what the charges will be. If your travel agent is not be familiar with all the small places in this guide (many are so tiny that they appear in no other major publications), you can loan him or her your book—it is written as a guide for travel agents as well as for individual travellers.

LETTER: If you start early, you can write directly to the hotels and request exactly what you need. Clearly state the following: number of people in your party; how many rooms you desire; whether you want a private bathroom; date of arrival and date of departure; ask rate per night and if a deposit is needed. When you receive a reply, send the deposit requested and ask for a receipt. NOTE: When corresponding with Italy, be sure to spell out the month. Do not use numbers since in Europe they reverse our system—such as 6/9 means September 6, not June 9. Allow six weeks for an answer—mail to Italy is very slow. Although most hotels can understand a letter written in English, you will find on page 241 a letter written in Italian with an English translation. Photocopy it and use it for your actual request letters.

TELEPHONE: Our preference in making reservations is to call direct. The cost is minimal if you direct dial and you can have your answer immediately. If space is not available, you can then decide on an alternate. Ask your local operator when to call for the lowest rates. Also consider what time it is in Italy when you call (even the most gracious of owners are sometimes a bit grouchy when awakened at 3 am). Basically, the system is to dial 011 (the international code) 39 (Italy code). Compose these five numbers then dial the city code (dropping the 0 if dialing from the United States) and the hotel telephone number that appears under the hotel listings. Almost all of the hotels have someone who speaks English. There are a few exceptions and when very little English is spoken, we have tried to indicate this under the hotel's description. The best chance for finding the owner or manager who speaks English is to call when it is late afternoon in Italy.

FAX: If you have access to a fax machine, this is another efficient way to reach a hotel. The majority of hotels in Italy now have fax numbers which we have listed in the back of the book under each hotel listing. Again, be sure to be specific as to your arrival and departure dates, number in your party, and what type of room you want. And, of course, be sure to include your fax number for their response. You can photocopy and use the request letter written in Italian and English (see page 241) for your fax.

UNITED STATES REPRESENTATIVE: Some hotels have a United States representative through whom reservations can be made. Many of these representatives have a toll free telephone number for your convenience. This is an extremely convenient and efficient way to secure a reservation. However you might find it less expensive to make the reservation yourself since sometimes a representative makes a charge for his service, reserves only the more expensive rooms, or quotes a higher price to protect himself against currency fluctuations and administrative costs. Furthermore, usually only the larger or more expensive hotels can afford the luxury of a representative in the United States. Nevertheless, if you understand that it might cost you more, contacting the hotel representative is an easy way to make a reservation. If a hotel has a representative, the name and telephone number for the representative are listed in the back of the book under the specific hotel's description. The representatives are given solely as a source of information for you. We are in no way affiliated with any of the hotel representatives and cannot be responsible for any reservations made through them or money sent as deposits or prepayments.

INFORMATION

If you have questions not answered in this guide or need special guidance for a particular destination, the Italian Government Travel Offices can assist you. NOTE: These offices are usually open only from 9 am–1 pm, Monday through Friday.

Italian Government Travel Office, telephone: (212) 245-4822, fax: (212) 586-9249
630 Fifth Avenue, Suite 1565, New York, NY 10111, U.S.A.

Italian Government Travel Office, telephone: (310) 820-0098, fax: (310) 820-6357
12400 Wilshire Blvd. Suite 550, Los Angeles, CA 90025, U.S.A.

Italian Government Travel Office, telephone: (312) 644-0990, fax: (312) 644-3019
500 North Michigan Avenue, Suite 1046, Chicago, IL 60611, U.S.A..

Italian Government Travel Office, telephone: (514) 866-7667, fax: (514) 392-1429
1 Place Ville Marie, Suite 1914, Montreal, Quebec H3B 3M9, Canada

Italian State Tourist Office, telephone: (004471) 408 12 54, fax: (004471) 493 66 95
Princes Street 1, London WIR 8AY, England

ITINERARIES

In the itinerary section of this guide you should be able to find an itinerary, or portion of an itinerary, that can be easily custom tailored to fit your exact time frame and suit your own particular interests. If your time is limited, you could certainly follow just a segment of an itinerary. In the itineraries we have not specified number of nights at each destination, since to do so seemed much too confining. Again, personality dictates what is best for a particular situation. Some travellers like to see as much as possible in a short period of time and do not mind rising with the birds each morning to begin a new adventure. For others, just the thought of packing and unpacking each night makes them shudder in horror and they would never stop for less than three or four nights at any destination. A third type of tourist doesn't like to travel at all: the destination is the focus and he will use this guide to find the "perfect" resort from which he will never wander except for daytime excursions. So, use this guide as a reference from which to plan your personalized trip.

Our advice is, if possible, do not rush. Part of the joy of travelling is to "settle in" at a hotel that you like and use it as a hub from which to take side trips to explore the countryside. When you dash too quickly from place to place you never have the opportunity to get to know the owners of the hotels and to become friends with other guests. Look at the maps in the back of this guide to find the hotels in the areas where you want to travel. Read about each hotel in the hotel description section of this book and decide which places to stay sound most suited to your taste and budget. Then choose a base for each area you want to visit.

MAPS

With each itinerary there is a map showing the routing and suggesting places of interest along the way. These are artist's renderings and are not intended to replace a good commercial map. To supplement our generalized routings, you will need a set of detailed maps that will indicate all of the highway numbers, expressways, alternate little roads, expressway access points, exact mileages, etc. Our suggestion is to purchase a comprehensive set of city maps and regional maps before your departure, and with a highlight pen mark your own "personalized" itinerary and pinpoint your city hotels. If you live in a metropolitan area you should have no problem buying maps in a travel bookstore or else your local bookstore should be able to place a special order. Our personal preference for Italy are the Rand McNally HALLWAG maps (there are Rand McNally stores in many major cities so it the Hallwag maps are readily available). Depending upon your itinerary, you need either the Hallwag map of "Southern Italy" or their map of "Northern Italy"—or both (don't purchase the Hallwag map that covers the whole of Italy—it is too general). Each map comes with a small index booklet to help you find the towns you are seeking. Almost every town in our guide can be found on the Hallwag maps.

SECURITY WHILE TRAVELLING

The Italians are wonderful hosts. They are friendly, outgoing, gregarious and merry—no one is a "stranger". In fact, it seems every Italian has a brother or cousin in the United States, and so the warmth of camaraderie is further enhanced. In spite of the overall graciousness of the Italians, there are a few "misfits" who have instilled in some tourists the idea that theft is rampant in Italy. True, there are stories about cars being pilfered and purses snatched, but this happens all over the world. Just be cautious. Watch your purse. Don't let your wallet stand out like a red light in your back pocket. Lock your valuables in the hotel vault. Use travelers' checks. Don't leave valuables temptingly exposed in your car. In other words, use common sense. Unfortunately, we have heard of incidents of a group of gypsy children who flock to you, usually in congested, tourist areas, and attempt to steal your wallet or purse. If this should happen to you, shoo them away and call for the police. NOTE: Whenever you travel to any country, it is wise to make a photocopy of the pages of your passport showing your picture, passport number, where issued, etc. With this in hand, in case you lose your passport, it is much easier to get a replacement.

SHOPPING

Italy is a shopper's paradise. Not only are the stores brimming with tempting merchandise, but their displays are beautiful, from the tiniest fruit market to the most chic boutique. Each area has its "specialty". In Venice items made from blown glass and handmade laces are very popular. Milan is famous for its clothing and silk-wear (gorgeous scarves, ties and blouses). Florence is a paradise for leather goods (purses, shoes, wallets, gloves, suitcases) and also for gold jewelry (you can buy gold jewelry by weight). Rome is a fashion center where you can stroll the pedestrian shopping streets browsing in some of the world's most elegant, sophisticated shops where you can buy the latest designer creations and, of course, religious items are available, especially near St Peter's Cathedral. Naples and the surrounding regions (Capri, Ravello, Positano) offer delightful coral jewelry and also a wonderful selection of ceramics.

TRANSPORTATION

Trains: Italy has an excellent network of trains. The major express trains are usually a quick, reliable way to whip between the major cities. In contrast, the local trains stop at every little town, take much longer, and are frequently delayed. Each train station is well organized. There is almost always an information desk where someone who speaks English who will answer any questions and advise you as to the best schedules. There is another counter where you purchase your tickets. Still a third counter is where seat reservations are made. If you can possibly plan ahead, we strongly recommend purchasing your train tickets in advance since it quite time consuming to stand in two lines at each train station, only to find—particularly in summer that the train you want is already sold out. You can purchase open tickets in the United States; however, recently it has become almost impossible to purchase in advance your seat reservations. When this is the case, go ahead and buy the open tickets and then you can either purchase your seat reservations locally, or else pay the concierge at your hotel to handle this transaction for you. NOTE: Seat reservations cannot be made just before getting on the train—it is best to make them as far in advance as possible.

The very popular Eurailpass is valid in Italy. This is a pass that allows unlimited travel on most trains throughout Europe. However, if you are going to travel only in Italy, then you might want to buy instead one of the Italian Rail Passes that are issued for 8, 15, 21, or 30 days. They are available for either first or second class travel. You can purchase these passes through your local travel agent or, in the United States, you can contact the Italian

State Railways, 342 Madison Avenue, Suite 207, New York, NY 10173, U.S.A., telephone (212) 697-2100. Another note on trains—in the summer when rail traffic is very heavy, unless you make dining car reservations in advance you might not be able to have the fun of eating your meal en route. If you have not made these reservations, as soon as you board the train, stroll down to the dining car and ask to reserve a table.

BOATS: Italy has gorgeous islands dotting her shorelines, a glorious string of lakes gracing her mountains to the north, and romantic canals in Venice. Luckily Italy's boat system is excellent—enabling the tourist maximum enjoyment of some of Italy's most stunning destinations.

All of Italy's islands are linked to the mainland and serviced frequently by a wonderful maritime network. The many outlying islands often have overnight ferries that even offer sleeping accommodations and facilities for cars. The closer islands usually have a choice of conveyances—the hydrofoil that zips quickly across the water or the regular ferry.

One of the highlights of traveling in Italy is to explore her wondrous lakes by hopping on one of the ferry boats that glide romantically between the little villages clustered along the shoreline. Again, there is usually a choice of either the hydrofoil that darts between the hamlets, or the ferry that glides leisurely across the water and usually offers beverage and food service on board. The boat schedules are posted at each pier, or you can request a timetable from the Italian tourist office. NOTE: these little boats are punctual, to the minute, so be right at the pier with your ticket in hand so you can jump on board during the brief interlude that the boat huddles at the shore. If at all possible, try to squeeze in at least one boat excursion while in Italy. It is a treat you will long remember.

WEATHER

Italy is blessed with lovely weather. However, unless you are a ski enthusiast following the promise of what the majestic mountains have to offer in the winter, or must travel in summer due to school holidays, we highly recommend travelling in spring or fall. Travel at either of these times has two dramatic advantages: you miss the rush of the summer tourist season when all of Italy is packed, and you are more likely to have beautiful weather. In spring the meadows are painted with wildflowers. In fall the forests are a riot of color and the vineyards are mellow in shades of red and gold. Although the mountains of Italy are delightfully cool in summer, the rest of the country can be very hot, especially in the cities. (NOTE: many hotels are not air conditioned, and when they are, an additional charge is frequently included on the bill.).

WHAT TO WEAR

During the day informal wear is most appropriate including comfortable slacks for women. In the evening, if you are at a sidewalk cafe or a simple pizzeria, women do not need to dress up nor men to wear coats and ties. However, Italy does have some elegant restaurants, where definitely a dress and coat and tie are the proper attire. A basic principle is to dress as you would in any city at home. There are perhaps a few special situations: the churches are still very conservative, shorts are definitely inappropriate as are low cut dresses. Some of the cathedrals still insist that women have their arms covered. It is rare that a scarf on the head is required, but to wear one is a respectful gesture.

The "layered" effect is ideal for Italy. Because Italy's climate runs the gamut from usually cool in the mountains to frequently very hot in the south, the most efficient wardrobe is one where light blouses and shirts can be "reinforced" by layers of sweaters that can be added or peeled off as the day demands.

Introduction

Italian Highlights by Train & Boat

Riva
Lake Garda
MILANO
SIRMIONE
VERONA
Desenzano
Padua
VENICE
FLORENCE
ROME
Naples
Pompeii
CAPRI
SORRENTO

◉ OVERNIGHT STOPS

Italian Highlights by Train & Boat

This itinerary can be journeyed easily by car; however, just the thought of taking an automobile onto an Italian expressway can intimidate even the bravest breed of tourist. It is true that the Italians love cars and enjoy driving fast: it would seem that many are practicing for the Grand Prix. But an aversion to driving does not mean that your only alternative is a "package" tour. Italy can be seen splendidly by train and boat. This is a glorious way to travel and has many advantages: everyone can watch the scenery instead of the road, a bottle of wine can be savored with lunch, and you all arrive rested and ready to enjoy the sights. But maybe the best advantage of all is that while using public transportation you will make friends. Perhaps there will be just a smile at first, then maybe the sharing of a piece of fruit, and, later comes the admiration of each other's family photographs. Somehow barriers break down on a long journey and the universal warmth of friendliness—at which the Italians are masters—spans any language barriers.

This itinerary covers some of the most famous destinations within Italy. For a short holiday it is impossible to include all the places of interest, but following this pathway will easily provide you with a glimpse of some of the highlights of Italy and will hopefully tempt you to return quickly to delve more deeply into the wonders that Italy has to offer. This itinerary is woven around towns that are conveniently linked by public transportation. Of course, if your time is extremely limited, this itinerary lends itself well to segmentation. If you cannot travel with us all the way, then choose what fits into your schedule and what most appeals to you. No matter what portion you include, you will be treated to a delightful holiday.

In the following itinerary approximate train and boat times have been included. Please note that these are given only as a reference to show you how the pieces of this itinerary tie together. Schedules are constantly changing, so these must be verified. Also, many boats and some trains are seasonal, so be very meticulous in making your plans.

ORIGINATING CITY   MILAN

This highlight tour begins in MILAN, a most convenient city since it is the hub of airline flights from throughout Europe, plus it is blessed with non-stop air service from the United States. Also, Milan is strategically located for trains arriving from all over Europe. Into her busy station trains come rushing via the Gotthard, Simplon and Bernina passes. However, it is not location alone which makes Milan an ideal starting point. Although frequently bypassed as an enormous industrial city of little interest, Milan has, at its core, a truly charming metropolis which includes delights to please all tastes: some of the best shopping in Italy gorgeously displayed in glass-domed arcades, superb medieval squares snuggled unexpectedly within her boundaries, dazzling cathedrals, fascinating museums, gourmet restaurants, and of course, La Scala—one of the world's most famous opera houses.

The train for Desenzano (the station you want for your destination of Sirmione) usually departs from the Milan Central Station, but sometimes the trains leave instead from the Porto Garibaldi station, so it is vital that schedules be checked very carefully.

   12:00 noon depart Milan Central Station by train
    1:12 pm arrive Desenzano

When the train arrives in the ancient port of Desenzano, you can take a taxi to the pier where hydrofoils, steamers and buses leave regularly for Sirmione. However, although more expensive, we suggest you splurge and take a taxi directly to Sirmione (only about 10 kilometers away). This is definitely the most convenient means of transportation since you are taken directly to your hotel.

SIRMIONE is a walled medieval village fabulously located on a tiny peninsula jutting out on Lake Garda. The peninsula where Sirmione is located seems like an island because it is connected to the mainland by just a thread of land. To enter the ancient town you first cross over a moat then enter through medieval gates. If travelling by car (unless you are one of the lucky ones with a hotel confirmed for the night) you will not be allowed to pass within the town walls, since only pedestrians are allowed through the entrance. But if you have hotel reservations, stop near the entrance at the information office where you will be given a pass to enter with your automobile.

There are several hotels in the heart of Sirmione but the most glamorous choice, the VILLA CORTINE PALACE HOTEL, is located in a park-like estate on the outskirts of town. The entrance is absolutely "Hollywood." You must ring a bell at the impressive gates which then slowly swing open, allowing you to wind your way up through the truly beautiful park to the hotel that crowns the small hill. Previously, this was a sumptuous private villa. Now a new wing has been built which doubles the original size. Although the newer wing looks a bit sterile from the outside, the rooms are delightful and most have better views than those in the old section. Demi-pension (breakfast and dinner) are required if you are staying at the Villa Cortine Palace. In addition, reservations are usually taken only for stays of at least three nights. But neither should prove a problem—you will never want to leave such a romantic setting.

Villa Cortine Palace
Sirmione

From the Villa Cortine Palace Hotel you can easily walk to the wharf in the middle of town to study the posted schedule in order to decide which boat you want to take for your day's excursion. You can either glide around the lake all day and have a snack on board, or you can get off in some small jewel of a town and enjoy lunch at a lakefront cafe. There is a choice of transportation: either the romantic ferry boats or the faster hydrofoils.

There are also some Roman ruins on the Sirmione peninsula. These are located on the very tip of the peninsula and can be reached either on foot, or if you prefer, by a miniature motorized train which shuttles back and forth from the village to the ruins

DESTINATION II   VERONA

There are trains almost every hour that cover the half-hour journey between Desenzano and Verona. But if it is a beautiful day it is much more romantic to incorporate some sightseeing into your transportation and take a boat and bus instead of the train. If this appeals to you, the following gives an idea of how this can be done.

   9:50 am depart Sirmione by ferry
   1:25 pm arrive Riva

You can have lunch on board the ferry or else you can wait until you reach the medieval town of RIVA, located on the northern shore of Lake Garda. The outdoor terrace overlooking the lake at the Hotel Sole (located just across from where the ferry docks) provides a serene luncheon setting. The interesting ancient core of Riva is small, so it will not take long to stroll through the old city.

After lunch and a walk through the old part of town, depart Riva by bus for Verona (buses run every 15 minutes in summer).The scenic route follows the eastern shore of Lake Garda and then on to Verona. When you arrive in VERONA you will be delighted. This is a town that is all too frequently bypassed by the tourist, but what a prize it is. The city is filled with medieval charm and proudly boasts one of the most dramatic Roman amphitheaters in Italy. Luckily, Verona has several good hotels to complement her marvelous sights. A favorite is the HOTEL GABBIA D'ORO, which is brimming with charm and conveniently located near all the places of interest. Verona can only be appreciated by walking and happily the heart of the city is compact with narrow winding ancient streets just begging to be explored. You can easily see everything of interest by foot.

Hotel Gabbia d'Oro
Verona

DESTINATION III   VENICE

When you are ready to leave Verona, there is frequent train service to Venice so the following is just a suggestion. NOTE: As you approach Venice, be sure not to get off the train at the Venice Mestre station, but instead wait for the next stop which is the Santa Lucia station (about ten minutes further).

2:20 pm depart Verona by train
3:48 pm arrive Venice, Santa Lucia station

As you come out of the front door of the train station you will find that the station is directly on the Grand Canal and that it is a few short steps down to where you can board a boat to take you to your hotel. The Vaporetti are the most popular means of transportation and are very inexpensive. They are like "boat buses" that constantly shuttle back and forth from the train station to St Mark's Square. The Number Two ferry makes only major stops while the Number One ferry pauses at every stop to exchange passengers. Much more expensive, but a little faster, are the Motoscafi that are like a water-taxis and will deliver you right to the door of your hotel, provided there is a motor boat dock. The third choice is to take one of the gondolas, but these are much slower and very expensive, so we suggest saving your gondola ride for a romantic interlude rather than a train connection.

VENICE has many hotels in every price range. Look in the back of this guide for various suggestions of places that we recommend. If you want to splurge, stay at the very expensive, very sumptuous, GRITTI PALACE, a former home of the immensely wealthy Doge Andrea Gritti. It is easy to imagine the grandeur of days gone by as you arrive in style at the hotel's dock on the Grand Canal and descend onto the red carpet, past the diners enjoying a snack on the deck, and into the beautiful lobby. If money is no object, go all the way and request a room overlooking the canal.

Hotel Gritti Palace
Venice

Venice has so many sights: marvelous restaurants, beautiful boutiques, and fascinating little alleyways to explore, that you could happily stay for weeks.

Of course, you will want to savor all the ambiance of St Mark's Square and visit the Doges' Palace. See the Clock Tower whose huge bronze figures bang out the hours with massive hammers. Wander through the museums. Go either on your own or on a tour to the three islands: MURANO (famous for its hand-blown glass), BURANO (famous for its colorfully painted fishermen's cottages and lace making), and TORCELLO (once an important city but now just a small village with only its lovely large church to remind one of its past glories). A real bargain is to board the Vaporetto and enjoy the many wonderful palaces bordering the Grand Canal. A favorite pastime in Venice is wandering—just anywhere—exploring the maze of twisting canals and criss-crossing back and forth over some of the 400 toy-like bridges.

Another outing you will certainly enjoy is to take the Il Burchiello, named for a famous 17th-century Venetian boat, which leaves Tuesdays, Thursdays and Saturdays at about 9:20 am from Pontile Giarinetti pier at St Mark's Square and travels the network of rivers and canals linking Venice and Padua. (The schedule might change, so verify.) This little boat, with an English speaking guide on board, stops at several of the exquisite palaces en route. Lunch is served and there is time for sightseeing in Padua before returning to Venice by bus. It is a delightful excursion.

DESTINATION IV   FLORENCE

There are several direct trains each day from Venice to Florence: however, in summer, space is at a real premium, so be sure to reserve a seat in advance. Some of the express trains must have prior seat reservations and will require a supplemental fee. NOTE: During the busy season, if you want to dine on the train it is necessary to make advance reservations when you buy your ticket.

2:45 pm depart Venice, Santa Lucia station (reservations obligatory)
5:17 pm arrive Florence

In FLORENCE, a very good choice for accommodation is the LUNGARNO HOTEL, which rises directly from the banks of the Arno very near the Ponte Vecchio. The Lungarno is not an "old-world" hotel, but rather a modern, very tastefully decorated, charming hotel perched directly on the Arno only a few steps from the heart of Florence. Although new, the Lungarno happily qualifies without too much stretch of the imagination for this guide because it incorporates into its construction a 13th-century tower in which there are some romantic rooms. However, our preference would be a room in the front overlooking the river—a few even have balconies for those lucky travellers who book well in advance.

Lungarno Hotel
Florence

Be generous with your time and do not rush Florence—there is too much to see. You must, of course, pay a visit to Michelangelo's David in the Galleria dell'Accademia (located just off the Piazza San Marco), and you must not miss the fantastic museums and cathedrals—the world will probably never again see a city that has produced so much artistic genius. Travellers best appreciate Florence when they are simply roaming. Wander through the streets and poke into small boutiques. Stop in churches that catch your eye—they all abound with masterpieces. Sit to enjoy a cappuccino in one of the little sidewalk cafes and "people watch." Stroll through the piazzas and watch some of the artists at work—many of them incredibly clever—as they paint portraits and do sculptures for a small fee. End your day by finding the perfect small restaurant for delicious pasta made by "mama" in the back kitchen.

DESTINATION V   ROME

There is excellent train service from Florence to Rome. It is probably best to take one of the midday trains—a choice that will allow you to enjoy lunch as you soak in the beauty of the Tuscany hills flowing by your window. Remember that you will need both seat and dining reservations.

  12:05 pm depart Florence via train
  2:05 pm arrive Rome, Termini station

As the train pulls into ROME, you might feel overwhelmed by its size and confusion of traffic, but once you settle into your hotel, you will realize that Rome is really not as cumbersome as it looks. The ancient part of the city is manageable on foot—a fabulous city for walking with its maze of streets and captivating boutiques just begging to be explored. We recommend many places to stay in Rome. Look over our selection in the Hotel Description section in the back of this guide and choose one that suits your purse and your personality. Be forewarned, Rome is a very expensive city. If you are looking for a well-located small deluxe hotel, the Hotel d'Inghilterra is a superb choice.

Hotel d'Inghilterra
Rome

Rome is bursting with a wealth of fantastic museums, ancient monuments, spectacular cathedrals, gourmet restaurants, beautiful boutiques, colorful piazzas, whimsical fountains, inspiring statues, theater and opera—the city itself is virtually a museum. One cannot possibly savor it all. Either before you leave home or once you arrive in Italy, purchase a comprehensive guidebook and decide what is top priority for your special interests. There are many stalls along the streets as well as book stores throughout Rome where guide books are available. Also, every hotel has brochures available that tell about sightseeing tours. If there are several in your party, then a private guide might be money well spent since he will custom tailor your sightseeing. With a private guide you can squeeze much more quality sightseeing into a short period of time.

One could spend weeks discovering the museum that is Rome, but if you have time to add a few more highlights before your return, try to include Sorrento and Capri. There is frequent train service from Rome to Naples and from there it is a short Aliscafi (hydrofoil) ride to Capri. However, for the adventurous it is fun to include Pompeii and Sorrento en route to Capri. Please be advised that this makes a long day of travel and takes some manipulating of schedules, but the rewards are great.

You will need an early start to accomplish a tour of Pompeii on your way to Sorrento, but this is a must. How could you be so close without visiting this intriguing city of the Romans that was destroyed, yet preserved forever by the ashes of Vesuvius?

  8:30 am depart Rome, Termini station
11:06 am arrive Pompeii, Main station

You arrive in POMPEII at the Main station, but you will depart from Pompeii at the Villa d'Misteri station, located just across from the main entrance to the archaeological site. Since you will not want to lug your suitcases around while you do your sight-seeing, take a cab from the Main station to the Villa d'Misteri station where there is a place to check luggage. Then you can just walk across the street to the main gate of Pompeii. There is a nice terrace restaurant by the entrance and also a cafe inside. If you want to do your own touring, you can buy a guidebook in English from a stall, or else you can negotiate with one of the licensed guides for a personal tour. You may have heard that the earthquake of 1980 destroyed much of Pompeii. It is true that many of the sites were damaged, but by now, almost everything has been reconstructed. An aura of mystery lingers in the air as you wander the streets of Pompeii. All visitors are touched by this ancient city that, in one day, became frozen for all time. As you explore Pompeii, there is no need to watch your clock because there is a narrow gauge train departing from the Pompeii Villa d Misteri station about every twenty minutes for the half-hour scenic journey to Sorrento.

When you arrive in SORRENTO, stay at the GRAND HOTEL EXCELSIOR VITTORIA, a romantic old villa at the center of town in a prime cliff location overlooking the harbor. The hotel's once perfect grandeur is perhaps a bit faded, but as you sit on the terrace in the evening and watch the sun turning the bay to shades of red and gold, the atmosphere is perfection. There is also a pool for relaxing and sunning. Definitely ask for a deluxe room with a view.

Grand Hotel Excelsior Vittoria
Sorrento

DESTINATION VII   CAPRI

When it is time to leave Sorrento there is excellent service by either hydrofoil or ferry to Capri. Perhaps the following schedule will give you a suggestion:

5:45 pm depart Sorrento by hydrofoil
6:30 pm arrive Capri

Your hydrofoil will arrive at the Marina Grande where you will find major hotel representatives on the pier. They will relieve you of your luggage and take it directly to your room in the hotel of your choice, freeing you to take either a mini-bus or the funicular to the main town of CAPRI.

There are many small hotels on Capri but, if you want to splurge, a deluxe hotel choice is the GRAND HOTEL QUISISANA. A larger hotel than most recommended in this guide, it is an oasis at the heart of Capri where you can escape the heat of the day and relax by the beautiful pool. During the day, the island is swarming with tourists who come on day tours. You might surmise that in the evening the activity subsides; but it isn't so. The tour groups leave at dusk but then a new group of people emerge from the secreted villas and fancy hotels: guests in chic clothes and fancy jewelry strolling the streets—both to see and be seen.

*Grand Hotel Quisisana
Capri*

Capri has many wonders. The most famous is its submerged cave, the BLUE GROTTO, which can be reached by boat when the seas are calm. Large boats begin leaving the harbor every morning at 9:00 am for the short ride to the entrance to the Blue Grotto, where you are transferred into tiny rowboats. The excursion is an adventure in itself. As your little boat approaches the tiny cave opening it seems impossible that there will be adequate room, but suddenly the sea surges forward and in you squeeze. Like magic you see it—the mysterious stunning blue light reflecting from some hidden source which illuminates the grotto.

Capri is a superb island for walking. As you stroll the trails, all your senses will be treated by the fragrant flowers, the gorgeous vistas of the brilliant blue waters and the sound of birds luring you ever onward. There are many spectacular walks. Follow the trail winding down the cliffs to the small harbor MARINA PICCOLA, located on the opposite side of the island from where the ferries dock. There are lovely views of the shimmering aqua waters as you make your way to the small beach where you can enjoy a swim before your return. Instead of walking back up the hill, take the little bus which will deliver you quickly back to the main square.

Another absolutely spectacular walk—although a long one of at least 45 minutes each way—is to EMPEROR TIBERIUS' PALACE, perched high on the cliffs on the western tip of the island. From the palace there are stunning panoramic vistas. You have an overview of the whole island and can watch the ferries shuttling back and forth to the mainland. A much shorter walk, but one equally as beautiful, is to the CANNONE BELVEDERE. This path guides you near delightful private villas hidden behind high walls (you can get glimpses through the gates) and on to a promontory overlooking the sea.

When the real world calls and you must leave Capri, there is frequent ferry or hydrofoil service back to Naples. From there, you can take either a train to Rome or a plane to your next destination.

Romantic Hilltowns
of Tuscany & Umbria

FLORENCE

PANZANO
IN CHIANTI

San Gimignano Siena

Abbey of Monte
Oliveto Maggiore

Pienza

Arezzo

Cortona

SINALUNGA

Perugia

ASSISI

Torgiano

Spoleto
Monteluco

Orvieto

Todi

ROME

◎ **OVERNIGHT STOPS**

Romantic Hilltowns of Tuscany & Umbria

Nothing could possibly surpass the exquisite beauty of the countryside near Florence in the spring. It is breathtaking. But it is not only in the spring: if you meander into the hilltowns south of Florence any time of the year, all your senses will be rewarded with the splendors that this enchanting Italian region has to offer. Almost every hillock is crowned with a picture-perfect little walled village. The fields are brilliant with vibrant red poppies. The vineyards lace the fields in all their glory and promise. The olive trees dress the hillsides in a frock of dusky gray-green. Pine forests unexpectedly appear to highlight the landscape. As if these were not enough, this area is a treasure trove of some of the finest small hotels in all the world. And if this is still not sufficient to tempt you away from the normal tourist route, be reminded that the food and wines of Tuscany and Umbria are unsurpassed.

So, when you plan your trip to Italy, please allow time to treat yourself to a unique adventure. Save at least a few days to slip away from the cities and into the country. Perhaps you will not have time to follow this entire itinerary, but at least sneak in a few days in this special region of Italy. You will be well rewarded with a wealth of memories that will linger long after you return home.

ORIGINATING CITY   FLORENCE

Your journey begins in FLORENCE. Allow enough time to savor this marvelous city but, if you are reluctant to leave, be consoled. There are many treats in store for you in the delightful hilltowns that surround Florence. Magnificent art is not confined to the city limits of Florence and you will see impressive cathedrals and beautiful works of art throughout the neighboring areas. On page 29 we have a few sightseeing tips for Florence.

DESTINATION I   ASSISI

The traffic around Florence is difficult, so find the expressway to Rome and follow it until you come to the turnoff for Arezzo, which is located about 10 kilometers east of the highway. You might want to bypass Arezzo. Although it has a rich, medieval history dating back to the Etruscan era, it is a large city and it is not as quaint as some of its smaller neighbors.

If you follow the main road south from Arezzo, you soon arrive at CORTONA. This is a beautifully situated walled town climbing up a steep hillside covered with olive trees. Stop to enjoy the atmosphere of this medieval town with its crazy little twisting streets, jumble of small squares and colorful buildings. A mighty castle dramatically stands guard over this hillside town.

Leaving Cortona, continue south to Lake Trasimeno and follow its northern shore to PERUGIA, a large medieval city surrounded by ramparts. An important Umbrian city since Etruscan days, the heart of the old city is the Piazza IV Novembre, a beautiful square with an especially appealing fountain, the Fontana Maggiore, built in the late 13th Century.

Hotel Subasio
Assisi

It is only a short drive farther south from Perugia to ASSISI. Even if it were not for the lingering memory of the gentle St Francis, this would be a "must see" for Assisi is one of the most spectacular hilltowns in Umbria. Perhaps there are a few too many souvenir shops, but this is a small price to pay for such a very special place. The town walls begin on the valley floor and completely enclose the city as climbs the steep hillside, climaxing in an enormous castle. Assisi is a marvelous town for walking: you will need sturdy shoes to wind your way up and down the maze of tiny streets. It is great fun. You will come across intriguing little lanes which open into small squares. When you stop to rest, there are marvelous vistas of the breathtaking Umbrian fields stretching out below. While exploring Assisi, don't miss the fabulous St Francis' Basilica which includes a monastery with a beautiful arcaded courtyard.

To truly appreciate the beauty of Assisi, it is best to spend the night and, luckily, there are several good hotel choices. Beautifully situated with one of its walls forming a section of the piazza of the St Francis' Basilica is the HOTEL SUBASIO. This is not a deluxe hotel but it has much to entice the tourist. Perhaps its most impressive attribute is the view from the vine covered dining terrace over the undulating Umbrian fields which seem to glow with a special radiance. Some of the bedrooms, too, have splendid vistas from their balconies. Definitely splurge and request one of the best rooms so you can capture each possible moment of this very beautiful scene.

While staying at Assisi, take a side-trip to nearby TORGIANO where there is a splendid wine museum. One would never dream that such a tiny town could boast such a stunning museum, but it is not a coincidence. The Lungarotti family owns the vineyards for miles in every direction and, indeed, they must be a very clever and dedicated family for they also own a delightful hotel in the center of town, LE TRE VASELLE. A charming spot for lunch, Le Tre Vaselle has the ambiance of a lovely country manor house. In addition to overseeing the decoration of this exquisite hotel, Signore Lungarotti also furnished the museum with artifacts pertaining to every aspect of the production of wine from the earliest days. The collection is interesting and beautifully displayed, worthy of a detour by anyone interested in wines.

DESTINATION II   SINALUNGA

Get an early start this morning because it is going to be difficult to squeeze in all of the enchanting hilltop towns en route. Driving south from Assisi you soon come to SPOLETO, an intriguing town. Not only is medieval Spoleto dramatically perched atop a hill, but it also has an almost unbelievable bridge dating from Roman times. The bridge, spanning the deep ravine between Spoleto and the adjoining mountain, was built over a Roman aqueduct existing in the 14th Century. This incredible engineering wonder is 755 feet long and 262 feet high. It is supported by a series of ten Gothic arches and has a fort at the far end as well as a balcony in the center. The cathedral in Spoleto is also so lovely that it alone would make a stop here worth while.

Before leaving the vicinity of Spoleto, if you are a St Francis enthusiast, make a short detour to visit MONTELUCO, where St Francis came to live as a hermit. You will appreciate why he chose Monteluco after you twist to the top of the mountain and enjoy the glorious view of the surrounding hillsides covered with olive trees.

Make a brief stop, as you head west, at TODI, another of the tiny hilltop walled villages about midway between Spoleto and Orvieto. However, do not linger too long in Todi because the next town, Orvieto, is the real prize.

Locanda dell'Amorosa
Sinalunga

ORVIETO is spread across the top of a hill which drops down on every side in steep volcanic cliffs. One wonders how the town could ever have been built. At Orvieto's center is a glorious duomo dominating a large piazza. You may think you have seen enough stunning cathedrals, but this one is really special—brilliantly colored in intricate mosaic designs and accentuated by slender spirals stretching gracefully into the sky. Also of interest in Orvieto is ST PATRICK'S WELL. This well, over 62 meters deep, hewn out of solid volcanic rock to collect and store water in case of a siege. Pope Clement VII took refuge in Orvieto in 1527 and to ensure the town's water supply in case of siege, he ordered the digging of a 62 meter deep well. What makes it unusual are the 70 windows which illuminate it and the two spiral staircases that wind up and down without meeting.

After seeing Orvieto, it might be getting late in the day and you will need to head directly north on the A1 to your night's destination, SINALUNGA. But, if you have time, explore the small back roads, winding through the countryside as you head north. As a goal, mark on your Hallwag map the tiny hilltop town of PIENZA as your first target. It does not matter if you get a little lost. The scenery is beautiful and you will make discoveries of your own. An example of unspoiled beauty: Pienza has no modern developments to interrupt its charm. Within its walls, you will find quaint little squares and a church built almost on the edge of the ramparts affording a lovely terrace view. About 36 kilometers north of Pienza is the ABBEY OF MONTE OLIVETO MAGGIORE (also on Hallwag map), serenely situated among the cypress forest. Of special interest are the terra cottas adorning the entrance, created by the famous artist, Luca della Robbia. The cloisters contain frescos portraying the life of St Benedict.

From the abbey, drive east to the town of SINALUNGA where there is a delightful (though quite expensive) hotel, the LOCANDA DELL'AMOROSA. The lane leading to the Locanda dell'Amorosa is lined on both sides with tall cypress trees through which you glimpse an expanse of vineyards. The town walls mark the hotel's entrance, as the hotel is the town. Pass through the gate into a large courtyard (at its end is an exquisite little church). The wing of buildings to the left contains the bedrooms. The wing to the right houses the reception lounge and the attractive dining room which is well-known for its food. In this same little "hotel-town" a delicious wine is bottled which you can sample at dinner.

On your way to Panzano be sure to stop in SIENA, another of the strategically built walled hilltowns. This is an entrancing city and deserves many hours to savor all its attributes. The ramparts are perfectly preserved with a series of massive gates guarding a meticulously maintained medieval stronghold. Drive as close as you can to the main square, park your car, and set out to explore on foot. The giant piazza is a sight in itself: it is immense and, instead of being square, is fan shaped. All the streets surrounding the square end like the spokes of a giant wheel in the Piazza del Campo. The town hall monopolizes one side of the piazza with graceful arches embellished with the coat of arms of Siena. It is in this gigantic piazza that the colorful "Palio delle Contrade" takes place in July and August every year. The horse race is only a part of a colorful spectacle of medieval costumes, wonderful banners and parades. You can check for the exact dates, but the festivities extend beyond the actual date of the races. Also, Siena has one of Italy's most dramatic cathedrals, located a short walk from the Piazza del Campo. Not only is the cathedral striking with its bold patterns of black and white marble, but it also houses a museum.

From Siena, continue north on the expressway and take the turnoff for SAN GIMIGNANO. Although you might think you are weary of walled towns, San Gimignano is unique and definitely worth a stop. What is so dramatic about San Gimignano is that at one time this small walled village was surrounded by 72 towers. During the Middle Ages it was a status symbol for noble families to build personal towers for protection: the higher the tower, the greater the image of wealth and importance. It is amazing that fourteen of the original towers are still standing. They make a striking silhouette soaring like skyscrapers: on a clear day, you can see them on the horizon from miles away. San Gimignano is truly a jewel of a town—one of our very favorites. If you can squeeze in an extra night, we heartily recommend staying at the L'ANTICO POZZO, a charming small hotel. If you can't spend the night, plan to have a meal: the hotel La Cisterna on the main square, or at La Mangiatoia near L'Antico Pozzo, both serve excellent food.

Hotel L'Antico Pozzo
San Gimignano

If you don't overnight in San Gimignano, head almost directly east to PANZANO IN CHIANTI where the prize of your journey, VILLA LE BARONE, awaits you. This is an exquisite small hotel encompassing all the joys that are Tuscany. This villa is the home of the Della Robbia family, and today is owned by Duchessa Franca Viviani Della Robbia. The location is idyllic: the villa is set in lovely gardens and surrounded by vineyards. There is a welcoming pool. A terrace for dining overlooks a panorama of the Tuscany hills stretching for miles in the distance while another dining room is fashioned from the former stables. Breakfast and dinner are included in the price of a room and reservations during the high season are usually accepted only for a stay of several days: but this is no problem—you will want to stay forever.

Villa Le Barone
Panzano in Chianti

When it is time to complete your loop and return to Florence you will find it only about an hour's drive away in time but years away in mood from the tranquillity of the Villa Le Barone.

Mountain & Lake Adventures

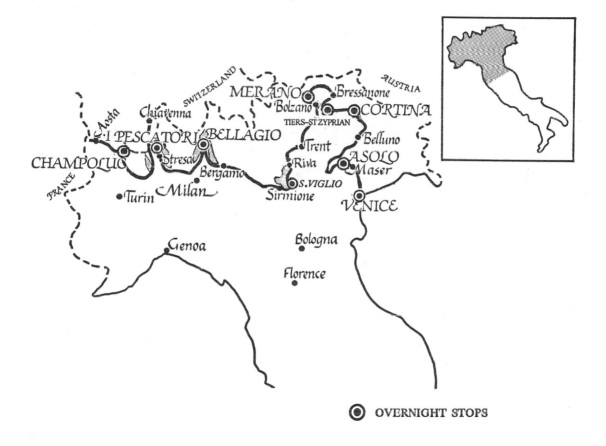

⊙ OVERNIGHT STOPS

Mountain & Lake Adventures

For the traveller who wants to combine the magic of seeing some of the world's most splendid mountains with the joy of visiting Italy's scenic northern lakes, this itinerary is ideal. Contrasts will heighten the impact of visual delights as you meander through lovely mountain passes, via lush green meadows laced with wildflowers, beneath giant mountains piercing the sky with their jagged granite peaks, and bordering lazy blue lakes whose steep shorelines are decorated with endearing little Italian villages wrapped in misty cloaks of wonderful siennas and ochre's. What a glorious holiday to wind across northern Italy enjoying some of its most beautiful landscapes. This itinerary can stand alone. However, it is also perfect for the traveller arriving or departing from neighboring countries. We have carefully shown detours for the tourist who will be leaving or entering from Austria, Switzerland, or France. All too often the tourist thinks he has "finished" Italy when his tour ends in Venice and he too quickly rushes north into Austria or Switzerland. What a waste. A very picturesque region still remains. Please linger to enjoy the mountains and lakes that truly are some of Italy's greatest natural treasures.

ORIGINATING CITY   VENICE

This itinerary begins in VENICE, one of the most romantic cities in the world. Her many narrow waterways are criss-crossed by storybook bridges and shadowed by majestic palaces whose soft hues reflect warmly in the shimmering water. Black gondolas quietly glide through the narrow canals as the gondolier in his red and white striped shirt softly serenades his romantic passengers with an operatic selection.

Venice is not a traditional city with streets and automobile traffic, rather an archipelago of 117 islands "glued" together by 400 bridges. There is a wealth of things to do while in Venice. Pick up a guide book at one of the tourist stalls to give you an idea of what you want to see. On page 27 we give a few sightseeing suggestions—our list is not long because a comprehensive one would merit a book in itself.

DESTINATION I   ASOLO

You need not rush your departure this morning. Venice is a city that should be enjoyed slowly and since your journey today is short, you can certainly have the luxury of a last leisurely breakfast before embarking on your next adventure.

Since all the "streets" in Venice are liquid, you will need to take a boat to your car. It will probably be at the Piazzale Roma where most of the car rental companies are located: in addition it is also where there are overnight car parks for storing your car if you drive into Venice. The choice of conveyance will depend upon your budget and your inclination. The Vaporetti are the most reasonable. Similar to river buses, the Vaporetti leave regularly from St Mark's Square for the approximately half-hour ride to the Piazzale Roma. The Vaporetto Number One stops at most of the little docks along the route whereas Vaporetto Number Two is an express boat that stops at only a few major points. The Motoscafi are motorboats that duck through the back canals and usually take about fifteen minutes to the Piazzale Roma. The Motoscafi are like private cabs and are much more expensive than the "bus", but can be very convenient, especially if your hotel has a private motor boat landing. The most deluxe mode of transportation is by private Gondola: however, these are very expensive and usually take about an hour to reach the Piazzale Roma.

Once you have retrieved your car from the parking garage, head north from Venice toward TREVISO, which requires about an hour's drive. If time allows, stop here. Stroll through this picturesque city spider-webbed with canals and surrounded by 15th-century ramparts. Perhaps have a cup of coffee or a bite of lunch before heading north toward Asolo. Treviso is famous for its arcaded streets, churches lavishly decorated with frescos, and many painted houses. You might want to climb the ramparts for a view of the Alps beckoning you on. From Treviso it is approximately another hour to Asolo. However, just a few miles before you reach Asolo you see signs for the town of MASER where the VILLA DI MASER (some of your books might use the name of VILLA BARARO) is located. This is a splendid villa designed by Palladio and fabulously decorated with frescos by Paolo Veronese. This elegant villa has erratic days and hours when it is open to the public—usually in late afternoons on Tuesdays, Saturdays and Sundays. However, it is only about one mile out of your way, so well worth a detour to investigate. There is also a very interesting museum of old carriages and antique cars at Villa di Maser.

Your prize tonight is ASOLO, a gem of a medieval village snuggled on the side of a hill with exquisite views of the countryside. As you drive toward Asolo the terrain does not seem to hold much promise—just modern towns and industry, but then the road winds up a lovely hillside and into the tiny village which encompasses a delightful combination of a "real" town of colorful fruit stands, candy shops, and the neighborhood grocer for those lucky few who live in Asolo; plus, gorgeous shops with exquisite merchandise for the tourist. Of course a castle adorns the hill above the village—mostly in ruins but setting the proper stage. Naturally, there is a wonderful cathedral dominating the square, just as it should. You will find all this plus vineyards and olive trees on the hillsides and the scent of roses in the air. No wonder Robert Browning fell in love with Asolo and chose it as his home. It might not be possible for all to live here, but at least you have the marvelous option of staying at the VILLA CIPRIANI, an enchanting, villa that was once Robert Browning's home. Here you can dream on the peaceful terrace in the evening and watch the soft lights paint the distant villa-dotted hills in mellow shades of gold.

Hotel Villa Cipriani
Asolo

DESTINATION II   CORTINA

There are a couple of towns that are worth seeing before leaving the Asolo area. If brandy holds a special interest for you, visit BASSANO DEL GRAPPA, an old town famous for its production of grappa (or brandy). The town is also a pottery center. However, it is rather large, and, in our estimation, much less interesting than MAROSTICA, a tiny town just a few miles farther. If you are in this area in September, check your calendar and consider a stop in Marostica because during the first part of September (in alternate years) the central square is transformed into a giant chess board and local citizens become the human chess pieces. Even if it isn't the year of the chess game, Marostica is a picturesque little medieval town encircled by ramparts whose pretty central square is formed by colorful buildings and castle walls. There is also a second castle guarding the town from the top of the hill.

As you head north into the Dolomites there are various routes from which to choose. The major highway heads north through Feltre and Belluno and then on to Cortina. However, if the day is nice and your spirit of adventure is high, there is really nothing more fun than the "back roads" through the mountains. Journey through tiny hamlets and gorgeous mountain valleys far from the normal tourist path; always keeping a map accessible so that you don't wind up hopelessly lost.

Hotel Menardi
Cortina d'Ampezzo

You might want to travel casually and choose your own little country inn in one of the lovely little valleys of the Dolomites, but if you are making reservations, a good choice for an overnight stop is CORTINA D'AMPEZZO. This is not a small town. It has grown into a large tourist center due to its excellent skiing facilities: however, the location is truly superb, with gigantic granite peaks ringing the town. In Cortina there are many hotels. One with a history that dates back far before the skiing craze is the Hotel MENARDI. According to the Menardi family, their small hotel was originally a peasant farm house located along one of the main mountain passes. Because so many travellers stopped seeking shelter for the night—more often than not in the hay loft—the house gradually became an inn. Times have changed. Today the Menardi is a proper hotel where the guests sleep in comfortable beds with fine linens and down comforters, and all the bedrooms have private baths. However, much of the original atmosphere remains, with beautiful country antiques cleverly incorporated into the decor. The dining room serves excellent meals and the total ambiance reflects the personal warmth and caring of the Menardi family. Although the Menardi was originally a farmhouse, civilization has crept in and today the inn is located on the north side of Cortina directly on the main highway heading toward Toblach.

DESTINATION III   TIERS–ST ZYPRIAN (*Tires–San Cipriano*)

When it is time to leave Cortina, take the Old Dolomite Road heading west from Cortina toward Bolzano. Quite frankly, we think this is one of the most stunning regions of Italy—the mountains are truly breathtaking. Our favorite treat on any research trip to Italy is exploring the tiny back roads in the Dolomites in an effort to add a wider choice of places for you to stay. Look on map 2 in the back of this guide to find our selection of hamlets where we have discovered small inns. Read about each of them and decide where you want to spend the night—anyone of them would make a good base for walking and soaking in the beauty of these soaring, saw-tooth mountain peaks. Before leaving Cortina, buy a very detailed map of the region because this is a confusing area for driving. Added to the confusion of finding your way is the fact that most of the towns have two names: one Italian and one Austrian (before the first World War this section of Italy belonged to the Austrian Empire and most of the towns have retained their original name along with their new one).

We suggest an overnight sojourn in the especially scenic village of St Zyprian (*San Cipriano*), tucked into the mountains just a few kilometers from Tires (*Tiers*). However, no matter which town you decide to choose for your mountain interlude, you will leave Cortina via the historic Dolomite Road originally used by the merchants of Venice on their way to Germany.

Pensione Stefaner
St Zyprian-Tiers
(San Cipriano-Tires)

From Cortina follow the highway S 48 is it leaves the valley floor and climbs over a windswept barren pass surrounded by towering granite peaks. The road then drops into a valley before climbing again to conquer the Pordoi Pass and then down into the Fassa Valley. About 12 kilometers beyond Canazei, highway S 48 splits off to the south. At this point, keep to your right and continue west on S 241 which goes through Vigo di Fassa. From the turnoff onto S 241, it is about 10 further to where you turn right on the road leading to Bolzano by way of Tiers (*Tires*). This road loops over the mountains and then drops down to an idyllic meadow where St. Zyprian (*San Cipriano*) located. As you drive into town, you will see a signpost on your right indicating the Pensione Stefaner, a simple chalet-style inn that is run by the gracious young Villgrattner family.

If you enjoy the out of doors, plan to spend at least several days in the Dolomites so that you can enjoy the splendor of the mountains. Join other travellers from throughout Europe who come to trek the well-marked trails that feather out into the hills. (At gift shops or tourist offices, you can purchase detailed hiking maps that show every little path available.)

DESTINATION IV   MERANO

When you depart St Zyprian, follow the road sign-posted to Bolzano. Before you reach Bolzano, watch for signs to the E6. Get on the expressway heading north in the direction of the Brenner Pass. Soon after getting on the expressway, there is an exit for BRESSANONE. Try to allow time to stop in Bressanone for lunch because this small city has much to offer: a walled medieval town ringed by mountains, it has a charming little village square plus a river (lined on both banks by promenades) meandering through its center. Bressanone hides another treasure, the HOTEL ELEFANT. This inn is famous for its exquisite cuisine. In its beautiful dining rooms only the freshest foods and wines are served—usually from the hotel's own farms and vineyards. But the hotel also has an intriguing tale: In 1550, King John III of Portugal sent, as a special gift, an elephant to Emperor Ferdinand of Austria Well, it seems this "gift" grew weary of walking by the time it arrived in Bressanone and so was housed at the local inn—you guessed it, the Elefant. The story alone merits a stop, but the joy is that the Elefant also retains so much character and serves such excellent food.

From Bressanone continue north for a short distance on the expressway toward the Brenner Pass. Then near Vipiteno, exit and head southwest along a twisting road that maneuvers along the Monte Giovo Pass as it twists its way through the mountains and then drops down into the valley to follow the Passiria River which winds a path into Merano.

NOTE: If your destination is Austria, then at Vipiteno continue north on the expressway for the short drive to the Brenner Pass leading into Austria.

In MERANO the CASTEL FREIBERG is an enchanting fairytale castle that majestically dominates the surrounding countryside from its hillside perch. This fabulous castle has everything: setting, view, marvelous architecture, gourmet food, beautiful rooms, priceless antiques, pool, tennis, and an efficient, friendly management.

Castel Freiberg
Merano

DESTINATION V   SAN VIGILIO

It is a short drive south from Merano to Bolzano where you will join again the expressway (E7), but this time head south toward Trent, best known as the town where the Catholic council met in the 16th Century to establish important articles of faith that emphasized the authority of the Catholic church.

Locanda San Vigilio
San Vigilio

Leave the freeway at Trent and head west on 45 toward the small, but lovely, green LAKE TOBLINO that is enhanced by a superb castle on its north shore where you can stop for lunch. From Toblino head south on the pretty country road, lined with fruit trees and vineyards, heading directly south toward Lake Garda, Italy's largest lake. When you come to ARCO, the road splits. Take the road to the left and continue south to Lake Garda and then follow 249 as it curves along the eastern shore of the lake.

About 4 kilometers beyond the town of Torri d'Benaco, turn right when you see San Vigilio sign posted. There is a gate where you will be stopped by an attendant who will want you to pay for parking (San Vigilio is also a park). Say you are a guest at the hotel and you will be allowed to pass. Drive as far as you can and then park your car. Walk down the path. Turn left at the stately villa (glimpsed through tall gates), and follow the lane until it dead-ends at the LOCANDA SAN VIGILIO, a 16th-century stone building, so close to the water's edge that waves lap beneath the windows. With such a setting, it is not surprising that Winston Churchill used to come here to paint. Inside, you will not be disappointed. The rooms are tastefully decorated with country antiques complemented by color coordinated fabrics. If you want to splurge, ask for a suite overlooking the lake, but no matter which room you choose, they are all most appealing. There is a romantic dining room where you can eat in your own little niche by a window overlooking the lake.

When you are ready to sightsee, drive a few kilometers further south along the lake to GARDA. Park your car and take one of the ferries or hydrofoils that ply the lake. If you have the time, choose a different destination each day—perhaps planning to have a bite of lunch at an enticing little lakeside cafe. If have time for only one adventure, visit SIRMIONE, a wonderful walled village at the south end of Lake Garda positioned at the end of a miniature peninsula that proudly pokes its head into the lake. During the summer this town is absolutely bursting with tourists, but you can easily understand why: this is another one of Italy's "stage setting" villages, almost too perfect to be true. If you take the ferry or hydrofoil to Sirmione, your boat will dock in the center of the town and you can stroll through the little boutiques, perhaps have lunch at one of the beautiful terrace cafes overlooking the lake, and explore the tiny island-like village. If you want to go to the tip of the peninsula, there are small motorized trams that take you there.

If time permits, take the ferry to RIVA on the northern shore of the lake. Although, much of the town is of new construction, the medieval core with its Piazza III Novembre and 13th-century Tower of Apponale is fun to see. A good place to eat lunch is on the terrace of the HOTEL SOLE, located directly across from the boat dock.

Another excursion is by car to GARDONE RIVIERA (on the western shore of the lake) to see a nearby museum, the VITTORIALE, once the home of Gabriele D'Annunzio, the celebrated Italian poet. (For those of us who love stories of romance, D'Annunzio is also famous for his love affair with Eleanora Duse.) While there, if you enjoy gourmet food, the pink and white VILLA FIORDALISO, located right on the lake, is a well-known restaurant. The Villa Fiordaliso also has a tidbit of historical romance—this was once the hide-away of Mussolini and his mistress, Claretta. For a simpler meal, just a few kilometers further north along the lake at Gargnano-Villa, you can enjoy a wonderful seafood lunch on the sun-drenched deck of the Baia d'Oro.

DESTINATION VI   BELLAGIO

It might be easier to leave the Locanda San Vigilio knowing that another beautiful lakefront hotel, the GRAND HOTEL VILLA SERBELLONI on Lake Como, awaits your arrival. The Villa Serbelloni will be a nice contrast because although both are on the lakefront, the Locanda San Vigilio is small and intimate whereas the Villa Serbelloni is grand and imposing.

On your way from Lake Garda to Lake Como, stop at BERGAMO, about an hour's drive west on the A4. As you approach Bergamo it will not look worth a stop—but it is. The shell of the city is deceiving because it hides a lovely kernel, the Cita Alta, or high city. The lower part of Bergamo is modern and congested, but the old medieval city snuggled on the top of the hill holds such treasures as the Piazza Vecchia, the Colleoni Chapel, and the Church of St Mary Major. Should you want to time your stop in Bergamo with lunch, there are several excellent restaurants. A suggestion would be at the Agnello d'Oro, a cozy, charming 17th-century inn in the Cita Alta.

From Bergamo it is a short drive on to BELLAGIO, a medieval port located at the tip of a peninsula dividing the lower section of Lake Como into two lakes, Lake Como on the west and Lake Lecco on the east. Your hotel, the GRAND HOTEL VILLA SERBELLONI, is found behind gates opening onto the main square of Bellagio. It is a large imposing "old-world" style palace hotel offering everything you could wish for in a lakeside interlude—tennis, swimming pool, boat excursions, private beach, and more. The Villa Serbelloni is very ornate, still retaining its glory of bygone days—it is almost overwhelming with its soaring, intricately painted ceilings, heavy chandeliers, and fabulous sweeping staircase. The setting of the Villa Serbelloni is superb and overshadows what might be perceived as the slightly "faded elegance" of the hotel's decor. NOTE: For a less expensive hotel, the family-owned and managed HOTEL FLORENCE in Bellagio is very pleasant.

Villa Serbelloni
Bellagio

Just a few steps from the hotel lies charming, medieval Bellagio where you can meander through the village or walk to the pier for one of the boats that will take you to all corners of the lake. What a wonderful excursion. Lake Como is absolutely beautiful—especially the lower eastern branch of the lake called Lake Lecco where cliffs enclose the shorelines like gorgeous walls and give a fjord-like beauty to the area. There are numerous romantic steamers that glide in and out of the picturesque, softly hued little hamlets dotting the lake shore. You can settle onto a steamer equipped with bar and restaurant and from your armchair lazily enjoy the constantly changing, but always intriguing shoreline as the boat maneuvers in and out of the colorful little harbors, past elegant private villas, by postcard-pretty villages. From Bellagio you can also step on board one of the swift hydrofoils that will whisk you about the lake. Or, you can put your car right on the ferry to either Cadenabbia on the western shore of Lake Como or Varenna on the eastern shore. With Bellagio as a base there are several sightseeing possibilities. An excursion to visit the VILLA CARLOTTA, a fairytale-like 18th-century palace—worthy of the Prussian Princess Carlotta for whom it was named—is enjoyable. You can take the car ferry from Bellagio to Cadenabbia on the western shore. From there it is just a short drive along the beautiful tree lined Via del Paradiso to the Villa Carlotta that is encircled by its own gorgeous park of terraced gardens.

DESTINATION VII   ISOLA DEI PESCATORI

NOTE: Should your plans call for ending your Italian sojourn and heading on into Switzerland this would be an excellent point to begin your journey. Head north along Lake Como and on to Chiavenna where you then turn east for the short drive (only about 10 kilometers) to the Swiss border. From there it is a lovely drive through the Engadine Valley to St Moritz.

Continuing on toward LAKE MAGGIORE, take advantage of the expressways to make your drive as easy as possible because there is usually heavy traffic in this part of Italy. It is best to head directly south from Bellagio to pick up the freeway in the direction of Milan. Keep on the bypass which skirts to the north of Milan and follow the freeway northwest to Lake Maggiore. When you reach the lake continue along the western shore to STRESA. It seems only suitable that for a "Mountain and Lake Adventure" one of your hotels should be located on an island in a lake—so we have chosen for you one of the Borromean Islands, ISOLA DEI PESCATORI (Fisherman's Island), located in Lake Maggiore. This is an enchanting little island with twisting, narrow alley-like streets and colorful fishermen's cottages. As the name implies, this is still an active fishing village. During the tourist season the island teems with people and the streets are lined with rather tacky souvenir shops, but it is hard to dull the charm of this quaint town.

Hotel Verbano
Isola dei Pescatori

Isola dei Pescatori can be reached by ferry from Stresa, Baveno, or Pallanza, but the most convenient of these is Stresa from where there are frequent scheduled departures to the island. Take one of the public ferries from Stresa to Isola dei Pescatori. The scheduled ferries are very reasonable in contrast to the private speed boats which are extremely costly. Your best choice for a place to stay here is the HOTEL VERBANO. This is not a deluxe hotel but its setting is superb, and over the years (since we first visited) the decor of this most romantic hotel has improved enormously. The bedrooms are pleasantly decorated, but lovely vistas are their most enchanting feature. The view from the terrace is also outstanding. It is here that guests enjoy dining while overlooking the lake. The food is delicious, and the service of the Zacchera family, who own and manage the Verbano, is warm and gracious. This tiny archipelago consisting of Isola Bella (Beautiful Island), Isola dei Pescatori (Fisherman's Island), and Isola Madre (Mother Island) are world-famous for their dramatic palaces and spectacular, fragrant gardens. How smug you will feel to settle into your room and then enjoy a drink on the lovely terrace while watching the last of the tourists hustle onto the boat for shore, leaving you to enjoy the sunset. NOTE: the closest island is Isola Bella—be sure to allow enough time to visit its sumptuous palace and glorious terraced gardens before returning to the mainland.

DESTINATION VIII   CHAMPOLUC

DETOUR: Should your next destination be Zermatt, Switzerland, then it is time to leave Italy by heading north in the direction of Domodossolo. About 16 kilometers beyond Domodossolo you arrive at Iselle where you drive your car piggyback style onto the train and ride in your car as you zigzag through the fabulous Simplon Tunnel and emerge about 20 minutes later in Brig.

From Verbano drive south to the main freeway and head west toward Turin. Before reaching Turin watch for the signs and take the branch of the expressway heading toward Aosta. When you come to Verres, leave the highway and take the small road north to CHAMPOLUC, an hour's drive. The road follows the Evancon River as it cuts its path through the mountains. At first the valley is quite steep and narrow and then opens up into wide meadows lazily stretching out on both sides of the river. In early summer the meadows are truly lovely, blanketed in brilliantly colored wildflowers.

Just before the road leaves Champoluc you will see a marker for the ANNA MARIA. At this sign turn to the right and follow the road for a very short drive up the hill until you see the hotel. It is beautifully located amid the pine trees and has views in every direction of the spectacular mountains. The Villa Anna Maria is a small chalet-style inn. The dining room is cozy and inviting with gay red checked curtains at the windows and rustic Alpine-style carved wooden chairs. The bedrooms, although small, all have private bathrooms and are very appealing with paneled walls and a country flavor.

Villa Anna Maria
Champoluc

When it is time to leave Champoluc you have two options if you want to travel into Switzerland. First you must drive back to the main expressway and head west. In about a half hour you will come to Aosta at which point you can leave the expressway for the road leading north to the San Bernardino tunnel and into Switzerland's Rhone Valley. Or, by continuing on the expressway west through the village of Courmayeur, you arrive at the Mont Blanc tunnel which delivers you briefly into France, and then on to Geneva within an hour via main highway. Of course, by taking the short drive to Milan you can easily "tie in" with another Italian holiday suggested in this guide.

Rome to Milan via the Italian Riviera

SWITZERLAND

AUSTRIA

FRANCE

MILAN
Pavia Carthusian Monastery

Genoa
Camogli
Chiavari
Carrara
PORTOFINO
Cinque Terre
La Spezia
LUCCA
FLORENCE
Pisa

ROME

⊙ **OVERNIGHT STOPS**

Rome to Milan via the Italian Riviera

This itinerary includes one of the most picturesque jewels of Italy, the Italian Riviera, where not only are there charming towns snuggled into small coves along the shoreline, but the road itself is a masterpiece of engineering. The coastal highway along the Riviera "bridges" for miles—high in the sky above the ravines—and "tunnels" in and out of the cliffs rising steeply from the sea. The original title for this itinerary was "Coastal Route from Rome to Milan," but after we personally experienced the drive, the route and the name were changed. There is an expressway partially following the coast from Rome to Pisa, but until this is finished the road is one of total frustration with a solid line of trucks and cars making the journey undesirable. Far easier, and actually more scenic, is to take the expressway north from Rome to Florence through the gorgeous Tuscany hills then to head west on to Pisa and finally travel on via the coast to Genoa and Milan. It is impossible to include all of the towns that dot the coastline, but after ducking on and off the freeway ourselves, we have tried to include some of the most charming.

ORIGINATING CITY   ROME

This itinerary begins in ROME, a favorite of all and a wonderful introduction to Italy. In the hotel section of this guide there are many suggestions for accommodations to suit your taste and budget. It would take this entire guide just to give you a taste of what Rome has to offer: the Roman Forum, the Colosseum, St Peter's Basilica, the Vatican, the Spanish Steps, the Arch of Constantine, the Pantheon—these are just a few of the places you must not miss. The whole of Rome is a virtual museum. Buy a paper-back guide book at one of the many bookstores or tourist stands to plan what you want to see and do.

Rome has a rich selection of places to stay. Browse through the hotel section in the back of this guide where we describe those hotels we think are especially appealing. Make a reservation in advance because space is very tight—particularly during the busy tourist season. Plan to stay in Rome for several days at least, then when you are saturated with the overwhelming sights and are ready to continue your journey, buy a detailed city map to assist you in maneuvering out of the city and onto the magnificent expressway heading north.

DESTINATION I   LUCCA

From Rome, take the A1 north toward Florence. This itinerary assumes that you have already visited Florence, certainly one of the highlights of any Italian holiday. If not, you will assuredly want to stop in Florence for several days—there are many wonderful places to stay suggested in the hotel section in the back of this guide. Otherwise, bypass to the south of Florence and take the A11 west and continue on toward PISA. You will probably want to stop in Pisa for a few pictures of the Leaning Tower, but frankly Pisa is somewhat overrated. It is such a solid mass of tourists and souvenir shops during the summer season that you can hardly find a place to park before trying to squirm your way to the central piazza. Admittedly, the duomo, gleaming white with its companion leaning tower, is impressive, so if you have never seen it, do stop. But even more interesting and not nearly so "touristy" is the extremely picturesque city of LUCCA located only a few kilometers to the north. This too is an ancient city, even more perfectly preserved than its neighbor, Pisa. Completely surrounding the city is enormous wall—a wall so wide that it even shelters pretty small parks and a road that runs along the top.

Villa la Principessa
Lucca

As you are driving from Pisa to Lucca along the old road, about 4 kilometers before you arrive in Lucca there will be signs to a handsome villa just to your left, the VILLA LA PRINCIPESSA. At one time a stately private villa, La Principessa now is a deluxe hotel set in a beautiful park with a pretty swimming pool (a welcome bonus after a long day of sightseeing). The inside of the villa could be considered somewhat flamboyantly decorated in terms of color schemes, but the setting is lovely and the building beautiful. The price tag is, however, a very expensive one, and if it does not suit your pocketbook, consider instead the BED & BREAKFAST OF TUSCANY in Montevettolini.

When you leave the Villa la Principessa, return to the expressway and head north on the A12 toward Genoa. Along the way you will see what appears to be a glacier shimmering white in the foothills of the Apuan Alps that rise to the right of the highway. This is not snow at all, but rather your introduction to the renowned white Italian marble. You might enjoy a detour to visit some of the marble mines. Exit the highway at CARRARA and take the winding drive up into the hills to the ancient village of COLONNATA—famous through the ages for its marvelous white marble. As you wander this tiny town you will be following the footsteps of Michelangelo, who used to come to Carrara to choose huge blocks of marble from which to carve his masterpieces.

Leaving Carrara you will enjoy an adventure of an entirely different kind—exploring the five little isolated towns on the coast called CINQUE TERRE. This area is quickly becoming linked with civilization so do not tarry if you love the thrill of discovering old fishing villages still untouched by time.

To begin this portion of your journey take the small road from Carrara west returning to the main highway and continuing on to the port of LA SPEZIA, a large seaport and navy town. From here you might want to take the short drive to the tip of the peninsula south of La Spezia to visit the old fishing village of PORTOVERERE that clings to the steep rocks rising from the sea. This was one of Lord Byron's haunts when he lived across the bay at San Terenzo. You will then need to return to La Spezia to continue your journey.

The Cinque Terre used to be five completely isolated fishing villages on a stretch of land between La Spezia to the south and LEVANTO to the north. First only a footpath connected these tiny villages, then a train was installed, and now real civilization is encroaching with a road under construction that will open them all to the world of tourism. Three of the towns are accessible now by road. From La Spezia you can travel to RIOMAGGIORE and then on to MANOROLA. From the northern approach of Levanto you can travel by road to the first town of MONTEROSSO. Still completely cut off from car traffic are the ancient fishing hamlets in between—VERNAZZA and CORNIGLIA. It is best to drive as far as possible from La Spezia stopping first at Riomaggiore and then on to Manorola. Upon arrival you can let your mood, the time, and the weather dictate your explorations. You can continue on by hiking the spectacular trails connecting the villages, by taking the small ferry between them, by using the train—or, best yet, by combining all these options. If you have time to see only one of the scenic towns, Vernazza, which clings perilously to a rocky promontory forming a tiny harbor, is perhaps the most scenic.

Hotel Splendido
Portofino

After Cinque Terre, continue north along the coast. If you are in a hurry, return to the freeway A12. Or, if time is not a problem, continue along the coast via the towns of SESTRI LEVANTE and CHIAVARI to SAN MARGHERITA. At San Margherita take the small road south for the short drive to the "picture book" village of PORTOFINO. This last section of the road, especially in summer, is jammed with traffic, but the plum at the end is worth the trials endured to reach it. Portofino is by no means undiscovered, but it is well-deserving of its accolades.

As you approach Portofino, watch for the entrance sign for the HOTEL SPLENDIDO. There is a guard at the entrance and only those with reservations are allowed to follow the lane as it winds up the hill to the magnificent villa-style hotel. Be prepared: the deluxe Splendido is a super expensive hotel whose prices include breakfast and dinner. But what a gorgeous setting. The hotel is perched in the hills above the Portofino with breathtaking views of the sea and the harbor. A swimming pool and tennis courts nestle below the hotel and enchanting little paths thread their way through the gardens, offering strategically placed benches for quiet moments to savor the stunning view. It is an easy walk into Portofino if you can bear to leave this haven.

Portofino is considered an Italian national treasure and it truly is a jewel. Her tiny harbor is filled with glamorous yachts, small ferries, and colorful fishing boats. In the center of town is a small square. Enveloping the harbor are colorful tall and narrow fishermen's cottages painted in warm colors of sienna, ochre, and pink and all sporting green shutters. Bright flower boxes accent the windows and the laundry flaps gaily in the breeze. Vivid reflections of these quaint little houses shimmer in the emerald water. Beyond the town the heavily forested, beautiful green hills rise steeply to complete this idyllic scene.

NOTE: While staying in Portofino, if you appreciate gourmet dining, drive south to one of Italy's finest restaurants, the CA'PEO, located in Chiavari a Leivi. You must make prior reservations because Franco and his wife Melly only take guests who call ahead since the food is specially prepared depending upon how many will be dining: telephone (0185) 319090. The Ca'Peo, whose origins date back to a very old farmhouse, is located high in the hills overlooking the coast. Be forewarned, the meals are *VERY* expensive, but the lodging rates are far more reasonable than at the Hotel Splendido, so if you enjoy fine food and wines and the price of dining is not a factor, you can visit Portofino instead of over-nighting there and stay at the Ca'Peo which offers a limited number of suites.

NOTE: For those of you travelling to the French Riviera, we wish you "adieu" in Portofino. From Portofino continue to follow the coastal highway west to Genoa along the Italian Riviera into the principality of Monaco and across the border to France.

For the rest of "our group", after leaving Portofino return to the main highway and continue west for about 30 kilometers to Genoa. Bypass Genoa and instead, as you circle the city, watch for the freeway A7 going north to Milan.

An interesting detour on the last leg of your journey is the PAVIA CARTHUSIAN MONASTERY (*CERTOSA DI PAVIA*). Probably the simplest way to find it would be to watch for the turnoff to Pavia (about 96 kilometers north of Genoa). At this point take the road east to Pavia and from there go north about 9 kilometers to the Carthusian Monastery. Lavishly built in the 15th Century, this splendid monastery is claimed by some to be one of the finest buildings in Italy. (Check carefully the days and hours open—it is usually closed on Mondays and for several hours midday.) The outside of the monastery is lavishly designed with colorful marble and intricate designs. Inside, the small cloisters are especially charming with 122 arches framed by beautiful terra cotta moldings. There is also a baroque fountain within, plus several small gardens. Next to the monastery you will find the former Palace of the Dukes of Milan that is now a museum. After your tour of the monastery it is approximately 26 kilometers farther north to MILAN.

The outskirts of Milan are not much fun: frustrating traffic and not too pretty commercial buildings. But the heart of Milan has much to offer. If you enjoy shopping (and Milan has some of the finest in Italy), the splendid glass-domed shopping arcade, lined with beautiful boutiques and cozy cafes, is outstanding. After a stroll through the arcade, you emerge into an imposing square dominated by the truly spectacular Duomo, the third largest cathedral in the world. Not only is the size impressive, but this sensational cathedral has a multi-colored marble facade enhanced by over 100 slender spires piercing the sky. Also, a must to see is Milan's opera house. Every opera buff knows about La Scala. Even if you have not been an opera enthusiast in the past, if you are in Milan during the opera season (which usually runs from December to May) write ahead and try to get tickets—the theater is stunning and an experience not to be missed. When it is not opera season, there is usually some other performance or concert featured. If you haven't purchased seats in advance, you can try to buy them the day of the performance (the ticket office is located down a flight of stairs to the left of the opera house).

Unfortunately, Milan does not offer a wealth of charming places to stay: most are modern, commercial hotels, seemingly way over-priced, with minimal old world appeal. Happily (if your budget can handle a deluxe hotel) there is an exception, the intimate, beautifully managed, HOTEL PIERRE MILAN, which abounds in antiques and charm.

Hotel Pierre Milan
Milan

Rome to Milan via the Italian Riviera

Highlights of
Southern Italy & Sicily

Rome
Anzio
Nettuno
Abbey of Monte Cassino
Dubrovnik
Corfu & Greece
Bari
Castellana Caves
Pompeii
RAVELLO
Naples
Salerno
ALBEROBELLO
Potenza
Capri
Matera
Taranto
Brindisi
Paestum
Sibari
TROPEA
Erice
PALERMO
Messina
Trapani
Villa San Giovanni
Cefalu
Marsala
Segesta
TAORMINA
Enna
Catania
Selinunte
Agrigento
Piazza Armerina
Siracuse

◉ OVERNIGHT STOPS

Suggested Side Trips — — —

73

Highlights of Southern Italy & Sicily

Having visited the famous trio of Rome, Florence, and Venice, most tourists think that they have "seen" Italy. If childhood geography lessons call forth such names as Pompeii, Herculaneum and Paestum, all too frequently the urge to visit these jewels of archaeological wonders is lost in the misconception that southern Italy is an uninteresting destination. What a waste. Southern Italy has fascinating ruins, gorgeous coastlines, beautiful medieval walled villages, lovely beaches, marvelous hilltowns, and some of the most unusual sights in Italy. Best yet, what fun to return home and casually mention to your dinner partner, who thinks he has been everywhere, that you think the Emerald Grotto on the Amalfi coast far exceeds the beauty of the Blue Grotto of Capri or that the Greek ruins at Paestum outshine many found in Greece or that you are still haunted by the mysterious town of Alberobello.

Therefore, for those of you who have already seen the fantastic highlights of northern Italy, we take pleasure in presenting to you the best of southern Italy. This itinerary makes a circle of southern Italy in order to suit the travel needs of a wide selection of tourists. Follow the entire route or select the portion best for you since this itinerary lends itself especially well for the traveller who wants to take only a segment. As an example, the journey from Rome to Brindisi is a popular one for the lucky tourist on his way to Greece. Or the west coast is a popular drive for the tourist who wants to visit Sicily and then return to Rome by air or ferry. And most popular of all is the segment from Rome to the Amalfi Drive. So, this itinerary allows you to custom tailor your journey and gives you many wonderful tips on what to see along the way.

ORIGINATING CITY   ROME

ROME is a most convenient starting point to begin a tour of southern Italy. Rome Airport is the destination of planes from all over the world and here passengers begin their "Roman Holiday." In Rome you can immerse yourself in a wealth of history, art, architecture, museums, and monuments—and build a foundation for the sights that will be encountered on your journey southward. Stop at a magazine stand or a book store and buy a map of Rome showing the major sights to see and a booklet describing the major points of interest, hours open, etc. Rome is virtually an open air museum—a fascinating ancient Roman city.

Because there is such a wide selection of accommodations in Rome in various price categories and locations, it seems most practical for you to choose the hotel that best suits your personality and budget from the hotel description section in the back of this guide. You will find that Rome has many excellent hotels and, even though the city is large, most of the hotels are still within walking distance of both shopping and sightseeing highlights. Or, if you do not like to walk, ask the concierge at your desk to call you a taxi or direct you to the nearest subway station. (Rome's main subway line stretches across the city—conveniently connecting most of the places of interest for the tourist.)

When leaving the city by car, bear in mind that Rome always has a monumental traffic problem. Within the city look for strategically placed signs that indicate that there is a expressway ahead. It might be quite a distance, but be patient as these signs will lead you to the outskirts of Rome to the highway encircling the city. Follow the expressway around to the exit for the major expressway heading south, highway A2. When you reach this expressway continue south for approximately 128 kilometers to the exit for CASSINO. Actually you will be able to spot your destination from several miles away because the ABBEY OF MONTE CASSINO crowns the top of a large mountain to the left of the highway as you drive south. When you reach Cassino turn off the expressway. The road that winds up to the summit of the mountain to the Abbey of Monte Cassino is clearly marked about midway through town. This abbey, founded by St Benedict in 529 AD, is extremely interesting both religiously and historically. For war historians the abbey is very significant because this is where the Germans held out against the Allied forces for almost a year in World War II. When the mountain was finally conquered in May 1944, it opened the way for Allied forces to move into Rome. As you read your history books it seems strange that one fort could hold out for so long, but when you see the abbey you understand. It is an enormous building on the crest of a precipitous mountain. In the siege the abbey was almost destroyed but it has been rebuilt according to the original plans.

NOTE: For those of you who for sentimental or historical reasons are especially interested in World War II, there is another destination you might well want to visit in this day's journey. ANZIO is a town on the coast about 56 kilometers south of Rome and could easily be included as a stop before Cassino. It was at Anzio that the British and the Americans landed in January 1944. The emotional reminder of this terrible war is a few kilometers south at NETTUNO where 8,000 white crosses and stars of David range—row after row across the green lawn. There is a circular drive around the beautifully manicured, park-like grounds where you will also find a memorial chapel and small war museum. For those who lost family or friends during the invasion, there is an information office to the right as you drive in. You can stop here to find out exactly where your loved ones are buried—you will need help because the park is very large.

From Cassino return to the expressway and continue south for about 59 kilometers until you see the sign for POMPEII. Unless you have absolutely NO interest in archaeology you must stop in Pompeii, the city of your childhood geography books, where time was frozen in the year 79 AD for the 25,000 people smothered by ashes from the eruption of Vesuvius. (If you are a dedicated student of archaeology you must also visit the National Archaeological Museum in Naples where many of the artifacts from Pompeii are housed in a magnificent museum.)

Time slips eerily back 2,000 years as you wander the streets of Pompeii and visit the temples, lovely homes, wine shops, bakery, and public baths. There is probably no other place on earth where you can feel so strongly the pulse of ancient days. Many of the private homes have been reconstructed so you can marvel at the lovely inner courtyards, beautiful dining rooms in Pompeii-red with intricate paintings on the walls, fountains, servants' quarters, bath rooms, and gardens. At the entrance to Pompeii there are souvenir stands where you can purchase a guide book to the city, or, if you prefer, you can hire a private guide at the entrance. Pompeii is so fascinating that you might well want to come back to spend a complete day visiting the city and the nearby ruins of Herculaneum that are also very interesting.

Leaving Pompeii, head to the coast in the direction of Sorrento where the AMALFI DRIVE, one of the most beautiful stretches of coast in the world, begins. Be sure to time your journey when there is sufficient daylight because you will want to be sure to glimpse every magnificent vista as well as safely negotiate this extremely twisty and precipitous road.

There are many excellent choices for hotels along the Amalfi Drive. Concentrated in just a few kilometers are some of the most splendid hotels, both budget and luxury, in all of Italy. It is hard to recommend just one town along the way since each is unique. A favorite is the cliff-clinging village of RAVELLO, reached by a road which twists and winds its way up and up and up and then suddenly delivers you in a little village high in the clouds with absolutely dazzling views.

Hotel Palumbo
Ravello

In Ravello there are several wonderful inns—all of which can be heartily recommended, but none can surpass the delightful PALUMBO. You enter into a light and airy reception room brimming with flowers and sunlight. Tucked throughout the inn are cozy little nooks filled with antiques. The inside dining room is charming, but usually meals are taken outside to enjoy the surrounding scenery to the maximum: steep hills covered with vineyards flowing down to the rugged coast where brilliant blue water dances between the rocks. The garden terrace of the Palumbo is an oasis of beauty and quiet enhanced by spectacular views. On an upper level is a rooftop terrace where the sun and views are again offered for the lucky guest. The Palumbo is a real jewel.

Before leaving Ravello you will certainly want to visit some of the other small fishing villages that dot the coast, such as POSITANO and AMALFI. These towns during the season are bursting with tourists, but fun to see.

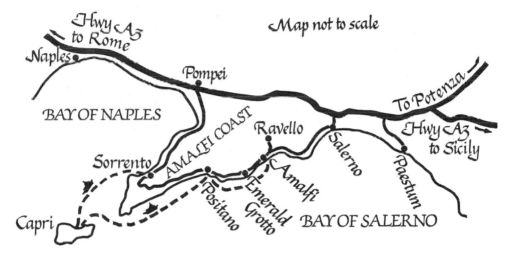

Also, if you have not been able to include an interlude on Capri during your Italian holiday it would be easy to arrange an excursion to this enchanted island from your location on the Amalfi coast. Steamers and hydrofoils depart regularly from Sorrento, Amalfi, and Positano. Ask at the tourist bureau or at your hotel for the schedule. (When the seas are rough it is more difficult to leave from Positano since there is no pier and it is necessary to take a small boat from the shore to the ferry.)

Also along the Amalfi coast is the EMERALD GROTTO, located between the towns of Amalfi and Positano. After parking, you buy a ticket and descend by elevator down the steep cliff to a small rocky terrace. Upon entering the water-filled cave, you will be rowed about the grotto in a small boat while your guide explains how the effect of shimmering green water is created by a secret tunnel allowing sunlight to filter from deep below the surface. The cave is filled with colorful stalactites and stalagmites that further enhance the mysterious mood. There is also a nativity scene below the water that magically appears and then drifts again from view.

DESTINATION II   ALBEROBELLO

When it is time to leave Ravello, there is an efficient expressway south to the "toe" of Italy. But for those who are en route to Brindisi or who have the luxury of time for another adventure, include a detour to the eastern coast, to the wondrous town of ALBEROBELLO.

Start early as there are several sightseeing stops recommended in route First of all, make the short side trip south to visit the spectacular ancient Greek city of PAESTUM. To reach Paestum take the Amalfi coastal road from Ravello to Salerno and then join the expressway for about 19 kilometers until the turnoff for Paestum that is located on a side road about a half-hour drive from the freeway. Magically, as soon as you go through the gates of the ancient city you enter a peaceful environment of a lovely country meadow whose grass is dotted with some of the world's best preserved Greek temples. As you walk the remains of the streets criss-crossing the city, your senses are thrilled by the sound of birds singing and the scent of roses. (Before leaving Paestum you might want to stop for a snack at the MARINI SEA GARDEN, a former villa set in a garden whose gates open onto the west side of the excavation.)

When you rejoin the expressway, continue east for about 22 kilometers until the highway splits. At this point take the left branch heading east toward Potenza. About 112 kilometers beyond the branching of the highway, watch for the exit leading to the town of MATERA. Located about a half-hour drive north of the expressway, Matera is a strange, spooky, ghost town with a weird setting amongst ravines and deep gorges. The old town of Matera clings to the side of a hill crowned by a modern city. To visit the lower "lost city" whose crumbling buildings melt into the rocks is a fascinating experience.

From Matera continue on the road leading northeast to Alberobello. Here are some of the strangest structures in Italy—the Trulli. These are circular stone buildings, usually built in small clusters, standing crisply white with conical slate roofs and whimsical twisted chimneys. Outside ladders frequently lead to upper stories. Often several of these houses are joined together to form a larger complex. The houses are intertwined with cobbled streets. What a strange and fascinating sight. These conical little houses form a jumble of a small village that looks as though it should be inhabited by elves instead of "real" people.

Trulli Houses

For a hotel choice, you should certainly choose the DEI TRULLI. This hotel is located on the outskirts of the trulli village and is made up of a cluster of ancient round houses. These conical dwellings have been made into guest cottages and are scattered around the large, park-like grounds, with pine tree lined paths leading between them. Each bungalow has a living room with fireplace, one or more bedrooms, a bathroom, and a small patio. One of the trulli houses has been transformed into the hotel dining room and another into the office. There is also a swimming pool and a tiny park with play equipment for children.

*Hotel dei Trulli
Alberobello*

The trulli houses are not confined to the town of Alberobello although this is where you will find them composing an entire village. In fact, the trulli houses you will see in the vicinity of Alberobello are sometimes more interesting than those in the town itself. As you drive along the small roads you will spot gorgeous villas cleverly converted from trulli houses that are now obviously the homes of wealthy Italians. Others are now farmhouses with goats munching their lunch in the front yard. Occasionally you will spot a charming old trulli home cozily nestled in the center of a vineyard. But most fun of all are the trulli homes of the free spirits. Their homes, instead of displaying the typical white exteriors, have been painted a brilliant yellow or pink or bright green with contrasting shutters.

As you are exploring the countryside around Alberobello you might want to take the short drive north to see the CASTELLANA CAVES where in a two-hour tour you will see many rooms of richly colored stalagmites and stalactites.

NOTE: Alberobello is about 72 kilometers from BRINDISI, the popular port from which to take the ferry to Corfu and on to Greece, and only about 56 kilometers from BARI, which is the port to use for ferries to Dubrovnik. So, if your plans are to continue your travel adventures by boat, then Alberobello is most strategically positioned. In both Bari and Brindisi you can turn in your rental car if your holiday in Italy has ended.

However, for the rest of "our tour" the itinerary continues on to the exciting destination of Sicily. When you leave Alberobello take the road south to the coast. Stop to see the ancient port of TARANTO that is connected by a bridge to the modern city of Taranto. Even if you are not interested in ancient history you might enjoy seeing the Italian naval ships—giant gray monsters sitting in the protected harbor.

From Taranto continue along the arch of Italy's boot until you come to Sibari where there is a road leading east to join the main expressway. When you are again on the Highway A3 continue south for only a few kilometers until you come to the exit for the tiny spur that juts up from the toe of Italy's boot, and then continue along the coast toward the town of TROPEA, located near the point of the peninsula.

Just before Tropea, a sign on the right of the road points to the HOTEL BAIA PARAELIOS, a very special hotel that allows you to create the wonderful combination of a beach holiday with a sightseeing tour. The hotel is a cluster of cottages, cleverly spaced at various levels leading down to the beach. Each cottage has a sitting room and one or more bedrooms plus a private terrace. Although the hotel is not old, a definite "inn" feeling prevails. The small reception room at the crest of the slope has pretty prints on the wall, baskets of flowers, a few antiques, and the definite flavor of good taste. The cottages are quite appealing with tiled floors and earth tone colors. On a small terrace as you walk down to the beach is an inviting swimming pool. Other amenities include a beautiful creamy-white sand beach dotted with lounge chairs and a cheerful dining room with an outdoor terrace. Just a few kilometers beyond the hotel (which is officially located in the town of Parghelia) is Tropea, an ancient fishing village perched on the cliffs overhanging the brilliant blue sea.

*Baia Paraelios
Tropea–Parghelia*

Sicily

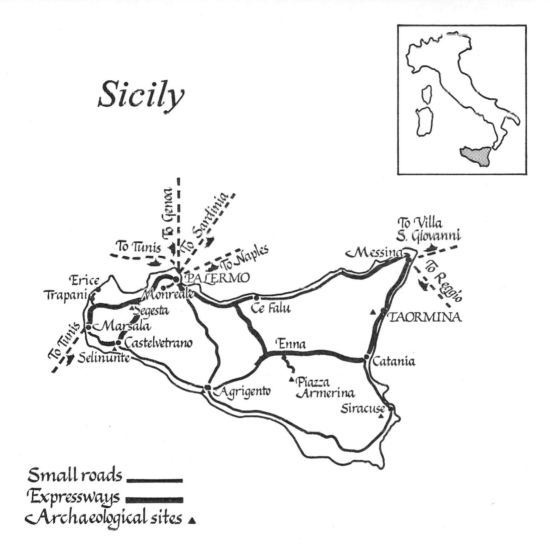

Small roads _____
Expressways ▬▬▬▬
Archaeological sites ▲

You can end your holiday savoring the beauty of Italy's southern coast, enjoying the tranquil beauty of the deserted beaches and the inviting clear water. However, if you are still in the mood to travel, Sicily beckons, just a short drive and boat ride away. Sicily is a treasure of ancient monuments—a must for those who love archaeology. The continuation of this itinerary crosses the narrow channel leading from the tip of the toe over to the island of Sicily.

Upon leaving Baia Paraelios, return to the expressway and continue south the short distance to the tip of the toe and take the exit to Villa San Giovanni. The route to the ferry is clearly marked. The boat ferries leave at least twice an hour for MESSINA, Sicily. After buying your ticket, drive your car to the indicated lane and wait with all the trucks, campers and other cars for the signal to drive onto the boat. When on board you may leave your car and go upstairs to a lounge area where snacks can be purchased while traversing the short channel. In half an hour, the large ferry draws up to the pier in Messina and you drive off to experience some of the most beautifully preserved Greek ruins to be found anywhere in the world.

When the ferry arrives in MESSINA follow the freeway signs to TAORMINA, about a half-hour drive south. Once in town watch for signs to the SAN DOMENICO PALACE which commands a dramatic perch overlooking the sea. The San Domenico Palace is a museum-quality monastery that has been exquisitely converted into a deluxe hotel. Stunning antiques, appropriate to the period, are seen in every nook and corner. If you listen carefully, you can almost hear the soft chant of hooded monks quietly meditating as they walk through the arcaded courtyard. However, the superb amenities of today have been discreetly interspersed with the relics of the past and even a swimming pool now nestles in the garden.

San Domenico Palace
Taormina

The town of Taormina is enchanting, seemingly glued to the top of a small peninsula, it juts out to the sea and then drops steeply to the coast below. Quaint, colorful streets wind through the town where you can browse in the gift shops, visit small churches, enjoy a cappuccino at a little cafe, or simply enjoy the view.

From Taormina follow the freeway south toward CATANIA and PALERMO. Instead of going directly to Palermo you might want to take the approximately 128 kilometer round trip excursion south to SYRACUSE which is an ancient Greek city dating back to 700 BC. The Greeks loved beauty and here overlooking a gorgeous blue bay they built their theaters, temples, and coliseums. Of special interest is an enormous theater over 400 feet across.

ENNA is about an hour's drive west from Catania. Should you want to include another short detour, about 32 kilometers south of Enna is the town of PIAZZA ARMERINA, about 6 kilometers southwest of which there are some excellent mosaics in the remains of an ancient Roman villa—the VILLA OF CASALE. Returning to Enna take the expressway north toward the coast and then head west to PALERMO.

Villa Igiea Grand Hotel
Palermo

Palermo is a large city with horrendous traffic and unsightly new construction. However, it makes a good base from which to explore some of the jewels of Sicily and luckily there is a splendid hotel here, the VILLA IGIEA GRAND HOTEL. Actually, the hotel is much more like a small castle than a villa and is an oasis in a bustling city. The hotel is located on the ocean right next to the harbor. The bedrooms are large and nicely furnished in a traditional motif and those in the rear have a lovely view over the back garden to the sea. There is a pool in the garden that even sports its own miniature Greek temple.

From Palermo there are many fascinating excursions. A circle trip from Palermo includes some of Sicily's finest archaeological wonders. To begin your journey take the expressway west toward TRAPANI. About 8 kilometers after the highway splits you will see a sign for SEGESTA which is located only a few minutes from the expressway. Here in a remote mountain area stands a sensational Greek Doric temple—practically perfect in its preservation. Many experts consider this to be one of the finest Greek Doric temples in the world today. But one of the most superb aspects of this temple is its setting: there is nothing to jar the senses. Reached by a path leading up from the parking area, the temple is located on a small hill with great natural beauty all around. After visiting the temple return to the parking area and follow the signs up the hill for another treat—a small, but splendid Greek theater. Again, the location is what makes this theater so special. What an eye the Greeks had for beauty. The stage is set in such a way that the spectators look out across the mountains to the sea.

Just north of Trapani is the ancient town of ERICE perched on rocks soaring over 2,000 feet in the clouds. This is a fascinating walled city filled with colorful medieval houses.

South of Trapani the road circles the island and passes through MARSALA which gives its name to the famous Marsala wine of the region. Then, on to the next destination, the great Greek ruins at SELINUNTE. As you near Castelvetrano watch for signs for the coastal archaeological site. Here by the ocean are the impressive remains of some of the most gigantic temples left by the Greeks. It is staggering to imagine how the Greeks, more than 2,500 years ago, could have pieced together the huge blocks of rock weighing over

100 tons each. From Selinunte the expressway heads directly north for your return to Palermo.

Another recommended side trip from Palermo is to visit the ancient fishing village of CEFALU built on a rocky peninsula about an hour's drive east from Palermo. Not only is this a very colorful fishing village, complete with brightly hued boats and twisting narrow streets, but there is also a splendid Norman cathedral built by King Roger II in the 12th Century in fulfillment of a promise he made to God for sparing his life during a storm at sea.

Two of Palermo's major sights are luckily only a few miles from the city. In MONREALE, about 8 kilometers south, is an awesome cathedral which is especially famous for its beautiful mosaic panels showing a strong Moorish influence. Reading from left to right, these 130 pictures depict the complete cycle of both the Old and the New Testaments. The bronze doors of the cathedral are beautiful, designed by Bonanno Pisano, a famous 12th-century artist. The other sight close to Palermo is MONTE PELLEGRINO, just west of the city. Here is a cave that has been transformed into a chapel commemorating Santa Rosalia, a Duke's daughter who became a hermit—living and dying in this cave.

There is still another very important archaeological site on Sicily—the ruins of the VALLEY OF THE TEMPLES at ARRGIGENTO. There is no doubt that this ancient Greek city, with the Temple of Juno, the Temple of Concord, the Temple of Hercules, the Temple of Jupiter and the Temple of the Dioscuri, is a marvelous example of the tremendous wealth, power and skills of the ancient Greeks. Because this excursion takes such a long drive (of which only a short portion is freeway) and because there is no excellent inn to recommend for the night, it seems that the wealth of temples that are more easily accessible will probably suffice for all but the most ardent ancient Greek enthusiast.

When it is time to leave Sicily, Palermo is a convenient gateway. From here you can fly to Rome and make a connection to your homeward flight or else you can take a ferry back to Naples, Genoa, Sardinia, or even Tunis.

Hotel Descriptions

There is a fascinating section in southeastern Italy with a collection of strange round white buildings with gray stone conical shaped roofs. These ancient houses seem to be "left over" from some Moorish tribe that must have inhabited this part of Italy long ago. These houses are called "trulli" and are usually seen in groups of two or three. In the town of Alberobello there is actually a whole village of the conical little houses whose jumble of domed roofs, whitewashed walls, and crooked little chimneys create a most unusual sight. Fortunately there is a good hotel in the area that is located within walking distance of the trulli village. Not only is its location excellent, but the hotel captures the mood of the area since it is constructed within some of the trulli houses. Small bungalows are scattered around a large park-like area connected by winding pathways under the pine trees. Each bungalow is actually a suite with a modern bathroom, a living room with fireplace, one or more bedrooms, and a private patio. The suites are spacious but the decor quite simple. The dining rooms and the reception area each occupy their own "trulli". Within the grounds are a pool and children's play yard. If you are on your way to Greece or Yugoslavia you will find the Hotel dei Trulli a convenient choice: very close to Brindisi and Bari, the two major ferry ports.

HOTEL DEI TRULLI
Manager: Luigi Farace
Via Cadore, 28
70011 Alberobello (BA), Italy
tel: (080) 93 23 555 fax: (080) 93 23 560
28 rooms: Double Lire 269,000
Open all year
Credit cards: all major
Restaurant, open daily
68 km NW of Brindisi, 55 km SW of Bari

As the road twists and turns ever further into the wooded hills above Assisi, one can't help but wonder what treasure could await at the trail's end, or, if anyone could possibly have found it before you. What a surprise then to finally turn off the graveled road and discover the parking lot filled with luxury cars. In this secluded hillside setting with a sweeping panorama of wooded hills, worldly cares quickly slip away. Although the hotel is built into a cluster of ancient stone houses (dating back to the 10th Century), all the modern day luxuries are present including a beautiful swimming pool on the right as you enter and, on a lower terrace, tennis courts. Behind the main building is a separate stone house where you find a most appealing lounge with deep green sofas and chairs grouped about a giant fireplace. Doors from the lounge lead into an intimate little bar and beyond to a dining room with honey-colored stone walls, beamed ceiling, and terra cotta floors with tables dressed in the finest of linens. The individually decorated bedrooms sport a rustic, yet elegant, ambiance. The well-equipped bathrooms offer enormous towels, fragrant soaps, hair dryers, and bathrobes. NOTE: to find Hotel "Le Silve di Armenzano" follow the signs from Assisi toward Gualdo-Tadino and immediately as you leave the town-walls of Assisi, watch for and take the road to the right sign-posted Armenzano. When you reach Armenzano, the hotel is well-marked.

ROMANTIK HOTEL "LE SILVE DI ARMENZANO"
Manager: Daniela Taddia
06081 Localita Armenzano, Assisi (PG), Italy
tel: (075) 80 19 000 fax: (075) 80 19 005
15 rooms, Double Lire 325,000*
*Rate includes breakfast and dinner
Closed January & February
Credit cards: all major
Restaurant open daily
Located 15 km E of Assisi
U.S. Rep: Euro-Connection 800-645-3876

The Villa Cipriani is just as I had envisioned in every dream of Italy: an old villa snuggled on a hill, her softly faded exterior emphasized by dark green shutters, masses of roses creeping over trellises, columns adorned with vines, lazy views over rolling green hills, faded ocher-colored walls half hidden by tall cypress trees dotting nearby hilltops, birds singing in the garden, the sentimental rhythmical peal of church bells, a pianist on the terrace playing old love songs, the fragrance of flowers drifting through the air like the finest perfume, a balmy night under the stars—perfection. My impression of a romantic paradise must not have been a unique experience for in the garden was a wedding party. A beautiful bride, a handsome groom; they had fallen in love at the Cipriani and had returned with family and friends from the United States for their marriage. The Villa Cipriani is located in Asolo, a charming, small, medieval, walled hill town less than two hours northwest of Venice. It has an atmosphere so delightful that Robert Browning chose it as a residence. And the home he chose? The Cipriani. Luckily, the home is now a hotel and you, too, can "live" in Asolo. Although the Villa Cipriani is a sophisticated, polished hotel, the warmth of reception is as gracious as in a small, family run inn: the manager, Giuseppe Kamenar, personally sees that all of his guests are properly pampered.

HOTEL VILLA CIPRIANI
Manager: Giuseppe Kamenar
Via Canova, 298
31011 Asolo (TV), Italy
tel: (0423) 5 54 44 fax: (0423) 5 20 95
31 rooms: Double Lire 390,000–430,000
Open all year
Credit cards: all major
Restaurant open daily
65 km NW of Venice, 14 km E of Bassano
U.S. Rep: CIGA 800-221-2340

Asolo is a beautiful medieval town in the low lying hills northwest of Venice, dominated by castle ruins on the hillside above, and filled with charming streets, gothic arcades, and frescoed facades. It is here in this magical town where one of our favorite hotels in Italy, the Villa Cipriani, is secreted in a garden just a short stroll from the center of the village. But since the price tag at the Cipriani does not fit every-one's budget, it is wonderful to now be able to recommend an alternate choice, the Hotel Duse, which had been highly recommended to us by several readers. We were eager to take a look and, when we did so, were pleasantly surprised: this little inn is indeed a "keeper". The location is superb—right in the very center of town, surrounded by romantic little streets lined with elegant shops. The Hotel Duse's management is very personalized yet very professional—friendly, helpful, and eager to please in every way. There is just a tiny reception lobby leading up to the guest rooms, which although not outstanding in their decor, are quite pleasant, each with a private bath, air conditioning, television, direct dial phone and mini bar. All are adequately spacious and furnished exactly the same except for the color scheme–color coordinated fabrics with matching drapes, spreads and chairs, in reds, greens or blues. The bathrooms are nicely equipped, modern and spotlessly clean. Note, ten 10 new rooms are "in the works" which might have been completed by the time of your arrival.

HOTEL DUSE
Manager: Luigi Prudente
Via Browning, 190
31011 Asolo (TV), Italy
tel: (0423) 55 241 fax: (0423) 95 04 04
12 rooms: Double Lire 150,000
Open all year
Credit cards: all major
No restaurant, breakfast only*
*Hosteria Ca Derton restaurant, same ownership
65 km NW of Venice, 14 km E of Bassano

One of the joys of researching a guidebook is to discover a "jewel" of an inn—it is rather like a treasure hunt. Rarely though do we find an excellent hotel which we have not heard of previously. However, the Country House, located on a small lane less than a kilometer from the lower gates into Assisi, is just such a find. The inn is actually an ancient peasant's cottage which Silvana Ciammarvghi, the owner, has lovingly restored and transformed into a small pensione. It is not surprising that the hotel is so loaded with charm, for Silvana loves antiques and has an eye for beautiful wooden chests, tables, chairs, mirrors and beds. In fact, the first floor of this inn is an antique shop. Most of the furniture in the house is for sale but, no problem: when a piece is sold, another takes its place from the shop downstairs. All of the rooms have style and taste. When we first discovered the Antichita "Three Esse" Country House it had just opened, and each time we visit we find more improvements. Rooms are now available in a new wing overlooking the terrace, but our preference is definitely for those in the original farmhouse which we think have more character and pretty views overlooking the countryside. One asset never changes, the gracious owner, Silvana Ciammarvghi, who will be there to greet you. She speaks excellent English and will be happy to welcome you to her "home" which is an ideal location for exploring Umbria.

ANTICHITA "THREE ESSE" COUNTRY HOUSE
Owner: Silvana Ciammarvghi
S. Pietro Campagna 178
06081 Assisi (PG), Italy
tel: (075) 81 63 63 fax: (075) 81 63 63
12 rooms: Double Lire 110,000
Open all year
Credit cards: all major
No restaurant, breakfast only
177 km N of Rome, 26 km E of Perugia

The Hotel Subasio is located in Assisi with one wall forming part of the ancient square in front of the Basilica of St. Francis. In fact, the hotel is actually linked to the Basilica by an arched colonnade. The setting is marvelous, with the rear of the hotel facing the beautiful Umbrian countryside. On the lower level there are several delightful view terraces romantically shaded by vines. Many of the rooms also have splendid vistas over the Umbrian valley. Request one of the deluxe rooms with a balcony—these are delightful. The public rooms of the Subasio are pleasant, but rather stilted and formal. However, you will not be inside much anyway. The terraces are magic: to sit and watch the lovely fields mellow in the evening sun with that very special glow which is so characteristic of Umbria is certainly one of life's real pleasures. It is no wonder that many celebrities have chosen the Hotel Subasio for residence when visiting Assisi; such famous names as Charlie Chaplin and James Stewart grace the guest book. Andrea Rossi personally oversees the management of the hotel and there is a friendliness in the air from the gentle maid who turns down your bed in the evening to the charming waiter who helps select your local wine with dinner.

HOTEL SUBASIO
Owner: Sergio Elisei
Via Frate Elia, 2
06081 Assisi (PG), Italy
tel: (075) 81 22 06 fax: (075) 81 66 91
56 rooms: Double Lire 210,000
10 suites: Lire 300,000
Open all year
Credit cards: DC VS
Restaurant open daily
177 km N of Rome, 26 km E of Perugia

For a moderately priced little inn just off the **Piazza del Commune** in the heart of Assisi, the Hotel Umbra is a wonderful choice. If you are expecting a luxury hotel with fancy decor, this will not be the hotel for you: although the public rooms have accents of antiques and a cozy ambiance, they are "homey" rather than grand. The bedrooms, although clean and fresh, are very basic in decor. Nevertheless, because of the absolutely delightful small terrace at the entrance which is oozing with charm, the Umbra would have won our hearts, no matter what was within. You reach the Umbra by way of a narrow little alley leading off from the Piazza del Commune. The entrance is through wrought iron gates which open to a tiny patio—a green oasis of peace and quiet where tables are set under a trellis covered with vines whose leaves provide shade and paint a lacy pattern of shadows. From this intimate terrace there is a lovely view. Some of the bedrooms, too, have a panoramic vista of the Umbrian hills and valley. There is an attractive dining room and several small drawing rooms. This small, family owned and managed hotel is a real asset to the wonderful medieval city of Assisi. NOTE: The owner, Alberto Laudenzi, has written to us that since our last inspection "many improvements have been made and there are now some very rich and spacious rooms". We are eager to visit again to see the renovations. In the meantime, we will be eager for reader feedback.

HOTEL UMBRA
Owner: Alberto Laudenzi Family
Via degli Archi 6-Piazza de Comune
06081 Assisi (PG), Italy
tel: (075) 81 22 40 fax: (075) 81 36 53
26 rooms: Double Lire 122,000–170,000
Closed mid-January to mid-March
Credit cards: all major
Restaurant closed Tuesdays
Central location off main square
177 km N of Rome, 26 km E of Perugia

The Hotel Florence is a moderately priced hotel in the charming ancient port of Bellagio. The location is prime—right on the main square. Across the street by the lake is a little tea terrace where you can have a snack while watching the boat traffic. If you are lucky enough to snare a front room with a balcony, you can step out through your French doors and be treated to a splendid view of Lake Como. There is a small reception area and, down a few steps, an intimate lounge with a fireplace, beamed ceiling and chairs set around tiny tables. A staircase leads to a guest dining room with a fireplace and ladder back chairs and to the guest rooms. On our last visit we were pleased to find many of the guest rooms have been redone—many with antique furnishings. Ours was a very cheerful, bright corner room with French doors opening onto a terrace where lounge chairs were invitingly set for viewing the lake. Another new item: jazz music is played every Sunday in the newly redecorated bar. The hotel is owned by the Ketzlar family, who are real pros: the inn has been in their family for 150 years and is now managed by Mrs Freidl Ketzlar and her daughter, Roberta. They both speak excellent English and are extremely gracious. Bellagio is such an atmospheric little town that we are happy to be able to recommend a pleasant, well-run, moderately priced hotel.

HOTEL FLORENCE
Owner: Ketzlar Family
Piazza Mazzimi 42
22021 Bellagio-Lake Como (CO), Italy
tel: (031) 95 03 42 fax: (031) 95 17 22
38 rooms: Double Lire 124,000–140,000
Open April 15 to October 15
Credit cards: EC, MC VS
Restaurant open daily,
Lakefront location
80 km N of Milan, 31 km NE of Como

The Grand Hotel Villa Serbelloni is certainly appropriately named. It definitely is GRAND. In fact, the public rooms are almost overwhelming, with intricately painted ceilings, gold mirrors, fancy columns, Oriental rugs, gilded chairs, heavy chandeliers, and a sweeping marble staircase. The bedrooms are quite nice, although I did not think the decor outstanding. However, the quality is superb: lovely percale sheets, soft down pillows, and large towels. The service, too, is excellent. Located in the gardens by the lake there is a large swimming pool. If you prefer sightseeing or shopping to swimming, the colorful old port of Bellagio is just steps from the hotel. If you tire of exploring the town of Bellagio, the ferry is only a few minutes away, or, if you want to be discreet, the concierge can arrange a special boat to pick you up at the private pier in front of the hotel. Perhaps the original grandeur of the Grand Hotel Villa Serbelloni has faded a little, but if ornate elegance and the feeling of living in a masterpiece of a palace appeals to you, I think you will enjoy your stay here. Pretend you are a guest at a weekend house party—given by royalty, of course. NOTE: Starting in May 1993, the Grand Hotel Villa Serbelloni has added a Fitness and Beauty Center, squash court and two tennis courts.

GRAND HOTEL VILLA SERBELLONI
Owner: Rudy Bucher
Manager: Giuseppe Spinelli
22021 Bellagio-Lake Como (CO) , Italy
tel: (031) 95 02 16 fax: (031) 95 15 29
95 rooms: Double Lire 370,000
Open April 10 to October 20
Credit cards: EC, MC, VS
Restaurant open daily
78 km N of Milan, 31 km NE of Como
U.S. Rep: Premier World Marketing 800-223-6620

Although surrounded by a sprawling, uninteresting concrete metropolis, the center of Bologna shelters a fascinating maze of ancient twisting streets, arcaded passageways, marvelous shopping under porticoed walkways and some of the best food in all of Italy. The Corona d'Oro, located in the heart of the medieval quarter, is a small, well-managed hotel whose elegantly designed construction conserves architectural elements of various periods. In the inner courtyard (covered over with a skylight which rolls back to allow the room to return to its original open-air status) you can admire a portico which dates back to the 14th Century. The hall and stairwell, exquisitely done in the liberty style of the early 1900s, leads up to the bedrooms which are individually decorated, mostly with modern furnishings, but with a touch of the traditional in the sedate color schemes and prints nicely displayed on the walls. Some of the rooms have recessed block panel ceilings with paintings of coat-of-arms and landscapes dating back to the 15th and 16th centuries. The hotel does not charge a premium for the few rooms that have small balconies or terraces.

HOTEL CORONA D'ORO 1890
Manager: Dr. Mauro Orsi
Via Oberdan, 12
40126 Bologna, Italy
tel: (051) 23 64 56 fax: (051) 26 26 79
35 rooms: Double Lire 350,000
Closed month of August
Credit cards: all major
No restaurant, breakfast only
Located in heart of Bologna

In 1550, King John of Portugal decided to give a little gift to the Emperor Ferdinand of Austria, so he purchased an elephant in India, shipped it to Genoa, then planned to "walk" it to Austria. This giant beast grew weary about the time it reached Bressanone and was stabled for two weeks at the Am Hohen Feld Inn. Young and old came from miles around to see this impromptu "circus". The proprietor of the Am Hohen Feld was obviously a master at marketing: to maintain the fame of his establishment, he promptly renamed his hotel—you guessed it—the "Elefant". A picture of our friend the elephant was painted on he front of the building commemorating the sensational event. But even without an elephant story this hotel is a winner. Although the bedrooms themselves are a little drab, they are immaculately clean and comfortable. In contrast to the simplicity of the bedrooms, the reception areas and dining rooms are fantastic, incorporating beautiful antiques, museum quality paintings and magnificent paneling. But, even if there were no elephant story nor an antique ambiance to the hotel, the Elefant would have another tremendous attribute: the food is fantastic. Most of the eggs, butter, milk, fruit, and vegetables, and even the wine, come from the hotel's own farms. NOTE: Bressanone is called Brixen on some maps.

HOTEL ELEFANT
Owner: Hotel Elefant, Inc
Manager: K.H. Falk
Via Rio Bianco, 4
39042 Bressanone (Brixen) (BZ), Italy
tel: (0472) 32 750 fax: (0472) 36 579
43 rooms: Double Lire 235,000–248,000
Open March to November and Christmas
Credit cards: VS
Restaurant closed Mondays
40 km NE of Bolzano, near Brenner pass

The Cenobio dei Dogi was formerly the summer home of the Genoese Doges, so it is no wonder that it has such an idyllic location nestled on a small hill which forms one end of Camogli's miniature half-moon bay. From the hotel terrace there is an enchanting view of the tiny cove lined with marvelous narrow old fishermen's cottages painted in all shades of ochre's and siennas. The hotel has a very nice swimming pool, plus a private (though pebbly) beach. Many of the bedrooms have balconies which boast romantic views of this storybook scene. For tennis buffs, there is a tennis court, although I cannot imagine anyone wanting to play tennis with all the beautiful walking trails which make enticing spider web designs on the peninsula. Although the Cenobio dei Dogi is larger than most hotels which appear in this guide and its decor does not radiate antique ambiance, it possesses a solid, comfortable, no-nonsense kind of charm. It is not chic in the "jet set" style of hotels frequently found on the Riviera, but if you relate to gorgeous flower gardens, exceptional views, and slightly faded, "old world" comfort in one of the most picturesque villages in Italy, then I think you will love this hotel.

HOTEL CENOBIO DEI DOGI
Manager: Franco Orio
Via Nicolo Cuneo, 34
16032 Camogli (GE), Italy
tel: (0185) 77 00 41 fax: (0185) 77 27 96
89 rooms: Double Lire 390,000
Closed January and February
Credit cards: all major
Restaurant open daily
Near Portofino–Italian Riviera
20 km SE of Genoa, 14 km NW of Portofino

The Albergo Vecchio Molino is a 15th-century mill which has been cleverly converted into an inn. Although it is very close to the busy highway that runs between Assisi and Spoleto, once you wind off the road and down the lane to this small inn, you drop out of the modern-day world and slip back into the tranquillity of days long past. The mill has been meticulously renovated with taste and style, retaining its original massive stone walls, heavy wooden beams, vaulted ceilings and even the old wooden gears and giant grindstone. Best of all, the river still wraps itself around the mill, a constant reminder of the building's origins. Perched on the hillside above the inn, a 14th-century stone church with handsome columns gives the impression of a Greek temple just a short walk away. Inside, the inn is nicely furnished using many antiques whose dark wood handsomely sets off stark white walls. The bedrooms we saw were not large, but appealingly furnished using antique beds and chests. The decor throughout the inn lends an air of uncluttered sophistication. On the day we arrived, we had the impression that not many Americans stay at the inn and that perhaps there might not be an especially warm welcome to English speaking visitors. But we always have a soft spot for old mills and could not bear to leave this one out ... please give us some feedback.

ALBERGO VECCHIO MOLINO
Owner: Anna Maria Flagiello
Manager: Massimo Clememtimi
Via del Tempio, 34 Localita Pissignano
06042 Campello sul Clintunno (PG), Italy
tel: (0743) 52 11 22 fax (0472) 27 50 97
17 rooms: Double Lire 195,000
Open April 1 to November 1
Credit cards: all major
No restaurant, breakfast only
141 km N of Rome, 11 km N of Spoleto

The newly-renovated Hotel Flora in the center of Capri is truly a delight. Just beyond the landmark Quisisana Hotel is the stark white building reflecting the sun's rays and trimmed with lush deep purple bougainvillea vines. Signora Vuotto runs her hotel with great care and attention—striving to make her guests feel the Hotel Flora is their "home away from home". She has succeeded. The small 24-room hotel has become known above all for its impeccable yet friendly service. The prim dining room with its smart striped yellow and green armchairs and colorful ceramic plates lining the walls, opens out to a large terrace overflowing with potted Mediterranean flowers and miniature palms. Guests linger over their morning cappuccino to take in the view over the San Giacomo ancient monastery to the sea from cushioned wicker chairs. Chef Giorgio practices his culinary expertise for dinner guests in the well known restaurant. There is a fresh, perfumed air about this elegant jewel of a hotel which is carried out through the luminous bedrooms and suites finely decorated with antiques, and colorful Pierre Deux fabrics. Each of the bedrooms has television, a small refrigerator and, best of all, a terrace with a view of the famous "Faraglioni" rocks. Spotless bathrooms are tiled in typical Caprese style.

HOTEL FLORA
Owner: Virginia Vuotto
Via Federico Serena, 26
80073 Capri (NA), Italy
tel: (081) 83 70 211 fax: (081) 83 78 949
24 rooms: Double Lire 230,000–350,000
7 suites: Lire 400,000
Open Easter to October
Credit cards: all major
Restaurant open daily
Island of Capri, ferry from Sorrento or Naples

The Grand Hotel Quisisana conjures up the image of a Hollywood setting where the jet-set gather. The women, adorned in jewels and the latest swimming ensembles, sit in the sun and gossip about the latest scandal while their husbands (or boyfriends?) sit pool-side drinking Scotch and playing the game of grown boys—discussing their latest business ventures. But it is all great fun and quite in the mood of Capri which has been a playground for the wealthy since the time of the early Romans. The Grand Hotel Quisisana is a deluxe hotel with a gorgeous oval pool overlooking the blue Mediterranean. The air of formal elegance appears as soon as you enter the lobby decorated with marble floors, soft green velvet chairs, Oriental carpets, ornate statues, crystal chandeliers and beautiful paintings. All the bedrooms are well appointed and the deluxe rooms even have separate "his" and "hers" half-baths. Room rates include breakfast and lunch or dinner and you can choose from almost anything on the menu. The Grand Hotel Quisisana most definitely provides a setting and atmosphere to reflect the image of, and cater to, their jet-set clientele.

GRAND HOTEL QUISISANA
Manager: Gianni Chervatin
Via Camerelle, 2
80073 Capri (NA), Italy
tel: (081) 83 70 788 fax: (081) 83 76 080
150 rooms: Double Lire 350,000 -580,000
Open April to October
Credit cards: all major
Restaurant open daily
Island of Capri, ferry from Sorrento or Naples
U.S. Rep: LHW 800-223-6800

The Hotel Luna savors one of the most beautiful locations on the Island of Capri. It is just a short walk from the main town yet, in atmosphere, it seems miles away from the bustle and noise. The hotel is perched on the cliffs overlooking the spectacular coastline of green hills that drop straight into the sea and from which emerge giant rock formations. There is an outside terrace for dining which captures this view, and the premium rooms have balconies overlooking the sea. Just a short stroll from the hotel there is a very large pool surrounded by flowers which also has a splendid view. We always loved the location of the Hotel Luna, but felt that it was in need of a fresher decor. However, just as we were going to press, the manager, Luisa Vuotto, advised us that a vast improvement program is underway: all the rooms will be redecorated: the restaurant, the garden, the open air restaurant—always in a cozy friendly atmosphere. We will be eager to visit the hotel again. By the time you arrive, the accommodations might be perfect. But, no matter what the decor, the cliff-top setting is so lovely that we think the hotel is one of the best on Capri. The overall mood at the hotel is set by its delightful approach, a covered trellis pathway which, in summer, is completely shaded by brilliant bougainvillea and grape vines and bordered by flowers: a wonderful introduction to the Hotel Luna and to a restful interlude by the sea.

HOTEL LUNA
Manager: Luisa Vuotto
Viale Giacomo Matteotti, 3
80073 Capri (NA), Italy
tel: (081) 83 70 433 fax: (081) 83 77 459
44 room, Lire 205,000–410,000
Open April to October
Credit cards: all major
Restaurant open daily
Island of Capri, ferry from Sorrento or Naples

The Villa Brunella is a small jewel located on the most picturesque and peaceful street of Capri, the Tragara, only a 10-minute walk to the center of town. The modern hotel, overlooking the Marina Piccola, squeezes the greatest advantage from its narrow, very deep lot. The hotel is built on levels starting at the street level with the terrace restaurant and "stepping down" the steep hillside to the blue swimming pool—at this point, only halfway down to the sea level (the beach is only about a 5-minute walk down the hill). The hotel is run more like a private home than a commercial hotel. The ever-gracious Vencenzo and his wife Brunella take great pleasure in entertaining guests and making them feel welcome. The 20 bedrooms, each with private bath, telephone, frigo-bar and air conditioning, are tastefully put together with pretty pink or powder blue floral bedspreads and matching curtains. The cool ceramic tiled floors, creamy white walls and potted plants add to the charm. Decoration in the rooms is really superfluous as the eye can hardly be torn away from the spectacularly dramatic views of the sea and island from one's own terrace. Simply heavenly.

VILLA BRUNELLA
Hosts: Vincenzo and Brunella Ruggiero
Via Tragara 24
80073 Capri (NA), Italy
tel: (081) 83 70 122 fax: (081) 83 70 430
20 rooms: Double Lire 295,000
Suites Lire 380,000
Open: Easter to October
Credit cards: all major
Restaurant open daily
Island of Capri, ferry from Sorrento or Naples

If you are approaching Florence from the west, perhaps on your way from Milan to Florence, we highly recommend stopping en route, just before you reach Florence, at the Paggeria Medicea. The hotel's address is Artimino, but the town is so small that I doubt you will find it on any map, so mark Carmignano instead on your map and when you arrive there you will find signs to Artimino, only a few minutes' drive farther on. The hotel is cleverly incorporated into what were once the pages' quarters for the adjoining 16th-century Medicea villa "La Ferdinanda". The long, narrow structure has been cleverly restored, preserving the many original chimneys which adorn the heavy, red-tiled roof. An open corridor whose heavily beamed ceiling is supported by a stately row of columns forms a walkway in front of the rooms. All of the guest rooms are simple, but very inviting, with tiled floors, pretty prints on the white walls, hand-loomed-looking white drapes hanging from wooden rods above the windows, and attractive antiques or copies of antiques as accents in each room. There is a snack bar in the same wing as the hotel, but the main restaurant, Biagio Pignatta (which serves simple but delicious Italian cooking), is located in a nearby building which at one time housed the butler for the villa. If you are a guest at the hotel, you have access to a delightful small Etruscan museum situated in the vaults of the adjoining Medicea villa "La Ferdinanda".

PAGGERIA MEDICEA
Manager: Alessandro Gualtieri
Viale Papa Giovanni XXIII
50040 Artimino (FI), Italy
tel: (055) 87 18 081 fax: (055) 87 18 080
37 rooms: Double Lire 240,000
Open all year
Credit cards: all major
Restaurant closed Wednesdays
20 km SW of Florence, 15 km S of Prato

The Villa Gaidello Club is located in the Emilia-Romagna, a region renowned for its cuisine—considered by many to be the finest food in Italy. Whether this is true or not, I do not know, but without a doubt the delicious pasta prepared by Paola Giovanna Bini (the owner) of the Villa Gaidello Club was the best I have EVER tasted. Paola Giovanna Bini, who inherited the farm from her grandmother, assumed the awesome task of reconstructing the 250-year-old farm house and adding three apartments (suites) which have been restored and decorated with care, keeping in mind the original character of the country home. These suites vary in size, accommodating from two to five persons. There are three suites in all: one accommodates 2-3 persons, one accommodates 3-4 persons, and one accommodates 4-5 persons. Although the rooms are pleasant, it is the food which makes this inn so very special: only the freshest vegetables and fruits are served; all the pasta is prepared the same day; the wines come from the farm's own vineyard; even the liqueur served after the meal is made from walnuts picked from the orchard. However, Paola Bini wants me to stress that it is ABSOLUTELY NECESSARY to make reservations for the restaurant: time is needed to prepare the food—all of which is strictly prepared the same day by hand.

VILLA GAIDELLO CLUB
Owner: Paola Giovanna Bini
Via Gaidello, 18
41013 Castelfranco Emilia (MO), Italy
tel: (059) 92 68 06 fax: (059) 92 66 20
3 apartments: Lire 140,000 for 2 persons
Credit cards: none accepted
Restaurant open daily, only for guests
26 km W of Bologna, 13 km E of Modena

Castelrotto, a medieval village abounding in old world character, is located in the heart of the Dolomite mountains in north-eastern Italy. In the center of town, the Hotel Cavallino d'Oro faces the market square which highlights an especially quaint, colorfully painted fountain. The entrance to the hotel is sign-posted with a Golden Horse, reflecting the name of this 14th-century inn. The facade is a deep-mustard-color highlighted by dark green shutters and flower boxes overflowing with cheerful geraniums. There is a traditional old world atmosphere throughout this small inn. All of the guest rooms are individual in decor, and nicely furnished in a typical Tyrolian style. Three rooms are especially pretty with light pine, four poster beds. From the beginning the Hotel Cavallino has always provided accommodations. When first documented in 1393, the inn was a coaching station with facilities to care for the horses, and also, of course, food and rooms for the weary traveller. The original hospitality is certainly on-going. Stefan and Susanne (both of whom speak excellent English) have now taken over as the third generation of the Urthaler family to run the hotel. Not only do they exude a boundless, youthful enthusiasm and a gracious warmth of welcome, they are also constantly upgrading their small hotel by incorporating more antiques into the decor and renovating guest rooms. The dining room was closed on the day of my visit, but Stefan tells me the kitchen is excellent with the chef specializing in regional dishes.

HOTEL CAVALLINO D'ORO
Owners: Susanne and Stefan Urthaler
39040 Castelrotto (Kastelruth)(BZ), Italy
tel: (0471) 70 63 37 fax: (0471) 70 71 10
24 rooms, Double: Lire 88,000–143,000
Open all year
Credit cards: all major
Restaurant closed Tuesdays
140 km NW of Verona, 24 km NE of Bolzano

We happened upon this newly opened inn during our latest exploration of Italy's glorious Tuscany region, well known for its rolling, vineyard covered hills. Just as the road curved into the small town of Castellina in Chianti, we noticed an inn we had never seen before and stopped for an inspection at the Hotel Il Colombaio. The building is very old—probably at one time a farmer's home with its typical heavy tiled roof, thick walls and courtyard. This comfortable inn is owned by the Baldini family and Roberta Baldini, the gracious daughter, is the manager. She speaks very good English and gave us a complete tour of the small hotel. The guest rooms are quite inviting, many with wrought iron beds and antique accents giving an appealing country flavor. There are 15 rooms and one suite in the main house, plus a small annex across the street with 6 more rooms. All have private bathrooms and are fresh and pretty. The dining room is especially cozy, again decorated with a rustic motif in keeping with the Tuscany countryside. A continental breakfast is the only meal served here, but Roberta is happy to recommend a good local ristorante for dining. On hot summer days, a welcome bonus is the swimming pool, located on a terrace behind the inn. (As a reader pointed out, the pool is nice, but not as dramatic as the one depicted in the hotel brochure). For a reasonably priced place to stay with an old-world ambiance, the Hotel Il Colombaio is a welcome addition to the Tuscany region.

HOTEL IL COLOMBAIO
Owner: Baldini Family
Via Chiantigiana, 29
53011 Castellina in Chianti (SI), Italy
tel: (0577) 74 04 44   fax: (0577) 74 04 44
22 rooms: Double Lire 120,000
Closed November
Credit cards: EC, MC, VS
No restaurant, breakfast only
21 km N of Siena on road #222

I visited the Pensione Salivolpi with the idea of including it only in our guide featuring inexpensive places to stay. However, the hotel is so very pleasant, that for those of you looking for a "budget" hotel while roaming the Tuscany hills, we have included this small, attractive pensione. Although the address is Castellina in Chianti (in the heart of the famous Chianti wine region), you will actually find the hotel on the outskirts of town, on the left-hand side of the road leading from Castellina to the small town of Sant Donato. The old, weathered stone farmhouse sits almost on the road. It is only when you pull into the parking area that the lovely position of the inn is revealed—behind the main building there is a beautiful view terrace featuring a lovely large swimming pool. It is a pleasant surprise to find such a swimming pool in a such a reasonably-priced place to stay. The bedrooms are pleasant, reflecting the nice taste of the Salivolpi family. With Florence only 40 minutes north and Siena 30 minutes to the south, the Pensione Salivolpi provides a simple, but very pleasant, base of operation.

PENSIONE SALIVOLPI
Owner: L. Salivolpi
Via Fiorentina–Localita Salivolpi
53011 Castellina in Chianti (SI), Italy
tel: (0577) 74 04 84 fax: (0577) 74 10 34
19 rooms: Double Lire 95,000
Open all year
Credit cards: EC, MC, VS
No restaurant, breakfast only
21 km N of Siena on road #222

The Tenuta di Ricavo, a member of the Romantik Hotel group, is unique—not a "hotel" at all in the usual connotation, but rather a tiny village with peasants' cottages which have been transformed into delightful guest rooms. The stables are now the dining room and the barn is now the office. Unlike many of the "Hollywood" hotels in Tuscany which have sprung up from literal ruins so that what you see is almost 100% new, Ricavo is *ALL* real, an authentic Tuscan hamlet. You enter the park like setting through a huge pine forest where small cottages are nestled in amongst the trees. Gardens are everywhere and roses embellish the weathered stone cottages giving them a fairy-tale appearance. The total effect is absolutely enchanting. Originally the village was the summer-holiday-home of a Swiss family, who, after World War II, transformed it into an exquisite resort. The family seeks no publicity. They do not need it: the hotel is always filled with fortunate guests who have discovered this paradise. However, the Tenuta di Ricavo is not for everyone. It is quiet. It is remote. It is unstructured. But it is a haven for the traveller for whom a good book, a walk through the forest, a swim in the pool, a drink at sunset, and a delicious dinner are fulfillment. Excellent English is spoken: Christine Lobrano lived in the United States as a child.

TENUTA DI RICAVO
Owner: Lobrano-Scotoni Family
53011 Castellina in Chianti (SI), Italy
tel: (0577) 74 02 21 fax: (0577) 74 10 14
23 rooms: Double Lire 220,000-340,000*
*3 night minimum
Open March 15 to end-October
Credit cards: EC, MC, VS
Restaurant closed Mondays
21 km N of Siena on road 22, 50 km S of Florence
U.S. Rep: Euro-Connection 800-645-3876

If the many magnificent old villas dotting the countryside near Venice, some have fallen into disrepair, some are still maintained as private residences, and a few have been converted into hotels. We looked at many of these fascinating villa-hotels but because of the expense of maintaining them, many are just too shabby to include. One however, the Villa Corner della Regina, still has an elegant, though slighted faded, appeal. Once home to Caterina, Queen of Cyprus, the villa dates from the beginning of the 16th Century and was later reconstructed around 1700 in the well-known Palladian-style. It is set in extensive manicured formal gardens and surrounded by vineyards. A pool is located to the left of the main building while the wing to the right, which originally housed the stables, has been converted to guest rooms and also some time-share condominiums. The decor in the side stable annex is nothing special, just standard hotel-like furnishings, but the suites in the villa abound with antiques—very grand and ornate, even somewhat overly fussy for my taste. There are several dining rooms in the villa: my favorite is a charming room with salmon-colored marble walls enhanced by color-coordinated tablecloths and draperies—formal yet cozy and not the least bit intimidating. The food served at the villa is excellent and the wines are produced on the estate. NOTE: Cavasagra is located between the towns of Ospedaletto and Albaredo on the Hallwag map.

VILLA CORNER DELLA REGINA
Owner: Count Dona delle Rose
Via Corriva, 10
Near Ospedaletto
31050 Cavasagra (TV), Italy
tel: (0423) 481481 fax: (0423) 451100
23 rooms, 7 suites: Lire 200,000–430,000
Open all year
Credit cards: all major
Restaurant open daily
45 km NW of Venice, 3 km W of Ospedaletto

A book on the most charming hotels in Italy could not be complete without including one of the queens of the world, the Villa d'Este. Originally the hotel was a private villa built in 1568 by the Cardinal Tolomeo Gallio. He obviously had elegant (and expensive) taste, for the Villa d'Este is truly a fantasy come true. From the moment you enter the enormous lobby with the sweeping staircase, marble, crystal, soaring ceilings, statues, and columns surround you. Everything is elaborate and ornate. The bedrooms are all elegantly furnished—no two are alike, but all are beautiful with color-coordinated carpets, wall-coverings and bedspreads. Some of the bedrooms have prime locations overlooking the lake. Although the interior is lovely, it is the outside where the fun really begins. The hotel opens onto a large terrace where guests relax with refreshing drinks. Just a short distance beyond the terrace is the lake where there is a dock for boats and a very large swimming pool which extends out over the water. Tucked away in the park there are eight tennis courts and within the nearby area, seven golf courses. However, the most stunning feature of the Villa d'Este is the park which surrounds it with lovely pathways winding between the trees, a jogging course, glorious flower gardens, statues and even a formal garden with dramatic mosaic colonnade.

VILLA D'ESTE
Manager: Marco Sorbellini
22010 Cernobbio, Lake Como (CO), Italy
tel: (031) 51 14 71 fax: (031) 51 20 27
158 rooms: Double Lire 550,000–870,000
Open March 1 to November 30
Credit cards: all major
Restaurant open daily
53 km N of Milan, 5 km N of Como
U.S. Rep: LHW, 800-223-6800

The Anna Maria is located in Champoluc which is a small town at the end of the beautiful Ayas Valley which stretches north into the Alps almost to the Swiss border. The glaciers of the Monte Rosa (one of the 4,000 meter peaks of the Alps) provide a glorious backdrop as you drive up the valley. Champoluc is a well-known ski center in winter as well as a favorite mountain summer resort. As you drive through Champoluc you will see a small sign for the Anna Maria on the right side of the road just before you leave town. Turn right on this little lane which winds up the hill and look for the Anna Maria on your right, set in a serene pine grove. The Villa Anna Maria is not a luxury hotel, but rather an old mountain chalet which is now a simple, but very charming, inn. A large deck for sunning stretches across the entrance. Inside there is a lovely dining room—my favorite room—which exudes warmth and coziness with its wooden Alpine-style country chairs, wooden tables, and gay red checked curtains at the windows. Upstairs the bedrooms are not luxurious but most agreeable, with wooden paneling on the walls and a rustic ambiance, and each one with a private bathroom. The atmosphere is "homey"—wonderful for those seeking a friendly country inn in a mountain village.

VILLA ANNA MARIA
Owner: Miki Origone
Via Croues, 5
11020 Champoluc, Monte Rosa (AO), Italy
tel: (0125) 30 71 28 fax: (0125) 30 79 84
20 rooms: Double Lire 160,000
Open June 20 to mid-September
December 10 to mid-April
Restaurant open daily, only for guests
Mountain location–NW Italy
175 km NW of Milan, 100 km N of Turin

I was puzzled to receive a hotel questionnaire response postmarked St Simon's Island, Georgia. But quickly all was explained. It was from James Adams who had been living in Europe, perfecting his Italian cooking skills at one of the finest restaurant-hotels in Italy, the Locanda del Sant'Uffizio—Ristorante da Beppe. The owner, Giuseppe Firato ("Beppe"), speaks no English so when our request for information arrived, he asked his American protégé to respond. After visiting the hotel, I can only say that it was more perfect than anticipated. Below is James' wonderful letter describing so superbly his "home away from home". "Originally in the 1500s the Locanda del Sant'Uffizio was a Benedictine monastery and served as such up until the mid 1800s after which time it passed into private hands serving as a farm. In 1972, Signore Giuseppe Firato (Beppe), a man from the village, bought the farm and slowly began converting it into its present form. Naturally at first there were only several rooms while the rest of the buildings were used for farming and wine growing. Through the years rooms have been added very carefully, with great respect for the traditional aesthetics, and now there are 35 guest rooms. All furnishings are antique and every detail of the decor has been rigorously overseen personally by Signore Beppe and his wife, Carla, with the result being a very tasteful, elegant, yet relaxed hotel cozily nestled amongst the vineyards in the hills of Monferrato. Other features include a tennis court, a swimming pool (in front of which one can have breakfast and lunch in the warm months) and, last but not least, there is the Ristorante da Beppe, an exquisite restaurant serving the finest of Piemontese cuisine. It is of course owned and operated by the Firato family, and, in fact, the restaurant preceded the hotel. It has earned one Michelin star and has been rated highly in notable Italian guides such as Espresso and Veronelli. When one combines the charm and relaxation of this elegant hotel with the pleasures of such a refined table, one is left with a very memorable experience."

There are many features that make the Locanda del Sant'Uffizio very special, but, without a doubt, the Firato family is responsible for the ambiance of warmth and hospitality which radiates throughout the hotel. Signore Beppe was born in the tiny village (population 50) where the hotel is located. When his father who owned a small bar died, Signore Beppe took over—although he was only a boy at the time. The rest is history: the bar grew into a restaurant, the restaurant into a tiny hotel, the small hotel into a delightful resort. Such a success story is not surprising when you meet Signore Beppe. He speaks no English. He does not need to. His charismatic charm transcends all language barriers. It is no wonder his restaurant—isolated in the countryside—is filled each night with chicly dressed Italian clientele: Beppe greets each of them with an exuberant warmth, and the food is outstanding, truly a gourmet delight. Since we originally visited the Locanda del Sant'Uffizio, Beppe and his wife have been joined in the operation of the Locanda del Sant'Uffizio by their two sons: Fabio, a chemical engineer, collaborates with the chef and Massimo, an architect, assists his father in the welcoming of guests. Happily for the visitors from abroad, both sons speak English and French.

LOCANDA DEL SANT'UFFIZIO
RISTORANTE DA BEPPE
Owner: Giuseppe Firato
Near Moncalvo
14030 Cioccaro di Penango (AT), Italy
tel: (0141) 91271 fax: (0141) 916068
35 rooms: Double Lire 440,000
Rate includes breakfast and dinner
Hotel closed January and August 10-20
Credit cards: EC, MC, VS
Restaurant open daily
5 km SE of Moncalvo, 60 km E of Turin
21 km N of Asti toward Moncalvo

The Ca'Peo, a well known restaurant serving some of the finest food in Italy, is located high in the coastal hills south of Genoa. You might think you will never arrive as the road winds ever upward through groves of olive and chestnut trees. But the way is well sign-posted, and just about the time you might be ready to despair, you will find a wonderful old farmhouse, owned by Franco Solari, who is host and in charge of the wines, and his wife, Melly, who is the chef. As we checked in, the entire family was in the kitchen busily chopping vegetables, rolling out pastry and preparing the fish for the evening meal. The dining room, enclosed on three sides by large arched windows, takes advantage of a sweeping view to the sea. Be aware that the meals are VERY expensive, but if you appreciate fine food and wines, superb. Dining is definitely the main feature; however, in a modern annex there are five suites available for guests who want to spend the night. The decor here is not antique, but each of the large suites is pleasant, and after lingering over a wonderful meal accompanied by delicious wines, how nice to walk just a few steps to your bed. A final note: the Ca'Peo is only about half an hour's drive from the popular resort of Portofino, so you might want to stay here instead or at least treat yourself to a memorable meal—but call ahead as reservations are necessary.

CA'PEO
Owners: Franco and Melly Solari
Via dei Caduti, 80
16040 Chiavari a Leivi (GE), Italy
tel: (0185) 31 96 96 fax: (0185) 31 96 71
5 suites: Lire 160,000
Closed November
Credit cards: VS
Restaurant closed Mondays
6 km N of Chiavari toward Leivi
44 km SE of Genoa, 22 km NE of Portofino

The Hotel Menardi dates back 200 years. Originally it was a peasant's farmhouse, but as Cortina's popularity as a fabulous ski center has spread so has the town, and now the "farm" is located right on the outskirts of town on the main road heading north. Nevertheless, the Menardi family, who have owned the home for a century and a half, have managed to maintain the country flavor through the use of many antiques, nostalgic prints on the walls, old clocks, giant dowry chests, Oriental carpets, and beautiful hanging cupboards—all set off by the warmth and gaiety of flowers everywhere. The dining room is appealingly cozy and the delicious food is impeccably served. The individually decorated bedrooms are all attractive. In addition to the original inn which has 40 bedrooms, there is a new house in the back garden with an additional 15 rooms. It seems that, due to its location on the main road, the Menardi farm just naturally evolved into a hotel. At first it gave shelter to the men carting loads over the Cimabanche Pass who needed a place to sleep—more often than not in the hay loft. Today the inn is a simple, but wonderful, small hotel whose special ingredient is the old-fashioned warmth and hospitality of the gracious Menardi family who personally see that every guest is made to feel welcome.

HOTEL MENARDI
Owner: Menardi Family
112 Via Majon
32043 Cortina D'Ampezzo (BL), Italy
tel: (0436) 24 00 fax: (0436) 86 21 83
55 rooms: Double Lire 140,000–280,000
Open July to September
  Christmas to March
Credit cards: VS
Restaurant open daily
133 km E of Bolzano
71 km N of Belluno

Corvara, a mountain village in northeastern Italy, is popular with guests who enjoy walking through high alpine meadows in summer and skiing down snow covered slopes in winter. Although the Dolomite region is one of the most beautiful in Italy and offers many hotels, there is not a rich choice for visitors who prefer small inns with an old-world, antique ambiance. Luckily, La Perla, located in the center of Corvara, offers not only a convenient place to stay, but also a cozy ambiance. This small inn is owned and managed by the Costa family who lovingly oversee every detail. The day I visited, Mrs. Costa was busily engaged in supervising the table arrangements to be sure everything was perfect. One enters into a large reception lobby where heavy wooden beams, Oriental carpets on tiled floors, fresh plants and country-patterned drapes set the mood. But the real winners are the dining rooms. There are a series of lovely places to eat: each with its own personality—all absolutely oozing with cozy charm. Antique clocks, tiled ovens, low beamed ceilings, painted chests, warm antique wood paneling, abundant accents of copper plus handsome linens, fresh flowers and candlelight make each room a dream. The guest rooms have all the modern amenities, but do not display the old-world ambiance of the public rooms.

LA PERLA
Owner: Costa Family
39033 Corvara (BZ), Italy
tel: (0471) 83 61 32 fax: (0471) 83 65 68
50 rooms: Double Lire 198,000–352,000
Open July to September
  mid-December to Easter
Credit cards: VS
Restaurant open daily
65 km E of Bolzano, 47 km W of Cortina
U.S. Rep: Euro-Connection 800-645-3876

The 19th-century Castello di Pomerio dates from the 9th Century and has been renovated with exquisite taste and quality. As you roam the antique-filled rooms, you will be aware of the impact of their perfection. Each detail of restoration shows loving care: in fact, even ancient frescos have been meticulously restored. Some of the bedrooms are in the main castle and others are in a wing across the road that is cleverly connected to the castle by a tunnel so that you still feel a part of the main hotel. All of the bedrooms vary in decor, but all are outstanding. Most of the ones I saw had wonderful wooden beds and attractive heavy curtains; many had cozy fireplaces—all had charm. For the exercise enthusiast, there is a tennis court plus both an indoor and an outdoor swimming pool. Through the ages, this hotel has changed hands many times. At one point, its past even included use as a silk factory. How lucky for the tourist that now the building houses such a romantic hotel where one can stop for a few days and live like a king in his "own" castle.

HOTEL CASTELLO DI POMERIO
Manager: Mr. Carcelli
Via Como, 5
22036 Pomerio di Erba (CO), Italy
tel: (031) 627516 fax: (031) 628245
54 rooms: Double Lire 250,000–350,000
Open all year
Credit cards: all major
Restaurant open daily
Near Lake Como
44 km N of Milan, 14 km E of Como

The Punta Est is a lovely old villa perched on a hilltop overlooking the sea. When the home was converted to a villa an annex was added to provide more bedrooms. However, it still gives the friendly feeling of a private home. This warmth of reception and attention to detail are the result of the management of the Podesta family who own and manage the inn. They seem dedicated to making your stay as enjoyable as possible—even their German Shepherd seems to want to welcome you. There are little terraces with lovely views snuggled at various levels among the trees and on one of these terraces is a swimming pool. There is also access to the public beach of Finale Ligure which can easily be reached by walking down the path to the main highway and following the tunnel beneath the highway to the beach. The rooms in the main villa are smaller and more old-fashioned than those in the newer annex which are more reminiscent of an American motel. There is a small dining room for breakfast which is especially inviting with its blue and white English bone china service. This is just one example of a very nice touch offered by owners who really want to please.

HOTEL PUNTA EST
Owner: Podestà Family
Manager, Attilio Podestà
Via Aurelia N.1
17024 Finale Ligure, (SV), Italy
tel: (019) 60 06 11 fax: (019) 60 06 11
37 rooms: Double Lire 340,000*
*Rate includes breakfast and lunch or dinner
*3 night minimum
Open May to October
Credit cards: AX, VS
Restaurant open daily
72 km SW of Genoa, 75 km E of San Remo

The Grand Hotel Villa Cora is a mansion, originally built during the 19th Century by the Baron Oppenheim as a gift for his beautiful young bride. Among the many romantic tales of the Villa Cora is the one about Oppenheim's wife who, so the story goes, became enamored of one of her many admirers. The jealous baron was so enraged that he threatened to burn the entire mansion. Luckily for you and me, he was stopped in time from this mad endeavor by his friends, and today this magnificent villa is a stunning hotel. Although only about a 5-minute taxi ride from the center of Florence (or a 15-minute walk), the Grand Hotel Villa Cora is eons away in atmosphere. You feel more like a guest on a country estate rather than in a city hotel. The villa is set in intricate gardens and even has a pool. The interior of the hotel is rather ornate and sumptuous. You can almost hear the sounds of laughter and music drifting through the gardens, and indeed the mansion has always been famous for its dramatic parties: at one time the villa was the residence of Napoleon's wife, Empress Eugenia, whose gay entertaining was the talk of Florence. Now this grand palace-like home can be yours for days of dreams and romance. NOTE: There is free limousine service for guests to and from Florence.

GRAND HOTEL VILLA CORA
Manager: Valerio Rastrelli
Viale Machiavelli, 18/20
50125 Florence, Italy
tel: (055) 2298451 fax: (055) 229086
48 rooms: Double Lire 587,000
Open all year
Credit cards: all major
Restaurant open daily
15-minute walk from heart of Florence

After being closed for two years for complete renovation, the Hotel Helvetia & Bristol reopened in late 1989 and instantly became, in my estimation, the finest luxury hotel in the center of Florence. Nothing has been spared to make this show-place a true beauty. The decor is outstanding. The lounges, exquisitely decorated with an elegant, yet extremely comfortable, home-like ambiance, exude quality without flamboyance. Each of the guest rooms is also superbly decorated, and, as in a private home, no two are alike. Abundant use of exquisite padded fabric wall coverings, with color-coordinated draperies, upholstered chairs and bed-spreads along with lovely antiques makes each one special. I fell in love with each of the rooms, but my very favorites were mini suites: room 257 in gorgeous shades of muted green and room 363 in lovely golds, creams, and dusty pinks, sumptuous marble bathroom with Jacuzzi tub, heated towel racks, enormous towels, plus the added bonus of a tiny terrace. The dining room, cozy yet elegant with dark walls and soft lighting, specializes in Tuscan and Italian cuisine. For light refreshments, a cool drink or just relaxing, the "Giardino d'Inverno" (Winter Garden) is a marvelous retreat -light and airy with a domed, old-fashioned skylight, potted plants and nostalgic wicker furniture. The Helvetia & Bristol is expensive, but no more so than the other luxury hotels in Florence, and for those who appreciate quality and refinement, it is unsurpassed.

HOTEL HELVETIA & BRISTOL
Director: Franco Ensoli
Via dei Pescioni, 2
50123 Florence, Italy
tel: (055) 28 78 14 fax: (055) 28 83 53
50 rooms: Double Lire 443,870–550,970
Open all year
Credit cards: all major
Restaurant open daily
In the heart of Florence

Each time we visit the Loggiato dei Serviti, we are again impressed with what a pleasant small hotel this is for the money. Many of the hotels in Florence are lovely, but fabulously expensive: others are reasonably priced, but shabby and dark. So it is an exceedingly happy surprise to find a light, airy, antique-filled small hotel—at a reasonable rate. This is not a deluxe hotel, but we think you will be well pleased. The building dates back to the 16th Century when it was built for the order of the "Serviti" fathers. The character of the original building has been meticulously maintained adding greatly to the charm of the hotel. The location is superb: right in the heart of Florence on the historical Piazza SS. Annunziata. There is a small reception area as you enter, beyond which is an intimate little bar where snacks are served (there is no restaurant at the hotel). A miniature elevator—just large enough for two people to squeeze into—takes you upstairs to the spacious bedrooms, each with private bath and each individually decorated in excellent taste with liberal use of antiques. There are four suites, one of which even has two bedrooms and two bathrooms. Although of course more expensive than the standard double room, these suites are most attractive and a good value for a family.

LOGGIATO DEI SERVITI
Owner: Budini Gattai
Piazza SS. Annunziata, 3
50122 Florence, Italy
tel: (055) 21 91 65 fax: (055) 28 95 95
29 rooms: Double Lire 210,000
4 suites: Lire 270,000–450,000
Open all year
Credit cards: all major
No restaurant, breakfast only
In the heart of Florence

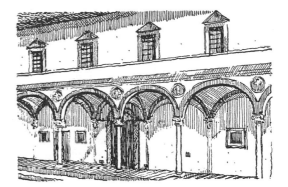

The Lungarno Hotel is superbly located directly on the Arno River and only a few minutes' walk from the Ponte Vecchio. Although most of the hotel is of new construction, the architect cleverly incorporated an ancient stone tower into the hotel so it is easy to rationalize including this hotel—one of my favorites in Florence—into this travel guide. The interior of the hotel is traditional rather than antique in decor, but the decorating is done with excellent taste and the effect is most pleasing. Lovely soft colors are used throughout with beautiful prints on the wall and many fresh flowers. The bedrooms are very comfortable and those who book well in advance can request one of the rooms overlooking the Arno. Those who really plan ahead might even be lucky enough to secure one of the few rooms with a balcony overlooking the river. What a treat to sit on your own little balcony in the evening and watch the Arno fade into gold and the Ponte Vecchio glow in the setting sun. There are several rooms in the tower itself, one of which is especially romantic with its remaining old stone wall and its staircase that leads up to a little balcony and a third bed. Several of the other rooms in the new portion of the hotel also have lofts which can be used as sleeping alcoves.

LUNGARNO HOTEL
Manager: Nedo Naldini
Borgo San Jacopo, 14
50125 Florence, Italy
tel: (055) 26 42 11 fax: (055) 26 84 37
66 rooms: Double Lire 270,000–340,000
Open all year
Credit cards: all major
No restaurant, breakfast only
Short walk to Ponte Vecchio
Directly on the Arno River

Mario's came highly recommended to us by several readers, and after seeing the hotel for ourselves, we agree that it is a delightful small hotel, moderately priced for Florence. It is conveniently located two blocks from the train station, and within easy walking distance to the city's major sightseeing. From the street, the appeal of the hotel is not readily evident as it is housed in a rather nondescript building, but after ascending the stairs to the second floor and stepping into the cozy, beamed-ceilinged lobby, you know you've arrived at a well-tended small hotel with an old Florentine ambiance. Facing the reception desk is an inviting sitting area with sofas arranged under a wall of pictures, Persian carpets enhancing the dark tile floors, and artfully arranged pictures and plants setting off the cream colored walls. Each of the guest rooms has a country fresh feeling with antique armoires, wrought iron headboards, rustic wooden desk and chairs and pretty bedspreads. The rooms are not large, but are very pleasing and immaculately tidy. A copious breakfast is served family-style at long dining tables in a charming room whose walls are hung with many pictures. Guests choose from a wonderful selection of breads, cheese, cereal, boiled eggs, coffee, tea, and chocolate. The nicest aspect of this hotel is the fact that it is small enough to be very personalized and Mario sees to it that every guest feels special.

MARIO'S
Owner: Mario Noce
Via Faenza, 89
50123 Florence, Italy
tel: (055) 21 68 01 fax: (055) 21 20 39
16 rooms: Double Lire 120,000–160,000
Open all year
Credit cards: all major
No restaurant, breakfast only
2 blocks from Florence train station

The Monna Lisa, located about a five-minute walk from the heart of Florence, is a real gem. Facing directly onto a small side street, the simple exterior gives no hint of the appealing small hotel secreted behind the heavy doors. The present owners, the Ciardi-Dupre family, are direct descendants of the very famous sculptor, Giovanni Dupre. This heritage undoubtedly accounts for the many art treasures found accenting every nook and cranny of this little inn. Many elegant, family heirloom antiques are also displayed throughout the Monna Lisa. The hotel has only 20 rooms, which are always occupied. They vary in size and decor—some with handsome antique beds and massive beamed ceilings. A few have balconies overlooking the lovely back garden. The exceptional appeal of the hotel, however, is not the guest rooms, but the public areas: the beautiful lounge, cozy bar, small parlor and spacious reception area from which a dramatic stone staircase gracefully sweeps up to the second floor guest rooms. The Monna Lisa is very home-like; in warm weather guests usually relax in the secluded back garden. Another real bonus if you are arriving by car: to the rear of the property is a parking area. The Monna Lisa was originally an elegant Renaissance palace and you will certainly feel like nobility while a guest at this hotel.

HOTEL MONNA LISA
Owner: Ciardi-Dupre Family
Manager: Riccardo Sardei
Borgo Pinti, 27
50121 Florence, Italy
tel: (055) 2479751 fax: (055) 2479755
20 rooms: Double Lire 225,000–325,000
Open all year
Credit cards: all major
No restaurant, breakfast only
5-minute walk from heart of Florence

The Regency is located on a small park-like square only a ten-minute walk from the heart of Florence. It is, however, a world away in atmosphere—instead of the noise of motorcycles and the bustle of tourist-filled streets, you have a peaceful, quiet, elegant setting. The mood of being "away from it all" is enhanced as you enter the hotel. Again you are protected: the front door is usually kept locked and only guests of the hotel are allowed inside. You ring the front door bell just as you would in a private home. Although small, the Regency is a deluxe hotel and, in fact, it is quite amazing that with only 38 rooms the Regency can offer so many of the luxuries that are usually found only in larger hotels, such as a concierge to assist you with any of your personal needs and an intimate restaurant in a gorgeous wood paneled dining room. A larger restaurant will soon be open in an adjoining townhouse. The bedrooms are spacious and luxurious, with excellent lighting and elegant bathrooms. I would prefer a few more antiques, but these are found mostly in the lounges and the dining room. At the present time, the Regency spreads into several adjacent "homes" with a garden connecting the wings.

HOTEL REGENCY
Owner: Amedeo Ottaviani
Manager: Pietro Panelli
Piazza Massimo d'Azeglio, 3
50121 Florence, Italy
tel: (055) 24 52 47 fax: (055) 24 52 47
38 rooms: Double Lire 420,000–540,000
Open all year
Credit cards: all major
Restaurant open daily
10-minute walk to heart of Florence
U.S. Rep: LHW 800-223-6800

For years I have heard about the charms of the Hotel Tornabuoni Beacci. In fact, on previous trips to Florence I tried to see the hotel, but the rooms were always completely occupied (as they usually are) and there was no one available to show me around. This time, in spite of it being a very busy season, I was able to take the "grand tour". It was worth waiting for. For those who want an excellent value in the heart of Florence, the Hotel Tornabuoni Beacci is quite special. The owner, Signora Beacci, manages the hotel and is ever-present. She cares about every detail of the operation, running this small hotel like she would her own home. An indeed, the appearance is like a family home, with cherished antiques creating a cozy ambiance in all the public rooms and also accenting the furnishings in the bedrooms. From the outside, one would never guess at the oasis within. Only a discreet sign alerts passersby that there is a hotel on the third floor of this nondescript building in the heart of the city. After entering a somewhat dismal lobby, a tiny elevator slowly rises to the third floor reception desk and the hallway which leads into the hotel. One of the nicest features of this little inn is its roof garden where, surrounded by fragrant flowers, tables are set up for guests to relax and enjoy a superb view over the rooftops of Florence.

HOTEL TORNABUONI BEACCI
Owner: Mrs. Lensi Orlandi Beacci
Via Tornabuoni, 3
50123 Florence, Italy
tel: (055) 21 26 45 or (055) 28 35 94
30 rooms: Double Lire 220,000–250,000
Open all year
Credit cards: all major
Restaurant open daily, only for guests
In the center of Florence

Florence is probably one of Italy's most romantic cities: Torre di Bellosguardo is definitely one of Italy's most romantic hotels. What a jewel. This is such a special inn that we are almost reluctant to share the secret. The Torre di Bellosguardo is housed in a sensational villa nestled on the shelf of a hill with a panoramic view of Florence—the tiled rooftops, steeples, towers and domes seem like a fairyland at your fingertips. I thought nothing could be more spectacular than when the setting sun painted Florence in a rosy glow at sunset. But then the twilight faded into darkness and the lights of the city seemed to dance below the starry sky and I decided this was almost more spectacular. It is not surprising the setting of the Torre di Bellosguardo is so fabulous. It was chosen by a nobleman, Guido Cavalcanti (a friend of Dante's) as the most beautiful site in Florence to build his villa. The villa is owned today by Amerigo Franchetti who inherited the fabulous property from his grandmother, a baroness. Each room is a treasure decorated with marvelous antiques. The garden is a meticulously groomed delight and highlights a splendid pool on the terrace overlooking Florence. Staying here is certainly like being the pampered guest of nobility: which of course you really are. The best surprise of all is the price. Though only a very short drive to the heart of Florence, the cost is much less than staying in the center of the city at a deluxe hotel—and more romantic.

TORRE DI BELLOSGUARDO
Owner: Amerigo Franchetti
Via Roti Michelozzi, 2
50124 Florence, Italy
tel: (055) 22 95 29 fax: (055) 22 90 08
16 rooms: Double from Lire 344,000
Suites to Lire 574,000
Open all year
Credit cards: all major
No restaurant, breakfast only
5-minute drive to heart of Florence

As an alternative to staying in downtown Florence, you might want to consider instead the Villa La Massa which is located on the banks of the Arno about a 15-minute drive from town. The Villa La Massa is actually composed of three buildings—each old and each having its own unique charm. This beautiful estate originally belonged to the rich and powerful Giraldi family: inscribed tombstones, underground tunnels and a chapel still remain from this period of the villa's ancient history. Although the Villa La Massa is very old, the hotel offers all of the modern amenities including tennis courts, a swimming pool, air conditioning, refrigerators in the guest rooms. The restaurant, Il Verrocchio, has a beautiful terrace for outdoor dining overlooking the Arno river and offers the best of Tuscan specialties. If you have a car, then the Villa La Massa might make an appealing alternative to staying in the heart of Florence: especially in summer when you can do your sightseeing during the day and return to a pool and garden setting at night:—there is free courtesy bus service to and from Florence.

HOTEL VILLA LA MASSA
Owner: Carlo Grillini
50010 Candeli (FI), Italy
tel: (055) 63 25 79 fax: (055) 66 61 41
40 rooms: Double Lire 420,000–490,000
Open all year
Credit cards: all major
Restaurant open daily
Located on bend of Arno River
7 km E of Florence

The Bencista is a real "find" for the traveller looking for a congenial, appealing, family run hotel near Florence which has charm and yet is reasonably priced. This delightful old villa, romantically nestled in the foothills overlooking Florence, is owned and managed by the Simoni family who are always about, personally seeing to every need of their guests. Simone Simoni speaks excellent English, and on the day of my arrival he was patiently engrossed in conversation with one of the guests, giving him tips for sightseeing. Downstairs there are a jumble of rooms, each nicely decorated with rather dark, Victorian furniture. Upstairs are the bedrooms which vary in size, location, and furnishings. Some are far superior to others; however, they are all divided into only two price categories: with or without private bathroom. Many people return year after year to "their own" favorite room. During the season, reservations are usually given only to guests who plan to spend several days at the hotel—this is an easy requirement because the hotel is beautifully located for sightseeing in both Florence and Tuscany. (If you do not have a car, there is a bus at the top of the road which runs regularly into Florence.) Two meals (breakfast and a choice of lunch or dinner of family-style Italian cooking) are included in the price. One of the outstanding features of the pensione is its splendid terrace where guests can enjoy a sweeping panorama of Florence.

PENSIONE BENCISTA
Owner: Simone Simoni -
50014 Fiesole (FI), Italy
tel: (055) 59 163 fax: (055) 59 163
43 rooms: Double Lire 170,000–200,000
Rate includes breakfast and dinner
Open all year
Credit cards: none accepted
Restaurant open daily, only for guests
8 km NE of Florence

It would be difficult to find another hotel with as many attributes as the Villa San Michele. In fact, almost impossible. How could one surpass a wooded hillside setting overlooking Florence, a stunning view, gorgeous antiques, impeccable management, gourmet dining, and, as if this were not enough, a building designed by Michelangelo. The Villa San Michele was originally a monastery whose inner courtyard dates back to the 15th Century. No expense has been spared in the reconstruction of this fabulous building to maintain the ancient ambiance. There are only 28 guest rooms, and, although not large, they are decorated with elegant taste. The lounges, dining rooms, terraces and gardens are also exquisite. Breakfast and either dinner or lunch are compulsory, but this is no problem since the food is delicious. Meals can be enjoyed either in a beautiful dining room or on a lovely veranda which stretches along the entire length of the building. A swimming pool has been built on a secluded little terrace above the hotel, and, as with every feature of the Villa San Michele, it is beautiful, perfectly situated to capture the view and surrounded by fragrant gardens.

VILLA SAN MICHELE
Manager: Maurizio Saccani
Via Doccia, 4
50014 Fiesole, (FI), Italy
tel: (055) 59451 fax: (055) 598734
28 rooms: Double Lire 774,000
Open April to December
Credit cards: all major
Restaurant open daily
7 km NE of Florence
U.S. Rep: LHW 800-223-6800

Across the street from the 12th century Abbazia di Follina, in the small town of Follina (less than an hour's drive north of Venice), there is a jewel of a small hotel, the Romantik Hotel Abbazia. As you enter into the spacious lobby with its subdued lighting, Oriental carpets, and fine antique furniture, you will feel as if you are entering a private home rather than a commercial hotel. There are only 17 guest rooms, each superbly decorated in an individual style reflecting an English country manor ambiance. All of the bedrooms are decorator perfect with color coordinating wallpapers, draperies, bed coverings and carpets. Accents of antiques, beautifully framed pictures, and bouquets of flowers make each room special. Particularly appealing are rooms 4, 5 and 6 which have large flower-decked terraces that overlook the garden in the central courtyard. There isn't a restaurant, but just a few-minute's-drive away is the superb Ristorante da Gigetto, a delightful villa, brimming with country antiques where, you can dine exquisitely. In the cellar is an outstanding wine collection—a truly incredible selection of priceless wines beautifully displayed in a museum-like setting—ask the owner, Gigetto, if he has time to give you the "tour." Just 20 km from Follina is the charming town of Asolo, plus, in the area there are numerous Palladian villas to admire.

ROMANTIK HOTEL ABBAZIA
Owners: Zanon family (Manager: Ivana Zanon)
Via Martiri della Liberta
31051 Follina (TV), Italy
tel: (0438) 97 12 77 fax: (0438) 97 00 01
17 rooms with private bathrooms
Double Lire 175,000, Suites: Lire 220,000
Open all year
Credit cards: all major
No restaurant, breakfast only
90 km S. of Cortina, 60 km NW of Venice
U.S. Rep: Euro-Connection 800-645-3876

The Hotel Villa del Sogno is perched on a hillside across the road from, and overlooking beautiful Lake Garda. I am not sure of the history of the villa, but apparently it was an estate—obviously of a family of means, for the hotel is a prime piece of property. A small private road winds up the hill through a grove of trees until the villa is spotted, a traditional ochre-colored, red-tiled-roof building set off with white trim and green shutters. As you enter the hotel, it is as if you were in a private home. A large wooden, open staircase leads to the upper floors where the spacious bedrooms are attractively decorated in traditional style furniture. The choice rooms of course are those in the front with a view of the lake. One of the very finest features of the Villa del Sogno is its especially large terrace in the back of the hotel which has a majestic view out over the trees to the lake. The day I visited, many of the guests were enjoying afternoon tea (the hotel seems to cater to small British tour groups) as they savored the view from the comfort of lounge chairs. Another favorite retreat is the swimming pool which is tucked onto a terrace nestled to the side of the hotel. The grounds surrounding the pool are quite lovely, with potted plants placed strategically about the various levels of park like grounds. Recently added is a new fitness center with solarium, sauna and Jacuzzi.

VILLA DEL SOGNO
Owner: Aldo Calderan
Lake Garda
25083 Fasano di Gardone Riviera (BS), Italy
tel: (0365) 29 01 81 fax: (0365) 29 02 30
35 rooms: Double Lire 260,000–320,000
Open April to December
Credit cards: all major
Restaurant open daily
2 km NE of Gardone Riviera
130 km E of Milan, 68 km W of Verona

I was enchanted with the Villa Fiordaliso (a fetching pink and white villa superbly located on the shore of Lake Garda) when I spent the night in one of its antique-filled bedrooms overlooking the lake several years ago. At that time, I wrote a glowing description of this beautiful little hotel, only to learn from the manager that I was one of the last guests—the villa was closing to the public. Nevertheless, when researching for a later edition, I went by the Villa Fiordaliso "for old times' sake" and, to my delight, found it open again as a small hotel. Although the emphasis now is definitely on dining (the meals are expensive, but excellent), there are seven bedrooms—each unique in decor, yet each with every modern comfort. The rooms facing the lake have a lovely view, and are quieter since they are away from the noise of the street. Throughout the interior there is a blend of antique and stylish modern furniture, nicely set off by ornate parquetry floors, cool marble pillars, and magnificent gilded and painted ceilings. For history buffs, the villa offers a bit of romance—the Villa Fiordaliso was a gift of Mussolini to his mistress, Claretta Petacci. In fact, Claretta's own bedroom is one of the rooms available and is a real winner with an enormous marble bathroom. The Villa Fiordaliso is owned and managed by the Tosetti family whose warmth of welcome mellows the sophisticated ambiance of this small hotel.

VILLA FIORDALISO
Owner: Giuseppe Tossetti
Via Zanardelli, 132
Lake Garda, 25083 Gardone Riviera (BS), Italy
tel: (0365) 20 15 8 fax: (0365) 29 00 11
7 rooms: Double from Lire 400,000
Suites to Lire 600,000 (Claretta's suite)
Rates include breakfast and a' la carte dinner
Open March to October
Credit cards: all major
Restaurant open daily
130 km E of Milan, 66 km W of Verona

When we first saw the Hotel Villa Giulia it was rated by the government as a third class pensione. However, the hotel is no longer a simple pensione. On our last visit we were pleased to note that all the rooms now have a private bathroom and even a swimming pool has been built into the garden. The inn is a Victorian-style villa in a large park which extends down to Lake Garda. A dramatic staircase at the end of the hallway leads to the simple bedrooms. In addition to the rooms in the main villa, guest rooms are available in a modern annex. On the same level as the entrance hall is a dining room which is quite appealing with enormous chandeliers and antique-style chairs. On a lower level, opening out onto the garden, is another dining room which is quite modern and lacking in charm. When the weather is warm, the favorite place to dine is on the terrace where tables are set to enjoy the sun and a view of the lake. Wherever you choose to dine, you will enjoy good home-style Italian cooking—it is not surprising that the food is well prepared since Signora Bombardelli, the owner, is usually bustling about in the kitchen personally overseeing the preparation of the next meal. She does not speak much English, but is extremely gracious and is always about seeing that her guests are happy. Not fancy, the Hotel Villa Giulia offers a very pleasant stay at reasonable prices with a superb lakefront location.

HOTEL VILLA GIULIA
Owner: Rina Bombardelli
Via Rimembranza, 20
25084 Gargnano, Lake Garda, (BS), Italy
tel: (0365) 71 289 fax: (0365) 72 774
30 rooms: Double Lire 150,000*
*3 night minimum
Open April to October
Credit cards: all major
Restaurant open daily
140 km E of Milan, 78 km W of Verona

The entrance to Baia d'Oro is off the narrow, cobbled street that runs through the quaint lake-side town of Gargnano-Villa. Once inside, there is a small lounge, intimate bar, and a dining room. To truly appreciate the attributes that make this small inn so very special, you must step outside to the terrace that stretches out over the water. In the daytime this sun-drenched oasis is a favorite with the luncheon crowd. In the evening as the sun sets, fresh flowers and candles are placed on small tables dressed with fresh linens: a romantic scene that will beckon you again and again to the Baia d'Oro. The food lives up to all expectations: the pasta is home-made in the kitchen, the fish is fresh from the lake. As you dine, here is a constant parade of beautiful yachts pulling up to the dock, unloading their cargo of laughing, chicly dressed, obviously well-to-do Italians who have come to dine. After dinner, you go a narrow staircase to the basic bedrooms which are perfect for the young of heart who are not expecting decorator perfect furnishings. Our favorite is 14, an old-fashioned room with an antique dresser, a fancy upholstered king sized-bed, a couple of frumpy little chairs, and two large windows opening onto the lake. The Baia d'Oro is owned by the Terzi family (Gianbattista Terzi is a well-known artist). In recent years, their son, Gabiele, has taken over the management. He does a superb job personally orchestrating the dinner each evening and seeing that all overnight guests are happy.

BAIA D'ORO
Owner: Terzi Family (Manager: Gabrielle Terzi)
Via Liberta, 25085 Gargnano-Villa
Lake Garda (BS), Italy
tel: (0365) 71 17 1 fax: (0365) 72 56 8
13 rooms: Double Lire 260,000*
* Rate includes breakfast and dinner
Open April to October
Credit cards: all major
Restaurant open daily
140 km E of Milan, 78 km W of Verona

Finally there is a very special place to stay near the Rome airport. However, to merely say that a void has been filled is totally inadequate for La Posta Vecchia without a doubt offers some of the most sensational accommodations in all of Italy ... in all the world. Not that everyone will be able to afford to stay here for this is an expensive small inn—very expensive, but if you have the money, it is a real bargain. For this is the opportunity of a lifetime for those who want to taste the life-style of the rich and famous. La Posta Vecchia was the home of the late John Paul Getty, his Italian villa nestled on the edge of the ocean just north of the Rome airport. Just imagine: there are only ten rooms, mostly suites, tucked into an enormous mansion, secluded by manicured gardens artfully created to emphasize the ruins of a Pompeii-like Roman villa whose beautiful mosaic floor peeks from between surrounding flowers and hedges. Within the villa, priceless antique furniture, statues, and fabulous fabrics adorn the rooms, artfully blended by Getty's interior designer to create an opulent, tasteful splendor. For Getty, nothing was too special, nothing too expensive. All has been retained as it was in Getty's day, the only changes being some cosmetic spiffing such as painting and new drapes (this was taking awhile because the factory in Paris where the original fabric had been woven had to be tracked down—but replacements were on the way at the time of our visit). The new owner has accomplished a remarkable feat of returning the villa to its original magnificence. The primary use of the villa is for small groups that book the entire hotel for private conferences, think tanks, seminars, and family reunions. If you want the entire villa for an exclusive holiday, you need have no worry about security since columns, discreetly positioned on each corner of the property, send out detector rays to keep anyone from the premises, plus of course bullet proof glass in the Getty bedroom and steel infrastructure in the walls. Also, should you want to bring your staff, the third floor is well equipped for your maids and butlers.

When Getty was renovating the villa for his personal use and installing the magnificent pool in the northern wing of the house, he found the villa dated back much earlier than he originally speculated. Beneath the house were the foundations of a Roman villa thought perhaps to be the weekend retreat of Julius Caesar. Getty, whom you know was profoundly interested in archaeology, spared no expense to preserve this antiquity. The Roman ruins now encompass the lower level of the home and guests can wonder at the gorgeous mosaic floors, walls and pottery displayed like in a living museum. Parts of the museum can be viewed from the upper level where a panel of glass has been installed in the floor so the mosaic under-flooring can be viewed. There is even a workshop in this subterranean museum, where archaeologists under the supervision of the Department of Fine Arts continue to piece together the puzzle of this fascinating villa. NOTE: Since La Posta Vecchia is ideally suited for small groups—such as an exclusive house party or summit meeting of heads of state—there will be times when the entire villa is rented and rooms won't be available for individual bookings. But, if you are lucky and can snare a room, this is truly an experience of a lifetime. NOTE: the latest renovation has added five more bedrooms, artfully tucked into the north tower wing.

LA POSTA VECCHIA
Manager: Mario Ciorciolini
00055 Palo Laziale
Ladispoli (Roma), Italy
tel: (06) 9949500 fax: (06) 9949507
17 rooms: Double Lire 500,000–700,000
Suites: Lire 1,200,000–2,000,000
Credit cards: all major
Lunch or dinner: Lire 120,000 per person
2 km S of Ladispoli at Palo, private road
25 km N of Rome Airport, Oceanfront
Relais & Chateaux Hotel

Limone sul Garda is a small town tucked into a pocket of a hillside at the edge of Lake Garda. This very old town of pastel colored houses adorned with bougainvillea and twisting cobbled streets attracts so many tourists that in high season it is wall to wall tourists. But, the town is nevertheless very quaint, and especially appealing a off season when you can avoid some of the crowds. There are several large, modern hotels on the hillside, but the Hotel Le Palme (in a building dating back to the 17th Century), is in the heart of town, directly on the lake. Whereas many of our suggestions in the Lake Garda area are intimate, family-operated inns, Le Palme is a hotel with more of a commercial ambiance. You enter into the lobby and go down a few steps to a small bar and an especially attractive dining room with handsome wooden, antique-style, high back chairs and beautifully set tables. From the dining room, French doors open onto an appealing outside dining room on a balcony overlooking the lake. Tucked along the side of the hotel is another, more casual place to eat in a garden terrace overlooking the lake. Here white wrought iron tables and chairs are set under the centuries-old palm trees with many plants and colorful flowers. The price is the same for all the guest rooms, but the ones overlooking the lake are prime. The rooms are pleasant and some have had a few antique pieces of furniture. The Risatti brothers who own Hotel Le Palme, own several hotels in town which is an advantage because guests can use the pool at their hotel La Pergola.

HOTEL LE PALME
Owners: Risatti family
Via Porto, 36
25010 Limone sul Garda (BS), Italy
tel: (0365) 95 46 81
28 room: Double Lire 120,000
Open Easter to end of October
Credit cards: all major
Restaurant open daily
160 km NE of Milan, 97 km NW of Verona

The Villa La Principessa is a stately, traditional country mansion surrounded by beautiful gardens. In a park-like setting behind the hotel is a large swimming pool with lounge chairs and umbrellas invitingly set for guests to relax and enjoy the sun. In the distance are lush, green hills. The entire effect is refreshing and serene. The interior of the villa does not maintain the same degree of quiet elegance as does the exterior: the entry hall has some fine antiques and a beautifully paneled ceiling, but the carpet is a loud plaid which would be better suited for a Scottish castle and in one of the lounge rooms, the carpet is purple and the walls and draperies a bright green. The dining room, however, tones down with more muted colors and is quite attractive. The Villa La Principessa is located approximately mid-way between the popular tourist destinations of Lucca and Pisa. As there are no deluxe places to stay in either Lucca nor Pisa, the Villa La Principessa makes an excellent choice for those seeking well-maintained, luxury accommodations in a resort-like setting. Note, under the same ownership and across from La Principessa is a newly opened small hotel, Principessa Elisa, an 18th-century country house with 10 suites decorated in antiques. We have not had the opportunity to visit yet, but this sounds like a lovely new possibility for accommodations.

HOTEL VILLA LA PRINCIPESSA
Manager: Giancarlo Mugnani
55050 Massa Pisana, Lucca (LU), Italy,
tel: (0583) 370037 fax: (0583) 379019
44 rooms: Double Lire 306,000–346,000
 Suites Lire 356,000–446,000
Closed January and February
Credit cards: all major
Restaurant closed Wednesdays
4 km S of Lucca on old road to Pisa
18 km N of Pisa, between Lucca and Pisa
Relais & Chateaux Hotel

The Albergo del Sole, located about an hour's drive south of Milan, came highly recommended to us as one of Italy's finest "restaurants with rooms" so we arrived eagerly for our first visit. Happily, this little inn surpassed our highest expectations, offering an elegantly rustic setting and delicious meals. This 600 year old farmhouse is now a food connoisseur's dream come true. From the moment you enter this old stone home you are enveloped in a country ambiance enhanced by fine antiques, heavy beams, copper pots hanging on the walls and extravagant bouquets of flowers. The heart of the inn is its kitchen, long famous as one of Italy's finest, and well-deserving of its Michelin star. The food, featuring regional specialties prepared from the freshest of locally produced ingredients, is very expensive, but outstanding. If you cannot overnight here, the inn is still worth a visit simply for its atmosphere and cuisine. However, if possible, plan to spend the night so you can linger over your dinner and savor the fine food and wines. Some of the guest rooms are in the main building, others are in rooms tucked around the back garden. Each of the bedrooms is nicely decorated, but with a much more modern mood than the dining rooms. Although the food and country style furnishings are outstanding, it is the traditional Italian welcome and caring warmth of the owners, Silvana and Franco Colombani, that make the Albergo del Sole so special. NOTE: very little English spoken.

ALBERGO DEL SOLE
Owners: Franco Colombani & family
Via Trabattoni 22
20076 Maleo (MI), Italy
tel: (0377) 58 142 fax: (0377) 45 80 58
7 rooms: Double Lire 272,000–320,000
Closed January and August
Credit cards: AX, VS
Restaurant closed Sunday evenings and Mondays
60 km S of Milan, 23 km W of Cremona

The Hotel Santavenere was a wonderful surprise. I had seen pictures of the hotel before I arrived and it looked rather like a motel—a long, narrow building with each floor a row of guest rooms. The photographs did not do it justice—the hotel is absolutely a knockout. From the moment you walk into the lobby, the gracious ambiance of an exquisite country home surrounds you. The living room is elegant, but not "stuffy"—soft, comfortable sofas and lounge chairs slipcovered in an attractive country print form cozy conversation nooks. Excellent antiques lend further charm. Plus, there are many nautical accents, such as models of sailboats, giving even more interest to the room. The dining room follows in excellent taste—a large, airy room with high-backed wooden chairs, fresh flowers on the tables, and white linen cloths. The bedrooms are beautifully decorated with excellent copies of antiques and have modern bathrooms. Each bedroom opens onto its own terrace or balcony with lovely sea views. The location too is exceptional: there is a beautiful green lawn adorned with a swimming pool which stretches to the side of the hotel. Beyond the lawn the cliffs drop down a steep wooded hillside to the sea and a small private pier.

HOTEL SANTAVENERE
Localita Fiumicello
85040 Maratea (PZ), Italy
tel: (0973) 87 69 10 fax: (0973) 87 69 85
44 rooms: Double Lire 654,000–730,000*
*Rate includes breakfast, lunch and dinner
Open June to September 26
Credit cards: AX, VS
Restaurant open daily, only for guests
220 km S of Naples, 5 km W of Maratea

Once in a while a hotel is so perfect that it is tempting not to include it—selfishly fearful that if everyone knows how exceptional it is there might not be "room in the inn" when we return. The Castel Freiberg is just such a hotel, but conscience dictates sharing our Shangri-La with you. This fantasy castle cresting a hilltop in the mountains near Merano exudes charm. All of the public rooms are a decorator's dream where priceless antiques abound. The bedrooms, each individual in decor, are all tastefully furnished and some have balconies overlooking the mountains. Even if the setting were not perfect, this castle would be a "winner" because of its enchanting decor, but add to this a gorgeous restaurant in a richly paneled room with gourmet cooking, and what else could you possibly desire? Well, there is more. If you talk to the masterful and professional concierge, you will find that surrounding the Castel Freiberg is a maze of splendid walking paths. Also, of course, there is a beautiful pool in a garden setting with the mountains as a dramatic backdrop, as well as an inside pool, clay tennis courts, an exercise room, and more—you must go to see for yourself.

HOTEL CASTEL FREIBERG
Owner: Bortolotti Family
Via Labers
39012 Merano, (BZ) Italy
tel: (0473) 24 41 96 fax: (0473) 24 44 88
35 rooms: Double Lire 280,000–310,000
Open April 22 to November
Credit cards: all major
Restaurant open daily
In the countryside 7 km S of Merano
28 km NW of Bolzano

Castel Labers (also called Schloss Labers) is a lovely old castle which dates back to the 11th Century. It has a picturesque setting on a hillside surrounded by vineyards and overlooking the beautiful Merano Valley which is framed by dramatic mountains. Although not luxurious, this castle has character and charm. Probably its major attribute is excellent management by the Stapf-Neubert family who oversee every detail of the operation and take personal responsibility to ensure that everyone is properly pampered. I spoke to Mr. Neubert who told me that his great grandfather came from Copenhagen in 1885 and bought the castle which became so popular with his visiting friends that it soon became a prosperous hotel. The lounges and dining rooms are not fancy, but have a lived-in, comfortable ambiance. Many fresh foods are included in the menu and both red and white wine, produced from the inn's own vineyards, are served with meals. The central staircase dramatically leads upstairs where many of the bedrooms have lovely mountain views. The setting of this old castle is peaceful and quiet, and if you enjoy being in the countryside, you will delight in the marvelous network of walking paths that abound in this area.

HOTEL CASTEL LABERS
Owner: Stapf-Neubert Family
Via Labers, 25
39012 Merano (BZ), Italy
tel: (0473) 23 44 84 fax: (0473) 34 14 6
32 rooms: Double Lire 170,000–190,000
Open end of March to November
Credit cards: AX, EC, MC
Restaurant open daily, only for guests
In the countryside 3 km NE above Merano
28 km NW of Bolzano

If you love picturesque chalet-style hotels in quiet, isolated surroundings, then the Hotel Vigiljoch will definitely be your cup of tea. There is absolutely no highway noise: there are no cars. The only way to reach the hotel is by cable car which you take from the town of Lana which is near Merano in the mountains of northeastern Italy. The cable car rises quickly from the floor of the valley and presents breathtaking views of the vineyards and apple orchards. When the cable car reaches the top and slowly joggles into the terminal you will see the Hotel Vigiljoch just to the left of the station. In summer, flowers cascade from every window box and umbrellas gaily decorate the front terrace. Inside you find quite simple bedrooms, many of which have balconies with a sweeping view of valley and mountains. The bedrooms are small but pleasantly furnished with furniture painted in an Alpine motif. A sprinkling of antiques highlights the lounges. My very favorite room is an intimate, wood-paneled dining room whose wonderful country prints of blue and red are complimented by attractive light-pine furniture. The gracious owner, Karl Gapp, is extremely knowledgeable about what to see and do in the area. He is very active with the tourist office and can assist guests with their various travel plans.

HOTEL VIGILJOCH
Owner: Karl Gapp
39011 Vigiljoch
Lana bei Merano (BZ), Italy
tel: (0473) 51 236 fax: (0473) 51 410
35 rooms: Double Lire 168,000*
*Rate includes breakfast and dinner
Open March 15 to November 15
Credit cards: none accepted
Restaurant open daily
Accessible by cable car
9 km S of Merano on route 238
24 km NW of Bolzano

The Villa di Monte Vibiano is unique: we have nothing else quite like it in our Italian guide. Not a hotel at all, but rather an exquisite private castle that opens its doors to paying guests. And indeed you will feel like a pampered guest from the moment you enter into the huge entrance hall and are greeted by the English butler. There are only six guest rooms so staying here is like being at a weekend "house party", especially since dinner (including wine) is included in the price and guests eat family style in the gorgeous dining room. Staying at the villa is expensive, but not when compared to the prices of deluxe hotels in Rome or Florence, and here you are getting the chance to truly live the life of nobility in an Italian castle. The Villa di Monte Vibiano is visible from miles around as it is spectacularly located on the crest of a wooded hilltop, affording sensational panoramic views of the countryside in every direction. While staying at Monte Vibiano, the castle is your home. You can wander through the gorgeously decorated rooms, literally a museum of stunning antiques, sit and read a book in one of the cozy nooks, play cards in the game room, swim in the refreshing pool, or walk in complete seclusion. There is also a very old garden maze, an outdoor theater, and even a tree house accessible to guests.

VILLA DI MONTE VIBIANO
Owner: Dr. Fasola Bologna
Monte Vibiano, 06050 Mercatello (PG), Italy
tel: (075) 87 83 371 not for reservations
6 rooms: Double U.S. $460.00*
* Rate includes breakfast, dinner and all drinks
Restaurant open daily, only for guests
Listed on Hallwag map under Monte Vibiano
25 km S of Perugia
1 km south of Mercatello
Reservations only through Solemar, Florence, Italy
tel: (055) 21 81 22 fax: (055) 55 28 71 57

Hotel Carrobbio is located on a narrow side street, just a few steps off the Via Torino—a major street leading to the Duomo. From the outside the hotel appears non-descript—a not-too interesting, modern, four-story building. However, I was glad I stopped to take a look because this small hotel has a lot to offer. Not that it can compare with its neighbor, the elegant Hotel Pierre Milan, but the prices are much lower. The reception area is small and guests are greeted warmly. According to the friendly reception manager, Franco Grassi, the hotel is small enough to know guests by name: they are never just a number. Beyond the reception area is a bar that leads into a lounge with the chairs and sofas upholstered in black leather. One end of the room is mirrored, reflecting puffy Austrian drapes and potted palms. A sky light, illuminating the core of the building, imparts a cheerful ambiance. A large buffet breakfast (served in a rather plain, white-walled room) is included in the room rate. Well-lit hallways lead to the bedrooms which are all similar in decor with built-in headboards, good reading lights, color coordinated bedspreads and chair coverings, mini bars, and television. Ask for one of the bedrooms on the top floor—three of these have spacious terraces with tables and chairs for sitting outside when the weather is nice. One of the nicest aspects of the Hotel Carrobbio is that it is so well kept. Everything looks fresh and new—not surprising as the hotel only opened in 1990.

HOTEL CARROBBIO
Manager: Franco Grassi
Via Medici 3
20123 Milan, Italy
tel: (02) 89 01 07 40 fax: (02) 80 53 334
35 rooms, Double: Lire 290,000
Open all year
Credit cards: all major
No restaurant, breakfast only
Located about 10-minute walk from Duomo

Milan, has very few deluxe small hotels with character. But, since the Hotel Pierre Milan came on the scene a few years ago, that need has been superbly fulfilled. The Pierre Milan is expensive, but no more so than other hotels in the same category. You walk under the canopy, through a large glass entry flanked by two handsome statues of prancing horses, and into the spacious reception lounge decorated in tones of beige accentuated by cream-colored marbles. Even when the hotel is fully booked, there is an air of quiet refinement. An inner courtyard provides a garden effect for the chic dining room with just a handful of tables, exquisitely set with fine linens. A hallway leads to the "American" bar, which opens onto a sophisticated, intimate lounge with black leather sofas and a grand piano. The guest rooms are not large (except for the suites), but each is individually decorated in impeccable taste: walls covered with fine fabrics, color coordinating with the carpets, drapes and bedspreads. On the bedside table a control panel allows you to call house-keeping, turn off the lights, turn on the television, put a "do not disturb" sign outside the door, and even electronically lower the window shades without getting out of bed. Many rooms have an antique desk or writing table, one of my favorites, room 210 (with French blue walls and drapes) has an antique, wooden, king-sized sleigh bed. The Hotel Pierre, located in the historically interesting Sant'Ambrogio district.

HOTEL PIERRE MILAN
Manager: Carlo Stanglini
Via De Amicis, 32
20123 Milan, Italy
tel: (02) 72 00 05 81 fax (02) 80 52 157
47 rooms, Double: Lire 390,000–570,000*.
*Weekend specials (on request) Double: Lire 290,000
Open all year
Credit cards: all major
Restaurant open daily
15-minute walk to the Duomo

During the 17th and 18th Centuries it was fashionable for wealthy Venetian noble-men to build palatial retreats along the cool banks of the Brenta River, thus the waterway became lined with sensational villas all the way from Venice to Padua. Today villages and commerce have built up in the area, but many of the mansions still survive, filled with statues, frescos, and Murano glasswork, attesting to the opulent life-style of days gone by. Some are now open as museums, but for those who really want to experience living the noble life as in the past, there is the lovely 17th-century Villa Margherita, an elegant small hotel. It is situated across the highway from the canal, just a short stroll from one of the villa museums, and a short drive from the others. Many converted villas in Italy are beautiful but faded, reflecting gentile neglect. Not so with the Villa Margherita where all is beautifully maintained; every detail is perfect. From the lounges with their elegant antiques to the guest rooms with color coordinated fabrics, each detail shows the care and involvement of the owner, Valeria Sabbadin, an expert hotelier. Far from the hubbub of Venice, yet only a 20 minute drive away, the Villa Margherita is an excellent hotel choice for those who prefer to avoid the hustle and bustle of the city. If you go into Venice to see the sights, it is best to take the bus, thus avoiding the congestion of traffic and high expense of parking.

HOTEL VILLA MARGHERITA
Owner: Valeria and Remingio dal Corso
Via Nazionale 416
30030 Mira (VE), Italy
tel: (041) 42 65 800 fax: (041) 42 65 838
19 rooms: Double Lire 200,000–220,000
Closed January 8 to February 8
Credit cards: all major
Restaurant open daily
On canal 2 km W of Mira
20 km W. of Venice

Of course, it is fun to be in the heart of Venice, but for half the price of what you would pay for a first class hotel there, you can stay twenty minutes to the north at the Villa Condulmer, a splendid 17th-century villa whose rooms more closely resemble a museum than a hotel. The rooms are grand, with fabulous wall frescos painted by Moretti Laresi. The eight rooms in the original villa are the most sumptuous in decor; however, in the heat of summer you might prefer the newer wing whose rooms provide the option of air conditioning. There are several lovely dining rooms for you to enjoy. In addition, when the weather is balmy, you may choose to have your meals served outdoors on the terrace. In the garden is a large pool and nearby a gym set which would appeal to children. For adult "play", there is a golf course adjacent to the hotel where arrangements can be made for you to play if you have a letter of introduction from your club in the United States. Should you like horseback riding this too can be arranged.

VILLA CONDULMER
Manager: Mr. Chinellato
31021 Mogliano Veneto (TV), Italy
tel: (041) 45 71 00 fax: (041) 45 71 34
45 rooms: Double Lire 176,000–270,000
Closed January 7 to February 15
Credit cards: all major
Restaurant closed Mondays
4 km NE of Mogliano toward Zerman
18 km N of Venice

Residence Castello di Gargonza is a romantic walled, storybook village, surrounded by forests and perched at the crest of a hill. The 900-year-old complex of stone buildings now receives guests. There are 7 guest rooms for overnight guests plus 19 picturesque farmhouses available for rent by the week. Most have one or two bedrooms plus a kitchenette and many also have a fireplace—perfect for chilly evenings. Each small cottage is named and when you make a reservation, the hotel will send you a map of the town and a description and a sketch of each of the houses so that you can choose what most appeals to your needs. If you prefer not to cook, there is a restaurant called "La Torre di Gargonza". The village oozes with charm: staying here is like stepping back to medieval times. The interior decor leaves something to be desired, with an extensive use of plastic furniture interspersed with more traditional pieces. However, the overall ambiance is terrific and the hotel is a fabulous bargain, especially for two couples travelling together or families with children who want a home base for exploring Tuscany. NOTE: The closest town on the Hallwag map is Monte Savino; the hotel is actually located about 8 kilometers west, on road 73 to Siena.

CASTELLO DI GARGONZA
Owner: Count Roberto Guicciardini
Manager: Giuliano Fucini
Azienda Castello di Gargonza, Localita Gargonza
52048 Monte San Savino (AR), Italy
tel: (0575) 84 70 21 fax: (0575) 84 70 54
7 rooms: Double Lire 160,000–210,000*
*3 night minimum
18 apartments: Lire 910,000–1,862,000 per week
Closed January
Credit cards: all major
Restaurant closed Tuesdays
35 km E of Siena, 8 km W of Monte Savino, rte 73

La Chiusa, nestled in the hills of Tuscany southeast of Siena, is an old stone farmhouse whose restaurant is so famous that guests come from miles away to enjoy the meals where everything is known to be fresh, homemade, and delicious. Dania and Umberto Lucherini are the gracious owners and Dania is the talented chef. Almost all the vegetables, olive oil, meats, wines, and cheeses either come from the inn's own farm or from those nearby. The original wood burning oven still stands in the courtyard in front of the inn, emitting delicious aromas of freshly baking bread. The dining room is large and airy, with an uncluttered simple elegance enhanced by windows overlooking rolling hills. When the weather is balmy, meals are also served on the back terrace which is ideally positioned with a sweeping view. The emphasis here is definitely on the exquisite meals, but happily there are also seven bedrooms for guests who want to spend the night. Like the dining room, the guest rooms are perfectly in keeping with the ambiance of the old farmhouse, lovely in their rustic simplicity yet with every modern convenience. If you appreciate and are willing to pay for gourmet meals, this is a perfect base for exploring Tuscany.

LA CHIUSA
Owner: Lucherini Family
Manager: Sodi Franco
Via della Madonnina 88
53040 Montefollonico (SI), Italy
tel: (0577) 66 96 68 fax: (0577) 66 95 93
12 rooms: Double Lire 280,000
2 suites Lire 420,000
Open mid-March to November 5
 December 7 to January 7
Credit cards: all major
Restaurant closed Tuesdays
60 km S of Siena
10 km NW of Montepulciano

Lucia Ana Luhan, whose parents came from Italy, grew up in a family rich in Italian tradition. She now lives in California where she is married to a busy surgeon, has a family of three, and operates several very successful fresh pasta restaurants plus a catering service. For most women this would keep them more than busy. But you don't know Lucia. A few years ago, while on holiday in Italy, she fell in love with a 500-year-old stone farmhouse, bought it on a whim, and converted it into the Bed & Breakfast of Tuscany. Now Lucia commutes back and forth between California and Italy. When Lucia is not at her Italian farmhouse, it is well-managed by Renata Cerchiari. However, if Lucia is in residence, that fact alone is reason enough to visit because pretty Lucia's radiant personality fills her small bed and breakfast. This seven bedroom inn is not luxurious, nor is it meant to be. All of the rooms are decorated in a homey, comfortable way—nothing contrived, just naturally pleasing and in keeping with the rustic nature of the simple stone house. When the weather is mild, guests enjoy a bountiful breakfast outside on the terrace. In the evening, homemade soup, cheeses and cold cuts are always available. A fancier dinner is served if requested in the morning, plus there are many restaurants in the world-famous spa town of Montecatini Terme, just a 6-minute drive down the hill. Since our first visit, a small pool has been added and there is a golf course 5 minutes from the inn.. Monsummano Terme is the closest town to Montevettolini on the Hallwag map.

BED & BREAKFAST OF TUSCANY
Owner: Lucia Ana Luhan
144 Via dei Bronzoli
51010 Montevettolini (PT), Italy
7 rooms: Double $150 U.S. dollars
tel and fax: (0572) 62 88 17
Open all year
Credit cards: none accepted
Dinner on request
55 km E of Florence, 3 km NW of Monsummano

In the competition for romantic Italian lake-side villages, none can top Orta San Giulio. It is truly a gem. Park your car and walk down a steep incline to discover a cluster of pastel-colored, very old buildings, hugging the shores of the lake. Just across the water the Basilica of San Giulio stands boldly on its own little island, creating a perfect picture for the avid photographer. This quaint town cries out for a wonderful place to stay. There is the Hotel San Rocco, a large deluxe hotel, beautifully positioned on the edge of the lake, but, in our estimation, the modern decor seems to jar with the medieval mood of the old town. Not nearly so deluxe, but with potential charm, is the simple Leon d'Oro, down a tiny lane just off the central plaza. The most outstanding features of this small hotel is its romantic outdoor terrace that stretches out to the edge of the water. Here excellent meals are served at small tables shaded by a trellis laden with grape vines. Signora Ronchetti personally oversees the meal service, insuring all the guests are well cared for. A more conventional dining room opens onto the terrace, but on balmy days, no one can resist eating outside. A flight of stairs winds up to the maze of corridors that lead to the various bedrooms where the decor is very plain. But, if you are a no-frills person you will be quite happy. Be sure to request one of the better rooms with a view of the lake. One of the most popular rooms is 33, a small room (with one wall of acoustical tile) with large windows looking out over a jumble of weathered tiled roofs to the lake.

ALBERGO LEON D'ORO
Owners: Sorelle Ronchetti family
28016 Orta San Giulio, Lake Orta (NO), Italy
tel: (0322) 90.56.66 (0322) 90 303
35 rooms, Double: Lire 170,000*
*Rate includes breakfast and dinner
Closed December and January
Credit cards: all major
Restaurant open daily
85 km NW of Milan, on Lake Orta

The town of Orvieto, just off the main expressway between Rome and Florence, is one of the most picturesque of all the Umbrian hilltowns. The small city crowns the top of a hill—an intriguing sight which can be viewed from miles away. Less than a 10-minute drive south of Orvieto is a 12th-century Gothic abbey which has been converted into a hotel. Here you can stay surrounded by the romantic ruins of yesteryear. We have overnighted at La Badia, enjoying the pool and the "old-world" atmosphere. Some readers have written they too liked their stay at La Badia, but we continue to receive some letters complaining of the aloof attitude of the personnel. Although **La Badia** does not seem to exude the caring management that makes staying at a hotel special, the location near the stunning town of Orvieto is excellent. The hotel itself is nice: the dining room is especially attractive with an enormous, high vaulted stone ceiling, wrought iron fixtures, heavy wooden beams, eye-catching copper accents and, at one end, a cavernous fireplace complete with a spit for roasting. The bedrooms are not large, but are comfortable and many have a stunning view of the town of Orvieto. In the meadows behind the monastery there is a pool which makes a welcome respite from a day on the road.

LA BADIA
Manager: Dot. Luisa Fiumi
05019 Orvieto Scalo (TR), Italy
tel: (0763) 90 359 fax: (0763) 92 796
24 rooms: Double Lire 283,000
Open March to December
Credit cards: all major
Restaurant closed Wednesdays
4 km S of Orvieto, 115 km N of Rome

The Villa Igiea Grand Hotel is an oasis of blissful tranquillity in the midst of the large and rather unattractive city of Palermo. With all the fabulous archaeological sites and marvelous cathedrals in the area it is wonderful to have such a splendid hotel to "come home to" at night. The approach to the Villa is not scenic, but from the moment you enter the gates you are in another world: a world of spacious lobbies, sweeping verandas, formal dining rooms, and generously sized, well furnished bedrooms with large modern bathrooms. Many of the bedrooms have private balconies overlooking the gardens to the sea. The hotel is called a villa, but it is much more like a small deluxe castle built right at the edge of the sea. A lovely freeform swimming pool fits itself onto a ledge which overhangs the water. Next to the pool the hotel has its very own ancient Greek temple—now how many hotels can top that? The most outstanding attributes of the hotel are the gardens which envelop the building in a nest of beautiful pines and masses of gorgeous flower beds intertwined with twisting pathways. Altogether, a most delightful spot.

VILLA IGIEA GRAND HOTEL
Manager: Franco Arabia
Via Belmonte, 43 (Acquasanta)
90142 Palermo, Sicily, Italy
tel: (091) 54 37 44 fax: (091) 54 76 54
117 rooms: Double Lire 390,000
Open all year
Credit cards: all major
Restaurant open daily
On northern coast of Sicily
U.S. Rep: Utell 800-223-9868

The Villa le Barone was once the home of the famous Tuscan family, Della Robbia, whose delightful terra cottas are still seen throughout Italy. Most of the estate now has been beautifully converted into a deluxe small hotel, but the present owner, Duchessa Franca Viviani Della Robbia, still maintains a charming vine covered cottage for her own use. Although she is now in her eighties, the Duchessa comes frequently to the villa to ensure that her impeccable standards and exquisite taste prevail. Staying at the Villa le Barone is very much like being the fortunate guest in a private, elegant home set in the gorgeous Tuscany hills. There are only 25 guest rooms, all of which vary in size and decor, but each with an individual charm. In addition, there is a lovely pool on a terrace overlooking the vineyards and out to the mellow hills beyond. Wonderful little terraces are found secluded in the park-like setting where guests can find a quiet nook to read or just to sit and soak in the beauty. The food is divine and in balmy weather lunch can be taken in the garden and dinner perhaps inside in a charming dining room which formerly housed the stables. Reservations are accepted for a minimum of three nights, but that should be no problem—three nights will be too short an interlude to spend in this romantic paradise. (Closest town on Hallwag map, Greve)

VILLA LE BARONE
Owner: Duchessa Franca Viviani Della Robbia
Manager: Caterina Buonamici
Via San Leolino, 19
50020 Panzano in Chianti (FI), Italy
tel: (055) 85 26 21 fax: (055) 85 22 77
25 rooms: Double Lire 300,000–340,000*
* Rate includes breakfast and dinner
Open Easter to October
Credit cards: AX
Restaurant open daily, only for guests
31 km S of Florence, 6 km S of Greve

My first introduction to La Scuderia, beautifully situated in the heart of Tuscany, was one idyllic evening while sitting outside in the garden with friends enjoying a simple, yet delicious dinner. Perhaps the magic was the balmy air, the delicate wine or just the home cooked meal. It was not until later that we learned that in addition to the restaurant (which is managed by a young local couple, Rossella and Marco), there are three apartments for rent. The suite in the back is one of my favorite hideaways in Tuscany. Here you will find a plain little old-fashioned parlor, a large bathroom (with a tiny little bathtub), a cheerful, well-supplied kitchen with a table tucked in the corner for dining, and a romantic bedroom which is simply, but attractively, furnished in family antiques with the added bonus of a "Romeo and Juliet" balcony overlooking the garden and vineyards. The apartments are best suited for a stay of a week (breakfast not included in weekly rate), but guests will be taken on a bed and breakfast basis for a three-day minimum. La Scuderia is not a sophisticated, luxurious hotel, but for those who enjoy simple accommodation and appreciate genuine, home-like hospitality, this is a real winner. NOTE: The closest town on Hallwag map is Sambuca.

LA SCUDERIA
Owners: Stella and Carlo Casolaro
Badia a Passignano
50020 Sambuca Val di Pesa (FI), Italy
tel: (055) 80 71 524
3 apartments: Lire 600,000 per week
Double Lire 80,000 by the night*
*3 night minimum
Open all year
Credit cards: none accepted
Restaurant closed Wednesdays
32 km S of Florence, 5 km NE of Sambuca

How smug I felt at "discovering" the Castel Pergine, for here is a picture book castle perfect for the budget-minded tourist. No need to forfeit romance and glamour for even though the Castel Pergine is inexpensive, it has a fabulous location dominating a hilltop above the town of Pergine. Luckily, this castle has been delightfully transformed into a small hotel with incredible views out over the valleys and wooded hills. From the tower you can even see two small lakes in the distance which invite a picnic. The Castel Pergine is more famous as a restaurant than a hotel, in fact the Michelin guide gives the kitchen a two fork rating. The dining room has an engaging medieval decor, gorgeous views, and good food. In another wing of the castle the guest rooms offer accommodation ranging from rather basic to comfortably charming. About half of the 21 rooms have private baths; these are more expensive but also more appealingly decorated with handsome wooden paneling and rustic, country-style furnishings. All the guest rooms are pleasant, most offering lovely views, but room #27, a corner room, is especially large and pretty. The Castle Pergine is a real bargain for the price-conscious traveller, its secluded hilltop ambiance definitely a winner—especially if you are travelling with children who will love their "own" Disneyland-like castle.

CASTEL PERGINE
Owner: Mario Oss
Manager: Verena Schneider-Neff
38057 Pergine (TN), Italy
tel: (0461) 53 11 58
21 rooms: Double Lire 145,000
Rate includes 3 meals a day
Open May to October 15
Credit cards: none accepted
Restaurant open daily high season
71 km S of Bolzano ,10 km E of Trento
2.5 km E of Pergine

I am such a romantic that, as the boat chugged across the lake from Stresa to the medieval fishing village of Isola dei Pescatori and I saw the Hotel Verbano with its reddish-brown walls, dark green shutters, and tables set on the terrace overlooking the lake, my heart was won—completely. To accommodate the many people who clamor off the excursions boats each day to visit the picturesque Isola Dei Pescatori (*Fisherman's Island*), the hotel has a large dining room with arched windows overlooking Lake Maggiore. However, when the weather is warm, the favorite place to dine is outside on the idyllic terrace overlooking nearby Isola Bella (*Beautiful Island*). In the evening, when most of the tourists have departed, the terrace becomes even more romantic—particularly a full moon reflecting on the rippling water. The food is excellent: featuring freshly-caught fish from the lake. There are twelve bedrooms, each with a view of the lake. When we first visited many years ago, their interior was a bit drab, but we are happy to report that they have been redecorated with a simple, old-fashioned charm. My favorite is Camelia, (number 11) a pretty corner room on the third floor with blue floral wall paper, writing desk, armoire, antique iron king-sized bed and shuttered doors leading out to a small balcony. NOTE: Take the public scheduled ferry from Stressa, the private water taxis are exorbitantly expensive.

HOTEL VERBANO
Owner: Zacchera Family
Manager: Alberto Zacchera
Via Ugo Ara, 2
28049 Isola dei Pescatori, Stresa
Borromee Isole, Lake Maggiore, (NO) Italy
tel: (0323) 30 408 fax: (0323) 33 129
12 rooms: Double Lire 140,000
Open March to November
Credit cards: all major
Restaurant open daily
80 km NW of Milan, ferry from Stresa

Taking a small road that winds up the hill from the non-descript hamlet of Pievescola, you soon see on your left a big gate leading into a large courtyard faced by a lovely old villa-castle and a church. You check into the inn across the street from the gate where, to the left of the restaurant, there is a small door with a sign, "Hotel Relais La Suvera—Reception". The noble Ricci family live in one part of the villa. The other section is efficiently managed by Hilda Zeri as an elegant bed and breakfast. Some parts of the palace date from the 14th Century, others from the 16th Century exhibiting a combination of styles, incorporating Renaissance arcades with older, more fortress-like architecture. The public rooms and bedrooms are furnished with dramatic family antiques and an astounding museum-quality art collection. There is not a feeling of this being a slickly run, sophisticated operation: as a result, guests have the sensation of actually living the noble life of a by-gone era. In addition to the guest rooms in the villa, there are others available in the former olive processing house (where you check in) and in the converted horse stables. Although very pleasant, these rooms are less stately than those in the main house. The restaurant, "Oliviera", is located in the former olive pressing building, and serves traditional Tuscan cuisine as well as other specialties. The wine cellar is extensive, featuring wines produced in vineyards dating from the 12th Century.

LA SUVERA
Owner: Marchese Giuseppe Ricci
Manager: Hilda Zeri
53030 Pievescola di Casole d'Elsa (SI), Italy
24 rooms: Double from Lire 260,000
12 suites to Lire 420,000
tel: (0577) 96 03 00 fax: (0577) 960220
Open all year
Credit cards: all major
Restaurant open daily
30 km W of Siena, 16 km E of Casole d'Elsa

POGGIO MIRTETO HOTEL BORGO PARAELIOS Map: 10

It is difficult to find a hotel in Rome with thick enough windows to keep out the ever-present buzz of traffic. Less than an hour's drive from the city, the Borgo Paraelios (a prestigious Relais & Chateaux hotel) offers the perfect solution: a luxurious country villa immersed in the lovely Tuscan-like hills of Sabinia. In this splendid villa, filled to the brim with elegant antiques, rich, warm-colored tapestries and period paintings, it is impossible to find a detail overlooked. It is a masterpiece of harmonizing old and new, as antique terra cotta tile floors, stone fireplaces, beamed ceilings and antique doors from castles and villas were actually brought here and cleverly incorporated into the building. The very inviting bedrooms, each with its own character and color scheme, look out over the lush garden where guests can breakfast among the flower-laden terra-cotta pots. Meandering through the gracious living room, two libraries, billiard and bridge rooms, one has the sense of having been invited to the country home of nobility for a weekend of absolute peace and tranquillity. An additional service is daily transportation to and from Rome, including an apartment near the Spanish Steps at guests' disposal for lunching and freshening up during the city's siesta hours. When you return from the bustle of the city, exquisite meals are served in the frescoed formal dining room. NOTE: Ask for driving instructions: Borgo Paraelios is tricky to find, but you will discover a true jewel at your journey's end.

HOTEL BORGO PARAELIOS
Owner: Signori Salabe
Localita Valle Collicchia
02040 Poggio Mirteto Scalo (RI), Italy
tel: (0765) 26 267   (0765) 26 268
13 rooms, 2 suites, from Lire 350,000
Open all year
Credit cards: AX, VS
Restaurant open daily
45 km NE of Rome, 2 km N of Poggio Mirteto
U.S. Rep: Hidden Treasures of Italy 708-853-1312

The Relais El Toula is a tiny, ten-room, super deluxe, exquisite inn located less than an hour's drive north of Venice. The Relais El Toula is not only a member of the prestigious Relais group and it is rated as one of their most deluxe Italian hotels. The villa has an idyllic, country setting. The original villa is flanked by two arcaded wings which stretch to the sides giving the building an elegant, long, low image. After driving through the vineyards you arrive at an iron gate through which you enter into a courtyard and the hotel. Inside there is an abundance of fresh flowers in the lounges and delightful bedrooms. In addition to the lovely park-like setting and the beautiful rooms, there is another bonus—the food and wines are superb. It is not surprising that the hotel is so exceptional, for it was owned by Alfredo Beltrame, a real pro in the inn-keeping profession. He was the founder of the Toula hotel chain.

RELAIS EL TOULA
Director: Giorgio Zamuner
Via Postumia, 63
31050 Ponzano (TV), Italy
tel: (0422) 96 91 91 fax: (0422) 96 99 94
10 rooms: Double Lire 355,000–440,000
Suites Lire 640,000
Open all year
Credit cards: all major
Restaurant open daily
2 km N of Ponzano Veneto toward Paderno
35 km N of Venice, 5 km NW of Treviso
Relais & Chateaux Hotel

The Al Vecchio Convento is a real gem, offering quality accommodation for a moderate price. Its several dining rooms are brimming with rustic country charm and serve delicious meals prepared from local produce. There are nine guest rooms, each with a private bathroom and each tastefully decorated with antiques. The town of Portico de Romagna is, like the inn, inviting yet unpretentious—a very old village surrounded by wooded hills and clear mountain streams. A stroll through medieval pathways that twist down between the weathered stone houses leads you to an ancient stone bridge gracefully arching over a rushing stream. The inn too is very old. At first I thought its origin must have been an old convent because of its name, but the wonderfully gracious owner, Marisa Raggi, told me that the name came from a restaurant, located in a convent, that she and her husband, Giovanni (who is the chef), used to operate. Later, when they moved the restaurant to its present location and added a few guests rooms, they kept the original name, Al Vecchio Convento. The restaurant is still their main focus, featuring fine meals beautifully prepared from local produce. Due to the winding, two lane mountain highway which leads to the village, it takes about two hours to drive from Florence, but if you enjoy the adventure of exploring Italy's back roads, this small hotel will certainly be one of your favorites as it is mine.

ALBERGO AL VECCHIO CONVENTO
Owner: Marisa Raggi and Giovanni Cameli
Via Roma, 7
47010 Portico di Romagna (FO), Italy
tel: (0543) 96 77 52 fax: (0543) 96 78 77
9 rooms: Double Lire 96,000
Open all year
Credit cards: all major
Restaurant open daily
75 km NE of Florence, 34 km SW of Forli

The Pitrizza is a tiny jewel of a hotel located on the Emerald Coast of the Island of Sardinia—the playground of the Aga Khan and the jet set of the world. From the moment you enter through the front gate, marked only with a discreet sign, you are in a world of tranquillity and beauty. There is a central clubhouse which has a beautiful lounge, a delightful dining room with hand-hewn wooden chairs, a card room, and a bar. A small protected patio extends from the dining room where meals are served when the weather is warm. French doors from the lounge open onto the terrace which leads down to a most unusual swimming pool, cleverly designed into the natural rock. Once in this wonderful pool, you have the impression that you are swimming in the sea, not a pool, because the water level matches that of the bay. The bedrooms are tucked away in small cottages which blend into the landscape. The rooms are not especially large, but beautiful, with every detail of the finest quality. If your idea of a vacation is a frenzy of activity and "things to do" then the Pitrizza is definitely not for you. There are no planned activities, no sports director, no loud music. Only lovely quiet, gourmet food, a beautiful pool, and a delightful small white sand beach.

HOTEL PITRIZZA
Manager: Pier Angelo Tondina
07020 Porto Cervo, Sardinia, Italy
tel: (0789) 91 500 fax: (0789) 91 629
51 rooms: Double Lire 1,190,000–1,280,000*
*Rate includes breakfast and dinner
Open mid-May to September
Credit cards: all major
Restaurant open daily
NE tip of Sardinia, airport Olbia
On the island of Sardinia

The Il Pellicano has been beautifully designed in the traditional villa style and, although not old, looks as though it has snuggled on its prime hillside position overlooking the Mediterranean for many years. The facade is of stucco, painted a typical Italian russet and set off by a heavily tiled roof. Vines enwrap the building, further enhancing its inviting look. One enters into a spacious, attractive lobby where the sun streams through the windows enhancing the white walls, terra cotta floors, and wooden beamed ceilings. The happy ambiance continues with pretty sofas, antique accents, and enormous displays of fresh flowers enlivening every conceivable nook and cranny. The overall impression is one of light and color—and great taste. Beyond the reception area is an outdoor dining terrace, a favorite place to dine when the weather is balmy. Frequently the chef serves elaborate buffets outside—(the food at Il Pellicano is expensive, but excellent.) From the terrace, a lawn dotted with trees extends down the hillside to where there is a beautiful pool romantically perched at the cliff's edge. From the pool a staircase leads to a pier at the water's edge. Along this path, small individual terraces with lounge chairs and mats for sunning have been built into the rocks. In front of the hotel is a tennis court, again surrounded by flowers. The Il Pellicano is expensive but superb—a truly idyllic retreat.

IL PELLICANO
Managers: Ennio and Nadia Emili
58018 Porto Ercole, Italy
tel: (0564) 83 38 01 fax: (0564) 83 34 18
30 rooms: Double Lire 220,000–600,0003
Open April to end September
Credit cards: all major
Restaurant open daily
South end of island, Hwy 1 exit Orbetello
160 km N of Rome, 4.5 km S of Porto Ercole

The Splendido is truly a luxury hotel. Located up a winding, wooded road high above the town of Portofino, it sits majestically above the beautiful blue Mediterranean and overlooks the boats which are moored in Portofino's lovely harbor. The hotel is much like a very stately, wealthy country home. On a terrace below the hotel is an enormous swimming pool. There is also a tennis court located in the gardens to the left of the hotel. The public rooms are charming with comfortable chairs covered with floral prints and fresh flowers galore. There is a delightful outdoor terrace where meals are served. The bedrooms too are lovely and many have balconies which overlook the sea. There are also romantic little pathways originating from the hotel. You can stroll the wooded grounds and stop along the way at strategically placed benches to enjoy incomparable views. The Splendido is deluxe and very expensive, but it is a beautiful hotel. If you love luxury and desire a resort setting in one of the most naturally scenic parts of Italy, you will certainly enjoy the marvelous Splendido.

HOTEL SPLENDIDO
Manager: Antonio Marson
16034 Portofino (GE), Italy
tel: (0185) 26 95 51 fax: (0185) 26 96 14
65 rooms: Double from Lire 693,000*
*Rate includes breakfast and dinner or lunch
Closed October 28 to April 8
Credit cards: all major
Restaurant open daily
5 km S of Santa Margherita Ligure
35 km E of Genoa

The Albergo Casa Albertina is a prime example of what a difference management can make. There is a wide choice of hotels in the picturesque little fishing village of Positano—many, like the Casa Albertina, with spectacular views, pleasant decor, and good meals. However, they don't have Michele Cinque who is an outstanding hotelier: gracious and warmhearted—willing to do whatever is required to make each guest feel very special. It is not surprising that Michele is such a pro—he has been in the hotel business for many years, having been the manager of one of Positano's most deluxe hotels (Le Sirenuse) before deciding to spend full time helping his wife and mother-in-law manage the Casa Albertina. The hotel is really a family operation: Michele is usually at the front desk ready to care for the guests, his mother-in-law is in charge of the kitchen while his wife helps out wherever needed. Two sons are also working at the hotel and one of them has already taken over its official management—and quite ably, I might add. The hotel (which is built into a 12th-century house) clings to the hillside above Positano, a position which affords superlative views, but also means a strenuous walk into town.

ALBERGO CASA ALBERTINA
Manager: Lorenzo Cinque
Via della Tavolozza, 4
84017 Positano (SA), Italy
tel: (089) 8 75 143 fax: (089) 81 15 40
20 rooms: Double Lire 240,000–280,000*
*Rate includes breakfast and dinner
Open all year
Credit cards: all major
Restaurant open daily, only for guests
55 km S of Naples, 17 km S of Sorrento

For those who want to be smack in the middle of the colorful fishing village of Positano, the Palazzo Murat might be just your cup of tea. It is superbly located—surrounded by shops and only steps down to the beach. The hotel consists of two parts: the original building (a 200-year-old palace) plus a new wing which stretches out as an extension to the side. The new section is a standard hotel—pleasant but not unusual. However, the palace is quite special, with a faded-pink patina whose charm is accented by wonderful arched alcoves, intricately designed windows and magenta bougainvillea clinging to the walls and cascading from the wrought iron balconies. The entrance to the hotel is through a sun-drenched patio, a favorite gathering spot for guests. Within, the "old-world" feeling is maintained with tiled floors, white walls and formal settings of antique sofas and chairs. My favorite bedrooms are the five located upstairs in the characterful palace section: especially appealing are those with shuttered French doors opening onto small balconies that capture a view of the bay. All the rooms are comfortable and have TV, radio, minibar, and air conditioning. In summer a large buffet-style breakfast is served outside on the patio. Breakfast is the only meal served, but this is no problem as there are many enticing restaurants nearby. The hotel has its own boat that three times a week takes guests for excursions along the coast.

HOTEL PALAZZO MURAT
Owner: Mario Attanasio
Manager: Carmine Pallone
Via dei Mulini, 23
84017 Positano (SA), Italy
tel: (089) 87 51 77 fax: (089) 81 14 19
28 rooms: Double Lire 200,000–280,000
Open Easter to October 15
No restaurant, breakfast only
Near the beach–heart of Positano
55 km S of Naples, 17 km S of Sorrento

The Il San Pietro di Positano is touted as one of the most delightful deluxe hotels in the world. It is. There is no question about it. From the moment you approach the hotel "class" is evident: no large signs; no gaudy advertising; just an ancient chapel along the road indicates to the knowledgeable that an oasis is below the hill. After parking in the designated area near the road, you take an elevator which whisks you down to the lounge and lobby. You walk out of the elevator to a dream world—an open spacious world of sparkling white walls, tiled floors, colorful lounge chairs, Oriental rugs, antique chests, flowers absolutely everywhere, and arches of glass through which vistas of greenery and sea appear. To the right is a bar and to the left is a marvelous dining room—again with windows of glass opening to the view, but with the outdoors appearing to come in, with the walls and ceilings covered with plants and vines. The bedrooms too seem to be almost a Hollywood creation—more walls of glass, bathrooms with views to the sea, and balconies on which to sit and dream. If you can tear yourself away from your oasis of a bedroom, an elevator will whisk you down the remainder of the cliff to the small terrace at the water's edge. If all this sounds gaudy, it isn't. It is perfect

IL SAN PIETRO DI POSITANO
Owners: Salvatore and Virginia Attanasio
84017 Positano (SA), Italy
tel: (089) 87 54 55 fax: (089) 81 14 49
55 rooms: Double Lire 590,000–740,000*
*Rate includes breakfast and dinner
Closed December to March 14
Credit cards: all major
Restaurant open daily, only for guests
2 km south of Positano on Amalfi Drive
55 km S of Naples, 17 km S of Sorrento
U.S. Rep: E&M: 800-223-9832

Le Sirenuse is a superb luxury hotel tucked smack in the middle of the picturesque ancient fishing village of Positano. It is no wonder that so many writers and artists have been attracted to this colorful town of brightly hued houses clinging to the precipitous hillside as it drops down to its own small bay. And it is also no wonder that so many of these men of fame have found their way to the oasis of Le Sirenuse. From the moment you enter the hotel lobby the mood is set with fresh white walls, tiled floors, oil paintings on the walls, and accents of antiques. The hotel cascades down the hill and so almost all the rooms capture a wonderful view out over the quaint rooftops and the tiled domed cathedral to the shimmering blue waters of the bay. It is only a short walk through the perpendicular streets until you are on the beach. The dining room has walls of glass which allow the maximum enjoyment of the vista below, but most diners prefer the splendor of eating outdoors where the deck is set with tables for dining. On another level of the hotel there is a small pool for sunning and dipping.

LE SIRENUSE HOTEL
Manager: Luigi Bozza
Via C. Colombo, 30
84017 Positano (SA), Italy
tel: (089) 87 50 66 fax: (089) 81 17 98
60 rooms: Double Lire 460,000–560,000
Open all year
Credit cards: all major
Restaurant open daily
Old fishing village on Amalfi Drive
55 km S of Naples, 17 km S of Sorrento
U.S. Rep: LHW 800-223-6800

The Villa Franca, with a commanding position overlooking the sea, is one of Positano's newly renovated classic hotels with an excellent quality/price rapport. There is an immediate warmth and charm as soon as you walk in to the redesigned and redecorated villa. The Russo family wanted to create an attractive full-service hotel without losing the friendliness and service of a small inn. It is just that. The fresh Mediterranean decor is most appealing with royal blue slip-covered armchairs, a profusion of plants, lacquered terra-cotta vases, white tiled floors and walls and arched windows everywhere, so that you don't miss a second of the mesmerizing views of the sea. The elegant glassed-in restaurant with floral tapestry chairs and blue tablecloths serves fresh local seafood. The food is exceptional: Mario Russo is himself a talented chef and personally oversees both the food and impeccable service. In the winter, the hotel sponsors a cooking school where Diana Folonari teaches her pupils the art of Italian-Mediterranean specialties. The bedrooms follow the same cheerful theme with colorful ceramic tiled floors, cream bedspreads with green and yellow striped trim and exquisite views. The cherry on top of the cake is the rooftop swimming pool surrounded by yellow chaise lounges and palms with a 360 degree panoramic view over "the world's most beautiful coastline."

HOTEL VILLA FRANCA
Owner: Mario Russo
Viale Pasitea, 318
Positano 84017 (SA), Italy
tel: (089) 875655 fax: (089) 875735
28 rooms: Double Lire 220,000–240,000
Open: Easter to October
Credit Cards: all major
Restaurant open daily
55 km S of Naples, 18 km S of Sorrento
U.S. Rep: E&M 800-223-9832

The Relais Fattoria Vignale is a very polished, sophisticated small hotel located in the heart of the Chianti wine region in the small town of Radda. The hotel was the manor house of one of the large wine estates where the family's wines are still produced and are readily available in a winery shop across the street. Although located right on the main street near the center of town, there is a country atmosphere because the back of the hotel opens up to lovely views of rolling hills laced with vineyards and dotted with olive trees. Capturing this idyllic vista is a large swimming pool with comfortable lounge chairs along the side. Inside, the rooms are all beautifully decorated with a combination of authentic antiques and excellent reproductions. Care has been taken in the restoration to preserve many of the nice architectural features of the manor such as heavy beams, arched hallways, decorative fireplaces, and painted ceilings. Only 300 meters from the hotel is the "Ristorante Vignale", which is under the same ownership as the hotel.

RELAIS FATTORIA VIGNALE
Manager: Silvia Kummer
Via Pianigiani, 15
53017 Radda in Chianti (SI), Italy
tel: (0577) 73 83 00 fax: (0577) 73 85 92
22 rooms: Double: Lire 220,000–300,000
Open April to October
Credit cards: AX, VS
Restaurant closed Thursdays
In the heart of Chianti wine region
52 km S of Florence, 31 km N of Siena

The Rasun di Sopra, built in 1578 by Count Heufler, is actually a castle, but not one of the large foreboding castles sometimes found high on mountain peaks. This is a friendly, almost chalet-like castle, located in a sunny mountain valley in north-eastern Italy. Although within a short drive of some of the most dramatic vistas in the Dolomites, the Ansitz Heufler's setting is pretty, but does not include dramatic jagged mountain peaks. However, in winter skiing is nearby and in summer walking trails beckon in every direction. The Ansitz Heufler does not seem geared to English speaking guests although we did find one of the staff with whom we could communicate. But even though language might be a problem, the reception is very friendly and everyone seems eager to please. The inn is popular as a restaurant and there is an especially cozy dining room with very old paneled walls and ceiling, planked wooden floors, leaded glass windows, tables set with pretty linens, and appealing chalet-style chairs with carved heart backs. In the summer, guests sit out on the terrace where refreshing drinks and snacks are served. The staircase leads up to a wide hallway off which are the bedrooms. The bedrooms are all different from one another, but are all attractively furnished in a simple, uncluttered style with a liberal use of dark antiques attractively setting off whitewashed walls and freshly scrubbed wooden floors.

ANSITZ HEUFLER HOTEL
Owner: Mediolalium Vita
Manager: Valentin Paul Huber
Valle di Anterselva
39030 Rasun di Sopra (BZ), Italy
tel: (0474) 46 28 8 fax: (0474) 48 19 9
9 rooms: Double Lire 110,000–170,000
Closed May and November
Credit cards: VS
Restaurant closed Wednesdays
90 km NE of Bolzano, 12 km E of Brunico

It is no wonder that the Hotel Caruso Belvedere has such an especially spectacular site in Ravello—it was built as a palace in the 11th Century by a noble family who probably had their pick of real estate. The views of the rugged Amalfi coast from the dining terrace perched high in the clouds is gorgeous. Many of the bedrooms too have vistas. Although the decor is rather drab, the views just can't be surpassed. If you choose the Caruso Belvedere, splurge and ask for one of their most deluxe rooms. These are simply decorated without much style BUT they have enormous balconies which stretch the width of the room to capture again the incredibly romantic coast below. You will wake in the morning to the sound of birds and the scent of flowers intermixed with the fragrance of the vineyards which drifts up from the terraces beneath your balcony. The Hotel Caruso has more to offer than just its marvelous views. The dining room offers excellent food including a divine specialty of the house—a delicious chocolate soufflé which will linger in your memory perhaps as long as the view. The meals are accompanied by wines from the Caruso family vineyards.

HOTEL CARUSO BELVEDERE
Owner: Caruso Family
Manager: Gino Caruso Via S. Giovanni del Toro, 52
84010 Ravello (SA), Italy
tel: (089) 85 71 11 fax: (089) 85 73 72
24 rooms: Double Lire 210,000–248,000
Open all year
Credit cards: all major
Restaurant open daily
Hilltown above Amalfi coast
66 km S of Naples, 6 km N of Amalfi

The Marmorata Hotel was cleverly converted from the shell of an old paper mill. Only a few of the old paper mills are still in operation, but at one time the Amalfi area was famous for its production of fine paper. The official address of the Marmorata Hotel is Ravello; however, it is not located in the cliff town of Ravello, but rather on the coastal highway. As you are driving north from Salerno to Ravello you will see the sign to the hotel which is snuggled in the rocky cliffs between the road and the sea. As you enter the hotel you notice the nautical theme carried throughout the decor from the chairs in the dining room to the mirrors on the walls. The interior is charming with comfortable leather lounge chairs and small Oriental rugs. There is a lovely terrace plus, on a lower level, snuggled into the rocks, a small swimming pool. The bedrooms are small, but nicely decorated, again with the seafaring motif: the beds seem to be built into captains' sea chests and nautical prints are on the walls. The bathrooms are also small, but modern and attractive. All of the bedrooms have radios, color televisions, telephones, air conditioning and small refrigerators. Many of the rooms have an excellent view of the water and rugged coast.

MARMORATA HOTEL
Owner: Camera d'Afflitto Family
Strada Statale, 163
84010 Ravello (SA), Italy
tel: (089) 87 77 77 fax: (089) 85 11 89
40 rooms: Double Lire 225,000–280,000
Open all year
Credit cards: all major
Restaurant open daily
On the coast below Ravello
62 km S of Naples, 23 km N of Salerno

There is something magical about the Hotel Palumbo, a 12th-century palace now one of the most special hotels in Italy, owned since 1875 by the charming Vuilleumier family. The location is perfect—up in the clouds overlooking the terraced vineyards and beyond to the brilliant blue sea which dances in and out of the jagged rocky coast. The Palumbo is a divine small hotel. The romance begins when you enter the beautiful lobby with its ancient atrium of arched colonnades, green plants flowing from every nook, masses of fresh flowers and beautiful antiques. Each small corner is an oasis of tranquillity from the intimate bar to the cozy antique filled tiny lounges. There is a beautiful dining room with a crystal chandelier, bentwood chairs and a fireplace, but usually meals are served on the breathtaking terrace which perches like a bird's nest in the sky. Wherever you dine, the food is superb and the elegantly gracious owner, Pasquale Vuilleumier, frequently pauses at each table—an attentive host seeing to the contentment of each guest. There is a charming garden in the rear with a vine covered terrace overlooking the Amalfi coast. Another tiny patio which captures both the sun and the view is tucked onto the roof of the villa. There are only 20 bedrooms, each individually decorated and appealing with its own personality. A few guest rooms are located in an annex.

HOTEL PALUMBO
Manager: Marco Vuilleumier ,
Via S. Giovanni del Toro 28
84010 Ravello (SA), Italy
tel: (089) 85 72 44 fax: (089) 85 81 33
20 rooms: Double Lire 530,000–630,000
Rates include breakfast and dinner
Open all year
Credit cards: VS
Restaurant open daily
66 km S of Naples, 6 km N of Amalfi

The Villa Cimbrone is not only a hotel: its gardens are one of Ravello's most famous attractions. The tourist office proclaims, "The Villa Cimbrone, essence of all the enchantment of Ravello, hangs like a swallow's nest on the cliffs." The villa is reached by a delightful ten-minute walk from the main square of Ravello (the signs are well marked to this favorite sightseeing prize). Once through the gates, the villa and its magnificent gardens open up like magic. The gardens are truly superb—if you have ever received a postcard from Ravello, chances are it showed the view from the terrace of the Cimbrone. Most dramatic of all is the belvedere with its stately Roman statues accenting the dazzling view. Luckily, this outstanding villa is also a small hotel. The rooms are of museum quality with furniture "fit for a king". We toured through the marvelous old building which is not open to the public—only to the guests. This fabulous villa was once the prized possession of an English Lord. Later it was sold to the present owner, Marco Vuilleumier, who told us the following romantic tale: toward the end of World War II, the English nobleman (who owned Villa Cimbrone) landed with the Allied troops in Salerno. Somehow he was able to find a jeep, and—you guessed it—wound up the twisting road to see once again his beloved villa.

VILLA CIMBRONE
Owner: Vuilleumier Family
84010 Ravello (SA), Italy
tel: (089) 85 74 59 fax: (089) 85 77 77
20 rooms: Double Lire 220,000–280,000
Open April to October
Credit cards: none accepted
No restaurant, breakfast only
10 minute walk to parking in town center
66 km S of Naples, 6 km N of Amalfi

The Villa Maria is perhaps best known for its absolutely delightful terrace restaurant which has a bird's eye view of the magnificent coast. Whereas most of the hotels in Ravello capture the southern view, the Villa Maria features the equally lovely vista to the north. The Villa Maria is easy to find because it is on the same path which winds its way from the main square to the Villa Cimbrone. After parking your car in the main square of Ravello (or at the Hotel Giordano which is under the same ownership) look for the signposts for Villa Maria. After about a 2-minute walk, you find the hotel perched on the cliffs to your right. The building is a romantic old villa with a garden stretching to the side where tables and chairs are set—a favorite place to dine while enjoying the superb view. Inside, there is a cozy dining room which overlooks the garden. The bedrooms have old-fashioned brass beds and antique furniture. The bathrooms have been freshly remodeled and some even have Jacuzzi tubs. The hotel is owned by Vincenzo Palumbo whose staff speaks excellent English should you call for a reservation. Vincenzo Palumbo also owns the nearby Hotel Giordano which has a heated pool that can be used free by guests at the Villa Maria. Many readers have written to us saying how gracious and warm a welcome they receive at the Villa Maria. How lucky to be able to have the best of all worlds should you be on a budget—a wonderful view and location plus a charming villa.

VILLA MARIA
Owner: Vincenzo Palumbo
Via S. Chiara, 2
84010 Ravello (SA), Italy
tel: (089) 85 72 55 fax: (089) 85 70 71
17 rooms: Double Lire 160,000–270,000
Open all year
Credit cards: all major
Restaurant open daily
66 km S of Naples, 6 km N of Amalfi

Only about a half hour's drive from Florence, easily accessible from the A1 to Rome, is the Villa Rigacci, once a private residence, now an inviting small inn. This 16th-century villa is a "picture-perfect" example of a Tuscan villa with its faded pink stucco facade, thick walls, heavy weathered red tile roof, green shuttered windows and park like gardens. The owner, Odette Mege Pierazzi, is personally involved with all aspects of running the inn: she is like a hostess overseeing the needs of her "house guests". In summer, after a day of sightseeing, guests relax in the back garden where a large pool, surrounded by lounge chairs and umbrellas, stretches out on a terraced lawn. Inside, handsome antiques adorn the sitting rooms and library. The dining room is especially appealing and, according to the guests staying at the inn, the chef is excellent. All of the bedrooms have direct dial telephone, color television, small bar and bathroom. Each is individually decorated with very attractive country-style antiques and lovely fabrics creating rooms that blend beautifully with the old world ambiance of the villa. Although I personally prefer the area of Tuscany that stretches directly south of Florence where the villages seem more secluded, the conveniently located Villa Rigacci offers easy access to the expressway and accommodation with charm, hospitality, and warmth. NOTE: Vaggio is a small town southwest of Reggello.

HOTEL VILLA RIGACCI
Owner: Odette Mege Pierazzi
50066 Vaggio-Reggello (FI), Italy
tel: (055) 86 56 718 fax: (055) 86 56 537
20 rooms: Double Lire 150,000–260,000
Open all year
Credit cards: all major
Restaurant closed January
mid-November to mid-December
30 km SE of Florence, 5 km S of Reggello

How could one possibly write about hotels in Italy and leave out the historical Albergo del Sole? Dating back to 1467, it is the oldest hotel in Rome—possibly one of the oldest still-operating hotels in the world. In addition to being of great historical interest, the hotel has the blessing of holding a prime location: looking across the ancient Piazza della Rotonda to one of Rome's masterpieces, the Pantheon, which was standing before the birth of Christ. The Albergo del Sole has been meticulously restored, faithfully reflecting its 15th-century heritage. You enter into an attractive long narrow lobby with arched ceiling, red tiled floor, white-washed walls and a very large, ornately framed antique oil painting over the reception desk. From the lobby, doors lead into the various lounges which maintain the same, elegantly simple, uncluttered look with white walls, white upholstered chairs and sofas and antique accent pieces. One floor up is a lovely interior garden-patio which opens onto an intimate breakfast room where the tables are invitingly set with pretty floral print table clothes. The bedrooms are each individual in decor, but similar in mood with color coordinating bedspreads and draperies. The suite is especially attractive with a beautiful antique wooden headboard.

ALBERGO DEL SOLE
Manager: Giancarlo Piraino
Piazza della Rotonda, 63
00186 Rome, Italy
tel: (06) 67 80 441 fax: (06) 68 40 689
26 rooms, Double: Lire 400,000
Open all year
Credit cards: all major
No restaurant, breakfast only
Located in the center of Old Rome

Hotel rates in the center of Rome are usually very expensive, but the Hotel Carriage, tucked into a tiny side street, is both moderately priced and conveniently situated just a short stroll from the bottom of the Spanish steps. From the outside it is a nondescript, sienna-colored building with green shuttered windows opening directly onto the street. The small entry lobby is flanked by a small breakfast room and a formal parlor with ornate furnishings including brocade chairs, an enormous gilt mirror, a fancy chandelier, and elaborately carved tables. The pretty soft blue walls of this room set the color theme for the hotel; the bedrooms I saw that had been redecorated were also done in varying shades of blue. Some of the guest rooms are very small so it is best to pay a bit more and request one of the best twin-bedded rooms. However, no matter what the size, all the rooms have air conditioning, telephone, radio, small refrigerator, and an old world flavor. One of the nicest features of the hotel is a rooftop terrace where on summer evenings guests may sit at tables and enjoy the view over a jumble of tiled roofs to the twin spires of the 16th-century church, Trinita dei Monti. The Hotel Carriage is not luxurious, but offers a less expensive alternative for lodging in Rome.

HOTEL CARRIAGE
Manager: Giampiero Cau
Via delle Carrozze, 36
00187 Rome, Italy
tel: (06) 69 90 124 fax: (06) 67 88 279
30 rooms: Double Lire 235,000
 Suites Lire 300,000–350,000
Open all year
Credit cards: all major
No restaurant, breakfast only
Located near bottom of Spanish steps

The Grand Hotel Plaza is aptly named. It is indeed a *GRAND* hotel. Although, it is larger than those usually featured in this guide, it is so interesting that we felt it definitely deserved a mention. The mood is established as you enter into an ornate, richly decorated lobby with colorfully patterned tiled floors, opulent multi-colored marble walls, paneled ceiling traced with gold, dramatic wall sconces, heavy crystal chandelier, and—what won my heart immediately—a larger-than-life, white marble lion stretched at the base of the elegant stair case at the end of the room. There are various elaborately decorated lounges, each with a Victorian ambiance established through the use of fancy wall papers, dramatic chandeliers, lavish moldings, dark paneling, and stained glass windows. However, I have left the best for last: Even if you do not stay at the Grand Hotel Plaza, drop in to stand in awe at its central lounge—a breathtaking gigantic formal room with a domed ceiling that is ornately decorated with richly frescoed paintings and intricate designs. Two identical, unbelievably huge, crystal chandeliers hang from the ceiling. Marble columns enclose the room forming an arcaded walkway. Beneath the domed ceiling, formal groupings of brocade-upholstered chairs with gold fringe, and old-fashioned potted palms in giant ceramic pots complete the scene. The bedrooms too have a turn-of-the century look. If you are not on a budget, ask for one of the suites with a private terrace overlooking the rooftops of Rome.

GRAND HOTEL PLAZA
Manager: Mr. Mariani
Via del Corso, 126
00186 Rome, Italy
tel: (06) 67 20 1 fax: (06) 68 41 575
204 rooms, Double: Lire 346,000
Open all year
Credit cards: all major
Restaurant open daily
Located in the heart of Rome

For location, the Gregoriana is superb: it is situated on Gregoriana Street which runs into the Piazza Trinita dei Monti at the top of the Spanish Steps. In spite of the perfect location, when I first saw the Gregoriana I just did not see how I could include it in our "inn" book because it has no antique ambiance: in fact, the decor motif might be classified as Chinese with a touch of art deco. However, after staying at this hotel, I just did not see how I could not include it—it is such a unique little inn and has such a sparkle of personality that it brightens the otherwise somewhat impersonal city of Rome. You will not be just one of thousands of tourists in Rome—upon arrival, the concierge will probably already know you by name and will continue to greet you personally as you come and go. Instead of feeling like a face which goes with a key hanging on the wall, you will feel a warmth and intimacy as if you were a guest in a private home. The rooms are simple but very pleasant and, like the lobby, are decorated with a touch of Oriental ambiance. Those at the rear are especially quiet and some enjoy a balcony with a view over the rooftops of Rome. Only breakfast is served. However, there is a concierge on duty twenty-four hours a day to cater to your special needs.

HOTEL GREGORIANA
Owner: Ernesto Panier-Bagat
Manager: Aldo Basso Bondini
Via Gregoriana, 18
00187 Rome, Italy
tel: (06) 67 94 26 9 fax: (06) 67 84 25 8
19 rooms: Double Lire 220,000
No restaurant, breakfast only
Located near top of Spanish Steps

The Hotel Hassler is a landmark in Rome. Located in the heart of the elegant shopping area, on the Piazza Trinita dei Monti at the top of the Spanish Steps, this small, elite hotel was once a palatial private home. Its entrance is sedate and elegant. The reception rooms are a little somber, but this mood is quickly relieved by an inner courtyard—a superb oasis with stone walls covered with vines, statues, flowers, cozy little tables, and a bar. You can linger in the garden, take a refreshment in the afternoon or perhaps meet a friend for an aperitif in the evening. The dining room at the Hassler is also spectacular, boasting one of the finest views in Rome: the entire panorama of the city surrounds you as you dine. As the evening deepens and the city lights begin to flicker, the scene will become one of romance. If money is no object, the Hotel Hassler offers some magnificent suites, some with enormous terraces and a view so beautiful that you will be sorely tempted never to set foot from this gorgeous hotel.

HOTEL HASSLER
Manager: Roberto E. Wirth
Trinita Dei Monti, 6
00187 Rome, Italy
tel: (06) 67 82 65 1 fax: (06) 67 89 99 1
100 rooms: Double Lire 612,000–802,000
Credit cards: AX, VS
Restaurant open daily
Located at top of Spanish Steps
U.S. Rep: LHW 800-223-6800

When we visited the Hotel d'Inghilterra a few years ago, the inside was most appealing although the exterior was quite drab. On our latest inspection, we were pleased to note that the entrance has been spiffed up and is now much improved. Inside, there is an ambiance of warmth and dignified charm enhanced by strategically placed antiques, lovely paintings decorating the wall, pretty Oriental carpets, antique mirrors and fresh flowers throughout. Down the hallway is a small bar which seems to be the rendezvous spot for everyone staying at the hotel. This appealing little bar has beautiful dark wood paneling adorned with colorful prints, intimate little tables, fine antique carpets, and comfortable leather sofas. The bedrooms are well decorated in traditional decor. The location of the d'Inghilterra is excellent. A short walk in one direction will lead you through lovely shopping avenues to the bottom of the Spanish Steps. A short walk in the other direction will lead you to the Trevi Fountain with its hubbub of activity. Originally, the Hotel d'Inghilterra was built as a guest house for the famous Torlonia Palace and you will certainly see and appreciate traces of grandeur which are still apparent throughout this once-regal residence.

HOTEL D'INGHILTERRA
Manager: Loredano Galligani
Via Bocca di Leone, 14
00187 Rome, Italy
tel: (06) 67 21 61 fax: (06) 68 40 82 8
102 rooms: Double Lire 450,000–500,000
Credit cards: all major
Restaurant open daily
Located near bottom of Spanish Steps

The Hotel Lord Byron is owned by a fascinating man and superb hotelier, Amedeo Ottaviani, who believes that "Hospitality is like an exquisite flower, it must be surrounded by a thousand delicate attentions"—a concept which transforms each of his hotels into far more than just a place to spend the night. Each is designed to be a "home away from home"—a quiet sanctuary, well-run and full of character. Ottaviani's chain of small, unique hotels includes the Lord Byron—tucked on a tiny lane surrounded by glamorous homes, it is much more like a private townhouse than a commercial establishment. The reception desk is discreetly located in the foyer which opens onto an elegant lounge. An elevator takes guests to the bedrooms, each individually decorated: fabrics, carpets, and the materials used on the custom-built pieces of furniture are carefully chosen to suit the personality and exposure of the room. Most of the furniture is new—modern yet traditional in feel. The colors used in fabrics, wall coverings, and carpets are mostly strong, bold colors—frequently with large, bright floral prints, but consistently of excellent quality. On the lower level is an intimate drawing room-bar where guests can relax before or after dining—adjacent is an elegant restaurant, the Relais Le Jardin, serving without a doubt some of the finest cuisine in Rome.

HOTEL LORD BYRON
Owner: Amedeo Ottaviani
Via G. de Notaris, 5
00197 Rome, Italy
tel: (06) 32 20 404 fax: (06) 32 20 405
37 rooms: Double Lire 380,000–540,000
Open all year
Credit cards: all major
Restaurant closed Sundays
Located on edge of Villa Borghese Park
U.S. Rep: LHW 800-223-6800

The Hotel Majestic Roma, located on the famous Via Veneto, has emerged from her recent renovation as one of Rome's newest jewels. Like other luxury hotels in Italy, the rates are very high, but so is the quality. From the moment you enter through the circular revolving doorway into the spacious, high-ceilinged lobby with a few well-chosen antiques and bouquets of fresh flowers, the mood of quiet elegance is established. Instead of one large lounge, there are a series of intimate parlors where guests can gather. In each room there are beautifully upholstered chairs, and opulent fabrics on the walls and richly draped windows. Be sure to peek in and see the fabulous frescoed ceiling of the 19th-century "Salone Verdi" which is used for special banquets. A wonderful old-fashioned wrought-iron elevator with polished brass trim takes guest to the bedrooms. As in a private home, each has its own personality, all are elegant in decor and traditionally furnished in an old world style, opulent style. On warm days, an outdoor terrace with a view of the city is a perfect place to pause for a cool drink. There is also a beautifully decorated, formal dining room specializing in typical Mediterranean dishes, as well as continental cuisine.

HOTEL MAJESTIC ROMA
Manager: Silvano Pinchetti
Via Veneto, 50
00187 Rome, Italy
tel: (06) 48 68 41 fax: (06) 48 85 657
98 rooms, Double: Lire 460,000–540,000
Open all year
Credit cards: all major
Restaurant open daily
In the heart of Rome on famous Via Veneto

La Residenza was recommended to us by several readers who claimed it to be their favorite place to stay in Rome, and after a personal visit, we are happy to be able to include it in our guide. This former villa really is quite different from most of the large, commercial places to stay in the center of Rome, appearing to be more like a private residence. Its facade looks very "Italian" with typical brown shuttered windows, greenery and flowers behind a small paved courtyard where guests may park their cars. The front hall has been converted into a reception area flanked by several guest lounges. The decor of these public rooms is not outstanding: some have contemporary, grass-cloth wallpaper, but others are more traditional in feeling and have a smattering of antique furniture. The breakfast room is spacious, although a bit dark, but the red bentwood chairs add a bit a sparkle. Because the hotel was fully occupied at the time of my visit, I was only able to see a few guest rooms, but those I did see were modern and seemed to be quiet adequate. The location just off the Via Veneto is glamorous, so even though the interior of La Residenza does not abound with charm, it is a good choice for travelers who want a small hotel in a good location without paying a fortune.

LA RESIDENZA
Manager: Mr. d'Arezzo
Via Emilia, 22
00187 Rome, Italy
tel: (06) 48 80 789 fax: (06) 48 57 21
27 rooms: Double Lire 230,000, Suite Lire 260,000
Open all year
Credit cards: all major
No restaurant, breakfast only
Located between Via Veneto and Spanish Steps

With every new edition of this guide we always add some new hotels; among these a few treasures always stand out, and the Hotel Relais Borgo San Felice is one such gem. Not only is it one of Italy's loveliest country hotels, it is also an outstanding value: a comparable hotel in any of the popular tourist targets would cost much more. Unless you are exclusively a "city person", you will love this hotel. Actually, the name is misleading because it is not a hotel at all in the usual sense of the word, but rather a very old village of beautiful stone buildings which have been cleverly converted into guest rooms, dining rooms, a restaurant and a bar. However, the village is not entirely consecrated to the hotel; local farmers still live in some of the houses and the winery is still housed in its original structure. The San Felice wines, produced on the 2,400 surrounding acres, are some of Italy's finest. All the guest rooms have every amenity and are decorated to offer a traditional ambiance of soft, pleasing colors, floral fabrics and many fine antiques. There is a beautiful swimming pool with a view terrace and also an inviting tennis court tucked into the vineyards. This hotel has no rough edges. It is superbly managed by the gracious Gualtiero Mancini who oversees every detail and welcomes guests with the warmth and friendliness usually only found at small inns. NOTE: The closest towns found on the Hallwag map are Castelnuovo and Pianella.

HOTEL RELAIS BORGO SAN FELICE
Manager: Gualtiero Mancini
San Felice
53019 Castelnuovo Berardenga, Italy
tel: (0577) 35 92 60 fax: (0577) 35 90 89
51 rooms: Double Lire 241,000–322,000
Open all year
Credit cards: all major
Restaurant open daily
20 km NE of Siena, 9 km NW of Castelnuovo

Finding the appealing Romantik Golf Hotel brought us an unexpected bonus: we discovered a niche of Italy which hugs the Yugoslavian border north of Trieste: an absolutely gorgeous region of wooded hills, rolling fields, and vineyards. The Castello Formentini, superbly positioned on a hillock overlooking the countryside, has belonged to the Counts of Formentini since the 16th Century. For many years there has been a restaurant within the castle called "Castello Formentini" which still serves excellent meals and a medieval banquet on Saturdays. Just outside the castle walls, one of the historic buildings of the castle complex has been converted into a small, charming luxury inn. The attractive, gracious owner, Isabella Formentini, says that all of the magnificent antique furnishings in the hotel are family heirlooms. Everything is authentic, even the wonderful prints and paintings. In fact, she says the furniture is more valuable than the castle. From the intimate lobby to each of the spacious guest rooms, everything is decorator perfect and exudes a delightful country manor ambiance. Only four of the rooms are within the castle, but all guests can stroll through the gate and into the castle grounds where the swimming pool lies invitingly on the shaded lawn. There is also a tennis court plus a nine hole pitch and putt golf course. NOTE: The closest town on the Hallwag map is Gorizia.

ROMANTIK GOLF HOTEL
Owner: Isabella Formentini
San Floriano del Collio
34070 Gorizia (GO), Italy
tel: (0481) 88 40 51 fax: (0481) 88 42 14
16 rooms: Double Lire 235,000
Open March to December
Credit cards: AX, VS
Restaurant closed Mondays
30 km N of Trieste, 7 km N of Corizia
U.S. Rep: Euro-Connection 800-645-3876

Without a doubt, San Gimignano is one of the most picturesque places in Tuscany: a postcard perfect hilltop village punctuated by 14 tall towers. During the day, the town bustles with activity, but after the bus loads of tourists depart, the romantic ambiance of yester-year fills the cobbled streets. For the lucky few who spend the night, there is a jewel of small inn, the Hotel L'Antico Pozzo. What a pleasure to see a renovation done with such excellent taste and meticulous attention to maintaining the authentic character of the original building. The name of the hotel derives from the an antique stone well (pozzo) which is softly illuminated just off the lobby. The fact that only the most affluent families could afford the luxury of a private well, indicates that this 15th-century town house was a at one time a wealthy residence. A worn-with-time stone staircase leads up to the bedrooms which are enchantingly tucked at various levels along a maze of hallways. Each one of the quietly elegant rooms has its own personality: frescoed walls, thick stone walls, terra cotta floors, and beautifully framed antique prints abound. One of my favorites was room 20—a large room with stone floor, the palest of pastel peach-colored walls, casement windows opening onto the terrace, and, a fabulous domed ceiling, richly painted with ancient Roman designs. Another that won my heart was 34—a small, but oh so romantic room with a large arched window capturing a fabulous view. Breakfast is the only meal served, but restaurants abound, including just around the corner, the superb "La Mangiataoia".

HOTEL L'ANTICO POZZO
Manager: Emanuele Marro
Via San Matteo, 87
53037 San Gimignano (SI), Italy
tel: (0577) 94 20 14 fax: (0577) 94 21 17
18 rooms, Double: Lire 125,000–190,000
Open all year
Credit cards: all major
No restaurant, breakfast only
55 km S W of Florence, 38 km N of Siena.

San Gimignano is one of the most fascinating of the medieval Tuscany hill towns. Most tourists come just for the day to visit this small town. As you approach, this looks like a city of skyscrapers: come even closer and the "skyscrapers" emerge as 14 soaring towers—dramatic reminders of what San Gimignano must have looked like in all her glory when this wealthy town sported 72 giant towers. If you are lucky enough to be able to spend the night, San Gimignano has a simple but very charming hotel, La Cisterna. The hotel is located on the town's main square, and fits right into the ancient character of the surrounding buildings with its somber stone walls softened by ivy, arched shuttered doors, and red tile roof. Once inside La Cisterna the medieval feeling continues with lots of stone, vaulted ceilings, leather chairs, and dark woods. The bedrooms are not fancy, but pleasant, and some have balconies with lovely views of the valley. Renovations in 1991 added air conditioning in the restaurant and satellite TV (for European channels). La Cisterna is probably more famous as a restaurant than as a hotel. People come from miles around because not only is the food delicious, but the dining rooms are delightful. Especially charming is the dining room with the brick wall, sloping ceiling supported by giant beams, and picture windows framing the gorgeous Tuscany hills.

LA CISTERNA
Owner: S. Salvestrimi
Piazza della Cisterna, 24
53037 San Gimignano (SI), Italy
tel: (0577) 94 03 28 fax: (0577) 94 20 80
50 rooms: Double Lire 119,000–144,000
Suites to Lire 174,000
Open March 10 to November 10
Credit cards: all major
Restaurant closed Tuesdays and lunch on Wednesdays
54 km SW of Florence, 38 km NW of Siena

The Castel San Gregorio is a sensational, small 12th-century stone castle just a short drive from Assisi, reached after following a winding road through a forest which emerges at the top of a hill to a truly romantic, secluded hideaway. There is a terrace to the side where tables and chairs are strategically placed to capture a splendid view of the valley far below. The castle, dating from 1140, has been meticulously reconstructed preserving its original appearance without, and maintaining a castle-like ambiance within. The interior of the hotel is quite dark due both to the character of the building and the wall coverings. The "old-world" ambiance is further enhanced by the bountiful use of excellent antiques. The reception desk is in the front lobby: to the left as you enter is an ornate living room; to the right is a dining room where one large table is set each night for the guests to eat together "family style". A restaurant is located on a lower level, open to the general public, where elegant dining is offered in a beautifully decorated room. The bedrooms I saw, although somewhat dark, were all quite outstandingly decorated with a collection of fine antiques. Surrounding the hotel are many walking paths leading through the quiet wooded hills. The Castel San Gregorio is an outstanding value for a hotel with so much character. NOTE: The closest town on the Hallwag map is Pianello—on a small road leading south from town.

CASTEL SAN GREGORIO
Owner: Claudio Bianchi
Via San Gregorio, 16
Near Pianello
06081 San Gregorio, Assisi (PG), Italy
tel: (075) 80 38 009 fax: (075) 80 38 904
12 rooms: Double Lire 110,000
Closed January
Credit cards: all major
Restaurant open daily, only for guests
16 km NW of Assisi, 2 km S of Pianello

The Residence San Sano is a small hotel in San Sano—a hamlet in the center of the Chianti wine-growing region. We were charmed by the hotel which is incorporated into a 16th-century stone building. The gracious young owners, Giancarlo Matarazzo and his German wife, Heidi, were both school teachers in Germany prior to returning to Italy to open a small hotel. They have done a beautiful job in the renovation and in the decor. A cozy dining room serves guests excellent meals—featuring typically Tuscan-style cooking. Each of 11 bedrooms is delightfully furnished in antiques and each has a name incorporating some unique feature of the hotel—the name evolving from the time during reconstruction when Heidi and Giancarlo remembered each room by its special feature. My favorite room was the "Bird Room": here birds had claimed the room for many years and had nested in holes which went completely through the wall. With great imagination, the holes were left open to the outside, but on the inside were covered with glass. Now the birds can still nest and guests have the fun of watching the babies. One room is named for a beautiful, long-hidden Romanesque window which was discovered and incorporated into the decor, another room for its very special view, and another for an antique urn uncovered during renovation. On our latest visit, the inn looked even lovelier than ever and a new pool now nestles in the vineyards. NOTE: The closest town on the Hallwag map is Radda.

HOTEL RESIDENCE SAN SANO
Owners: Heidi and Giancarlo Matarazzo
Localita San Sano
53010 Lecchi in Chianti (SI), Italy
tel: (0577) 74 61 30 fax: (0577) 74 61 56
11 rooms: Double Lire 120,000–130,000
Closed November to mid-March
Credit cards: all major
Restaurant open daily, only for guests
60 km S of Florence, 9 km S of Radda

The Locanda San Vigilio is truly special: our favorite among the tiny luxury inns in the beautiful lake district of northern Italy. And, although it is expensive, it costs less to stay here than at some of the famous well known "queens" along the lake. Not only is it a superb small hotel, but the location is unsurpassed. The Locanda San Vigilio is a 16th-century building romantically positioned fronting the water on an exquisite, park-like peninsula that juts out into Lake Garda. There is not much action here. If you want to see and be seen by the rich and famous, the glamorous Villa d'Este should be your hub, but if you desire tranquillity, accented by lovely accommodations, then try the San Vigilio. Here you will find understated luxury, nothing commercial at all. Hardly a sign marks the tree-lined entrance just a few kilometers north of the town of Garda. After parking your car in the designated area, you walk past a gorgeous Italian villa and then down a path to the hotel, a 16th-century sturdy stone building so close to the water that waves gently lap the walls. The dining room is lovely and if you are lucky, you can eat at one of the cozy tables overlooking the lake. The food is sensational and the decor is faultless. Upstairs the prize guest rooms overlook the lake. If you long for tranquillity, this is it. Churchill came here to paint, and after visiting the San Vigilio you may also be inspired to take up the art.

LOCANDA SAN VIGILIO
Owner: Conte Agostino Guarienti di Brenzone
Assistant Manager: Christina Weber
37016 San Vigilio, Lake Garda (VR), Italy
tel: (045) 72 56 68 8 fax: (045) 72 56 55 1
7 rooms: Double Lire 260,000–378,000
Open March to November
Credit cards: all major
Restaurant open daily, only for guests
154 km W of Venice, 3 km N of Garda

Having heard about a lovely little chalet tucked amidst the pines high in the Italian Alps near the French border, I was beginning to wonder what awaited me as the road wound through the ski town of Sauze d'Oulx with its unattractive jumble of modern concrete ski hotels. However, the road soon left the resort town and continued up, twisting higher and higher into the mountains until suddenly Il Capricorno came into view nestled in the forest to the left of the road. Just as you enter there is a tiny bar, and, beyond, a cozy dining room enhanced by dark wooden chalet-style chairs, rustic wooden tables, and a stone fireplace with logs stacked neatly by its side. There is not a hint of elaborate elegance—just a simple cozy country charm: the perfect kind of inn to come "home" to after a day of skiing or walking the beautiful mountain trails. The bedrooms, too, are simple but most pleasant with dark pine handmade furniture, neat little bathrooms, and, for a lucky few, balconies with splendid mountain views. However, the greatest asset of this tiny inn are the owners, Mariarosa and Carlo Sacchi. Carlo personally made most of the furniture and will frequently join the guests for skiing. Mariarosa is the chef, a fabulous gourmet cook. This is a very special little hideaway for very special people.

IL CAPRICORNO
Owners: Mariarosa and Carlo Sacchi
Les Clotes
10050 Sauze d'Oulx (TO), Italy
tel: (0122) 85 02 73 fax: (0122) 85 49 7
8 rooms: Double Lire 215,000
Open July to mid-September
Christmas to May
Credit cards: VS
Restaurant open daily, only for guests
2 km E of Sauze d'Oulx via small lane
60 km W of Turin, 28 km W of Susa

The Maremma, a beautiful area in the coastal foothills of southern Tuscany, quite undiscovered by tourists, offers a wealth of sightseeing possibilities: walled villages, Etruscan ruins, archaeological sites and lovely landscapes. Until recently there were few places to stay with charm. Happily this problem was solved when the Pellegrini family recently converted a 200-year-old stone farmhouse into a small hotel. Here you will find true Tuscany hospitality from the moment you enter. Although the Pellegrinis do not speak English, they have made sure to employ front desk personnel who do. The dining room is the heart of the inn and has tables set in a beamed-ceilinged room that is filled with sunlight from large French doors that open onto a terrace where meals are served on warm days. The guest rooms are small, but comfortable, immaculately clean and each with a private bathroom. The warmth and gracious country-style hospitality of this simple small hotel make a stay here special. Another real bonus is the food. It is wonderful. Everything is homemade, including marvelous pastas prepared by the talented chef, Tullio Sassi, and the hotel even produces its own wines which are served with the meals. A specialty of the inn is trekking (or, as we say, horseback riding). In the coral below the hotel, horses are groomed each day for guests' use; in fact, special room rates are offered which include the use of your own horse.

ANTICO CASALE DI SCANSANO
Owners: Massimo Pellegrini and Family
58054 Castagneta-Scansano (GR), Italy
tel: (0564) 50 72 19 fax: (0564) 50 78 05
16 rooms: Double Lire 115,000–140,000
Closed January 15 to March 1
Credit cards: all major
Restaurant open daily
30 km S of Grosseto, 2 km W of Scansano
U.S. Rep: Hidden Treasures of Italy 708-853-1312

Although the Berghotel Tirol is a new hotel, it happily copies the typical chalet style of the Dolomites. Inside too, the tasteful decor follows the delightful Alpine motif with light pine furniture, baskets of flowers, and a few antiques for accent pieces. However, what is so very special about the Berghotel Tirol is its marvelous location on a hillside looking over the lovely village of Sexten and to the fabulous mountains beyond. Many of the rooms have large balconies which capture the view and the warmth of the mountain sun. The Berghotel Tirol is not actually in the town of Sexten (Sesto), but in a suburb called Moos (Moso). This is one of the most scenic areas of the Dolomites and the town of Sexten one of the most attractive of the mountain towns. In addition to the natural beauty, there is a wonderful network of trails leading in every direction to tempt all into the crisp mountain air. When you return at night to the hotel it is rather like a house party. Most of the guests come for at least a week and table hopping is prevalent as the knicker-clad guests share their day's adventures. Acting as hosts to the "house party" are the extremely gracious, cordial owners, the Holzer family, who seem to be dedicated to seeing that everyone has a good time.

BERGHOTEL TIROL
Owner: Kurt Holzer Family
39030 Sexten (Sesto) (BZ), Italy
tel: (0474) 70 386 fax: (0474) 70 455
46 rooms: Double Lire 140,000–240,000*
*Rate includes breakfast and dinner
Open Christmas to Easter
 mid-May to October
Credit cards: none accepted
Restaurant open daily
Dolomites–near Austria
2 km SE of Sexton toward Moos
44 km E of Cortina, 116 km W of Bolzano

If you would like to combine your sightseeing of Siena with a luxury resort, then the Certosa di Maggiano might be "just your cup of tea". This is an expensive hotel, but delightful and quite unique. Outside, the hotel looks quite ordinary—just a wall facing the road—but when you step inside it is a fairyland. It doesn't resemble a hotel in the slightest. And it is no wonder: the hotel is built into the restored ruins of a 700-year-old Carthusian monastery. As you enter the arcaded courtyard you can almost see the ghosts of priests, their dark robes flowing, silently walking beneath the vaulted roof of the cloisters. On three sides of the courtyard are arranged the fourteen guest rooms, the lounges, the game rooms, the library, the bar and the exquisite dining room. The fourth side of the courtyard is formed by a small church. The guest rooms are spacious and pleasant but not outstanding in decor. However, the public rooms are smashing, with antiques galore, and all of the finest quality. Another bonus: there is a beautiful pool in the gardens which is never crowded since this is such a tiny hotel. In fact, there are so few people around, that it truly is like being a guest in a private estate.

CERTOSA DI MAGGIANO
Manager: Anna Recordati
Via Certosa, 82/86
53100 Siena, Italy
tel: (577) 28 81 80 fax: (0577) 28 81 89
5 rooms: Double Lire 495,000
12 suites: Lire 670,000–790,000
Open all year
Credit cards: all major
Restaurant closed Tuesdays
2 km E of Siena, near the Porta Romana gate

Although the Palazzo Ravizza is a much simpler hotel than we usually include in our guides, if you want to stay in Siena where you have the fun of walking to all the sights, this is the best choice. There are many other more luxurious places to stay in the vicinity, but they are outside the city walls. Even though the government has categorized it as a pensione, the Palazzo Ravizza definitely has some antique ambiance with the added bonus of being smack in the center of town. A 17th-century mansion, the Palazzo Ravizza has belonged to the same family for nearly 200 years. There are 30 bedrooms which all cost the same, even though they vary in their decor and location. Some of the rooms are very basic, so be sure to ask for one of the best rooms—if possible, try to get one of the rooms with antique decor overlooking the garden. The pretty back garden and terrace offer a panoramic view of the Tuscany hills, definitely one of the nicest aspects of this city hotel which fronts directly onto a commercial street. Siena is sadly lacking in a choice of hotels, and the Palazzo Ravizza remains as one of the best choices for accommodation within the city walls. The location is perfect: only a short walk from one of the most gorgeous cathedrals in Italy and only a stroll from the sensational fan-like plaza where the annual "running of the horses" takes place.

PENSIONE PALAZZO RAVIZZA
Manager: S. Iannone
Pian dei Mantellini, 34
53100 Siena, Italy
tel: (0577) 28 04 62 fax: (0577) 27 13 70
30 rooms, 21 with private bathrooms
Double: Lire 200,000–290,000*
*Rate includes breakfast and dinner
Open all year
Credit cards: all major
Restaurant open daily
Within the walled city of Siena

The Locanda dell'Amorosa makes a wonderful base for exploring the hill towns south of Florence. It is very accessible since it is located in Sinalunga which is just a few minutes from the expressway between Rome and Florence. From the Locanda dell'Amorosa it is an easy drive to such sightseeing delights as Siena, Pienza, Orvieto, Todi and Assisi. However, it is not location alone which makes this hotel so perfect: there is far more. Truly, the Locanda dell'Amorosa would be marvelous if there were nothing nearby—in fact, the hotel is a tiny town a few miles south of Sinalunga. The approach to "town" is a road lined by a majestic row of cypress trees. Park your car and enter the walls of the 14th-century medieval town where you are greeted by an enormous plaza with its own little church—exquisite inside with its soft pastels and its lovely fresco of the Madonna holding the Christ child. To the right of the main entrance to the courtyard are the stables which have been converted to a beautiful restaurant whose massive beams, natural stone and brick walls are original and tastefully enhanced by arched windows, thick wrought iron fixtures and wooden tables. The guest rooms, located in a separate building to the left of the main entrance, are tastefully appointed with a few antiques and matching bedspreads and draperies. The rest of this tiny village spreads out behind the main square and the buildings are used for other purposes—including the production of wine. A new swimming pool is scheduled for the summer of 1992.

LOCANDA DELL'AMOROSA
Manager: Carlo Citterio
53048 Sinalunga (SI), Italy
tel: (0577) 67 94 97 fax: (0577) 67 82 16
15 rooms: Double Lire 350,000-500,000
Closed January 20 to February 28
Credit cards: all major
Restaurant closed Mondays
80 km S of Florence, 45 km E of Siena

What a sense of impending grandeur you experience as you wait for the giant metal gates of the Villa Cortine Palace to swing open. Once inside the road winds and curves impressively past fountains and statues, flower gardens and mighty trees until you reach the summit where the Villa Cortine Palace reigns. This beautifully situated villa has been expanded so that the original wing now boasts a new section which appears to have more than doubled the size of the original castle. Some of the remodeling has a "too modern" feel: one rather wishes that perhaps more of an "old-world" ambiance could have been preserved. However, in the old section of the villa, which is to the left as you enter the lobby, the rooms still maintain their grandeur with incredibly ornate furniture, soaring ceilings and stunning paintings. Upstairs the guest rooms are large and are decorated with color coordinated drapes, chairs and bedspreads. What leaves absolutely nothing to be improved upon are the gardens—what a gorgeous sight. In fact, they are absolutely awe-inspiring. The villa is surrounded by graveled walkways which wind in and out amongst the fountains, ponds, statues, and glorious rose gardens, all overlooking the lovely lake.

VILLA CORTINE PALACE HOTEL
Manager: Sig. Roberto Cappelletto
25019 Sirmione (BS), Italy
tel: (030) 99 0 8 90 fax: (030) 91 63 90
55 rooms: Double Lire 350,000–420,000*
2 suites: Lire 700,000–820,000*
*Minimum stay 3 night
Open April to November
Credit cards: all major
Restaurant open daily
Park setting–overlooks Lake Garda
127 km E of Milan, 35 km W of Verona

Located about an hour's drive south of Milan's Linate airport, the Locanda del Lupo makes a convenient stop if you plan to drive directly south toward Florence. Soragna is a sleepy little town in the countryside whose main point of interest is a walled, medieval fortress. Around the central plaza buildings of great character are interspersed with modern construction. The Locanda del Lupo, built in the 18th Century by the noble Meli Lupi family, is easy to find—just a block off the plaza. The inn is best known as a gourmet restaurant: there are a series of beautiful dining rooms with gleaming copper hanging from white-washed walls, terra-cotta floors, dark beamed ceilings, antique clocks, and 17th-century oil paintings. To the left of the reception is a cozy bar and beyond a formal living room furnished in antiques. A flight of stairs leads to the guest rooms whose old world ambiance is enhanced by beamed ceilings, tiled floors and thick walls. Each guest room is individually decorated and exudes a refined, country-house ambiance. Authentic antique pieces of furniture (including fine wooden chests and wrought iron bedsteads) exude a feeling of quality. NOTE: From the Milan-Bologna expressway, take the Fidenza exit and follow signs to Soragna.

LOCANDA DEL LUPO
Manager: Alessandro Pezzani
Via Garibaldi 64
43019 Soragna (PR), Italy
tel: (0524) 69 04 44 fax: (0524) 69 350
46 rooms, Double: Lire 196,000
Suite: Lire 296,000
Closed August
Credit cards: all major
Restaurant open daily
100 km S of Milan, 118 km N of Bologna

The Grand Hotel Excelsior Vittoria has a superb location high on the cliff overlooking the port and bay of Sorrento and surrounded by an orange grove and park of about four acres with a swimming pool. The hotel is a grand old villa with a real "old-world" atmosphere, entered through a formal gate which is just a short stroll from the center of town. The furnishings, for the most part, continue the antique mood. The Excelsior Vittoria is a good place to splurge and reserve one of the superior rooms with a view of the sea. The ceilings in some of the reception rooms and in the marvelous airy dining room have gorgeous frescoed designs. The terraces and gardens surrounding the hotel offer wonderful views, as do the bedrooms which face the bay. When we first saw the Grand Hotel Excelsior Vittoria there was a gracious, though faded, elegance to the hotel giving it a slightly "worn" look. However, this magnificent villa has since been lovingly restored under the guidance of Lidia Fiorentino, the owner's wife, carefully retaining the unique turn-of-the-century mood. Staying here will certainly delight anyone who loves the feeling of reliving the grandeur of days gone by in a villa by the sea.

GRAND HOTEL EXCELSIOR VITTORIA
Owner: Fiorentino Family
Manager: Mario Damiano
Piazza Torquato Tasso, 34
80067 Sorrento (NA), Italy
tel: (081) 80 71 044 fax: (081) 87 71 206
125 rooms: Double Lire 277,000–340,000
Suites: to Lire 750,000
Open all year
Restaurant open daily
Credit cards: all major
48 km S of Naples, 250 km S of Rome
U.S. Rep: Susan Barber (212) 838-25511

It was "love at first sight" as I drove up the long graveled road through forest and vineyard and suddenly caught my first glimpse of the Borgo Pretale, a tiny cluster of weathered stone buildings nestled next to their 12th-century watch tower. My first impression was more than justified. This small inn is truly paradise. There is absolute serenity and beauty here with nothing to mar its perfection. Civilization seems miles away as the eye stretches over a glorious vista of rolling hills forested with oaks, juniper and laurel, interspersed with square patches of vineyards. But although this small village is seemingly remote, it is only a short drive south of Siena, thus a perfect hideaway from which to enjoy the magic of Tuscany. And although the buildings seem rustic, this tiny hotel, tucked into a 12th-century hamlet, offers some of the finest accommodations in all of Italy. Each room is a showplace of fine country antiques and splendid designer fabrics, blended together with the artful eye of a skilled decorator. Every piece is selected to create a sophisticated yet rustic elegance. The dining lounge beckons guests to linger after dinner by the roaring fire. A path leads to a groomed tennis court and further on to a swimming pool on a hillside terrace. (Note, Pretale is not on any map we could find, closest town on Hallwag map is Rosia, about 5 km SE of Pretale)

BORGO PRETALE
Manager: Sergio Corrado
53018 Localita Pretale-Sovicille (SI), Italy
tel: (0577) 34 54 01 fax: (0577) 34 56 25
26 room with private bathrooms
Double: Lire 350,000–450,000
Open mid-March to mid-November
Credit cards: all major
Restaurant open daily
18 km SW of Siena on Rte 73, N on 541
U.S. Rep: Hidden Treasures of Italy 708- 853-1312

The walled hill-town of Spoleto is a "must" for any trip to Umbria. What Spoleto has that is so outstanding is its Bridge of Towers (Ponte delle Torri), an absolutely awesome feat of engineering. Built in the 13th Century on the foundations of an old Roman aqueduct, this bridge, spanning a vast crevasse, is supported by ten Gothic arches that soar into the sky. Built into the hillside, the Hotel Gattapone (a mustard yellow building with dark green shutters) provides a box seat location to admire this architectural masterpiece. As you enter, there is a cozy reception area. To the left, is a bright, sunny lounge with modern black leather sofas, a long black leather bar, very pretty deep blue walls, large pots of green plants, an antique grandfather clock, and, best of all, an entire wall of glass that offers a bird's eye view of the bridge. To the right of the reception, steps sweep down to another bar and lounge where breakfast is served. This room is even more starkly modern with deep red wall coverings. The newer wing of the hotel houses the superior category bedrooms, each with a sitting area and large, view windows. In the original section of the hotel, the bedrooms are smaller, but also very attractive and every one with a view. Tucked below the hotel is a sunny terrace. Although most of the hotels in this guide have more of an antique ambiance, the Gattapone is highly recommended—a special hotel offering great warmth of welcome and a superb vistas.

HOTEL GATTAPONE
Owner-Manager: Hanke P. Giulio
Via del Ponte, 6
06049 Spoleto (PG), Italy
tel: (0743) 22 34 47 fax: (0473) 22 34 48
13 rooms with private baths
Double Lire 184,000–260,000
Open all year
Credit cards: all major
No restaurant, breakfast only
Located 130 km N of Rome, 48 km S Assisi

The San Domenico Palace is a super deluxe hotel cleverly incorporated into what was formerly a Dominican monastery. Don't let the monastery bit deter you: absolutely no trace of a life of denial remains. In fact, this is one of the most super deluxe hotels in Italy, catering to your every whim. As you enter the building the lobby opens onto the core of the hotel, the beautiful arcaded Renaissance cloister. Around this inner courtyard the vaulted walkway is now glassed in, but filled with light. Leading off the courtyard are various lounges, writing rooms and game rooms. The dining room is a masterpiece: it has high backed wooden chairs, enormous arched windows and a paneled ceiling. The chapel has been converted into a bar. Throughout the hotel there are priceless antiques of a quality which would make a museum blush with pride. Many of the bedrooms look out to the beautiful bay of Taormina. In the rear of the hotel there is a lovely garden filled with gorgeous flowers and laced by pathways with small nooks where you can stop to soak in the splendid sea view. A swimming pool is squeezed into the property just as it drops down to the road below. There is no doubt that this is a MOST dramatic hotel.

SAN DOMENICO PALACE
Manager: Luigi Menta
Piazza San Domenico, 5
98039 Taormina, Sicily, Italy
tel: (0942) 23 701 fax: (0942) 62 55 06
100 rooms: Double Lire 620,000–680,000
Credit cards: all major
Restaurant open daily
On northern coast of Sicily
U.S. Rep: E&M 800-223-9832

Instead of being located in the ancient cliff-top settlement of Taormina, the Villa Sant'Andrea is found in the village which clusters below. There is a cable car which can whisk you quickly back to Taormina for sightseeing or shopping. (The cable car is only a short block from the hotel so is very convenient.) If you are travelling with children the location is especially nice because the hotel is beautifully positioned at the end of a small swimming cove. In fact the property is built in levels which descend right to the beach where the hotel has its own private section for the guests. You enter the charming old villa from the street level where the reception desk is located. On a lower floor is the dining room which has an informal ambiance with white wicker furniture. The lounge maintains an "English country" look with sofas and chairs upholstered in cheerful floral prints which match the draperies. The bedrooms are simple but many have balconies with beautiful views across the small bay to the dramatic rocks jutting from the brilliant blue water. The hotel was originally built as a private residence for an English family in 1830 and it still maintains the ambiance of an English country estate.

VILLA SANT'ANDREA
Director: Francesco Moschella
98030 Taormina, Mazzaro
Sicily, Italy
tel: (0942) 23125 fax: (0942) 24838
67 rooms: Double Lire 300,000–380,000
Closed February
Credit cards: all major
Restaurant open daily
Own private beach
On eastern coast of Sicily

An especially glorious paradise in the Dolomites is the tiny hamlet of St. Zyprian (also called San Cypriano) near the village of Tiers (also called Tires). Here lush green meadows and pine forests are encircled by the soaring giant, tooth-like peaks of the Dolomites. The Pensione Panorama, located just above the town on a wooded hillside, captures to perfection the breathtaking view. The hotel is of new construction, but built in the regional chalet style of white stucco set off by shuttered windows, carved balconies and cascading geraniums. You enter directly into the dining room which has large windows looking out to the mountains. The dining room serves also as a lounge area with a ceramic tile stove cozily warming one corner of the room where the bar is located. Although new, the decor is a bit "dated" with heavily upholstered chairs and a swirley-design red carpet. The good-sized bedrooms, furnished with modern built-in wood furniture, are fresh and pretty—be sure to request one with a view of the mountains. What is absolutely outstanding about the Pension Panorama is its location: the views from its hillside perch are truly breathtaking. To reach the Pension Panorama, turn off the main highway at the beautiful small church and head up into the mountains, following the yellow signs leading to the Hotel Panorama. It is one of the last hotels, almost at the end of the gravel road.

PENSION PANORAMA
Owners: Robatscher family
39050 Tiers-St Zyprian (BZ), Italy
tel: (0471) 64 21 19
fax c/o tourist office (0471) 64 20 05
10 rooms, Double: Lire 130,000*
*Rate includes breakfast and dinner
Open June to October
Credit cards: none accepted
Restaurant open daily, only for guests
17 km E of Bolzano, 2 km of Tiers (Tires)

The road to the Pensione Stefaner winds up a tiny mountain valley in the heart of the Dolomites. The road is spectacular. As we rounded the last curve before St Zyprian (*San Cipriano*) the valley opened up and there spread before us was a sweeping vista of majestically soaring mountains. Across soft green meadows painted with wildflowers and dotted with tiny farm chalets rose an incredible saw-toothed range of gigantic peaks. A tiny church with a pretty steeple added the final touch of perfection to the already idyllic scene. There are many places to stay in this region. None are glamorous resorts, but rather small family run pensions. One of our favorites is the Pensione Stefaner, an attractive, chalet-style hotel with flower-laden balconies. There are a smattering of antiques, but most of the furniture is new. The hotel is efficiently, and warmly managed by the young, attractive Villgrattner family. Mrs Villgrattner is a genuinely gracious hostess and her husband (the chef) provides wonder home-cooked meals for the guests. The simple bedrooms are all impeccably tidy. Some have balconies with mountain views. NOTE: Tiers is called Tires on some maps. The town of St Zyprian (*San Cipriano*) rarely shows up on any maps, but it is just 3 km east of Tiers (*Tires*).

PENSIONE STEFANER
Owner: Villgrattner Family
39050 Tiers-St. Zyprian (BZ), Italy
tel: (0471) 64 21 75
fax c/o tourist office (0471) 64 20 05
15 rooms: Double Lire 120,000*
*Rate includes breakfast and dinner
Closed mid-November to mid-December
Credit cards: none accepted
Restaurant open daily, only for guests
NE Italy in Dolomites
17 km E of Bolzano, 3 km E of Tiers

Le Tre Vaselle is a very sophisticated inn located in the small wine town of Torgiano which is very near Assisi. The decor of the hotel is one of a lovely country manor. The owners are the Lungarotti family, famous for their production of superb wines: Mr. Lungarotti owns all of the vineyards around Torgiano for as far as the eye can see. The hotel probably evolved to fill the need for a place for business associates and friends to stay when visiting the vineyards. The accommodations are extremely comfortable and have all the amenities of a large city hotel. The most amazing aspect of Le Tre Vaselle is that it has stunning conference rooms furnished in antiques with intimate adjacent dining rooms. The Lungarotti family has thought of everything: to keep the wives happy while their husbands are in meetings, the hotel schedules cooking classes in one of the most professional kitchens I have ever seen. The Lungarottis also have a private wine museum which would be a masterpiece anywhere in the world. Not only do they have an incredible and comprehensive collection of anything pertaining to wine throughout the ages, but the display is a work of art. The museum alone would be worth a detour to Le Tre Vaselle.

LE TRE VASELLE
Owner: Lungarotti Family
Manager Romano Sartore
Via Garibaldi, 48
06089 Torgiano (PG), Italy
tel: (075) 98 80 447 fax: (075) 98 80 214
48 rooms, 6 suites: Lire 280,000–390,000
Open all year
Credit cards: all major
Restaurant open daily
27 km SW of Assisi, 158 km N of Rome

The Baia Paraelios is an absolutely delightful hotel tucked onto the spur of land that juts from the toe of Italy near the ancient port of Tropea. The hotel is actually a resort which follows the contours of the hillside from the highway down to the beach. The reception office is located at the top of the hill and the mood is set from the moment you register. The small office is tastefully decorated with plants and charming old prints on the walls and the personnel in the office are gracious and warm in their welcome. The rooms are all bungalows which are artfully terraced down the hill to capture the best view possible from each. Midway down is a lovely pool. At beach level is a beautiful dining room and a comfortable, inviting lounge. The bungalows each have one or more bedrooms, a sitting room and a deck or patio. The decor is simple but in excellent taste with tiled floors and earth tones used throughout. One of the most beautiful white sand beaches I saw in Italy stretches invitingly in front of the complex. The Baia Paraelios makes a nice stop along your route south. Not only will you have the benefit of a lovely break in your travels, but also the nearby ancient town of Tropea, which hangs on the cliffs above a beautiful bay, is fun to explore.

BAIA PARAELIOS
Owner: Adolfo Salabe
88035 Parghelia, Tropea (CZ), Italy
tel: (0963) 60 03 00 fax: (0963) 60 00 74
70 bungalows: Lire 530,000*
*Rate includes all meals
Open May 10 to September
Restaurant open daily
Southern Italy–near tip of toe
420 km S of Naples, 5 km N of Tropea

Susan and John Abbot hail from the East Coast of the United States, but they have lived in Italy for over 20 years, and it is now "home" to them. When they saw the Castello di Polgeto, it was love at first sight, and, according to John, they bought it in 20 minutes. I can certainly understand why. The castle is idyllically perched on a hillside with blissful vistas of vineyards, olive groves, green meadows and wooded hills—Umbria at its finest. When they purchased it, the castle was practically a shell: they had to install bathrooms, build proper roofs, add walls, tile the floors, wire for adequate electricity, plant artistic landscaping and on and on. It has been years of work, but John is both an artist and architect so it has all pulled together like a dream. Six spacious, self-catering apartments, individually decorated using native rustic materials, choice country antiques and simple fabrics, are artfully integrated with modern furniture and abstract paintings. A lovely pool is tucked into a secluded terrace below the castle. By the time you arrive, Susan and John might have completed their latest addition, a wonderful suite in the ancient tower. NOTE: The closest town to the Castello di Polgeto on the Hallwag map is Umbertide.

CASTELLO DI POLGETO
Owners: Susan and John Abbot
06019 Umbertide-Polgeto (PG), Italy
tel: (075) 94 13 719 fax: (075) 94 13 719
6 apartments: Double UK £400-£507 per week*
*No meals included in rates–3 night minimum
Open all year
Credit cards: none
No restaurant, apartments self-catering
No children under age 16
30 km N of Perugia, 4 km SW of Umbertide
Reservations only through:
  Harrison-Stanton, London, England
  tel: UK (071) 7365094 fax: UK (071) 3842327

The Gasthof Obereggen, located in the Val d'Ega (Ega Valley) is very simple, but quite wonderful. The inn is situated on the side of a hill overlooking a gorgeous mountain valley in one of the most beautiful mountain regions of northeastern Italy. The town of Obereggen is a ski resort and the lift is just a few minutes' walk away. From the sun-drenched deck which extends generously out from the hotel, there is an absolutely glorious vista across the green meadows to the mountains. Behind the hotel even more majestic mountains poke their jagged peaks into the sky. Inside there is a cozy dining room. Mr. Pichler must be a hunter, for trophies line the walls, and there is a typical tiled stove against one wall to keep the room toasty on a cold day. The inn has 12 bedrooms—those on the second floor open out onto lovely view-balconies. The greatest asset of this inn, and the real reason for its inclusion, is Mrs. Pichler: she is very special—running her little inn with such a warmth and gaiety that just being in the same room with her is fun. Mrs. Pichler speaks no English, but her hospitality crosses all language barriers, and her bountiful, delicious "home style" cooking speaks to all who love to eat. NOTE: Obereggen is almost impossible to find on any map, although the Val d'Ega is usually indicated. If coming from Bolzano head southeast through the Val d'Ega for approximately 16 kilometers watching for the turn to the right for Obereggen. The closest town on the Hallwag map is Ega (Ega is also called *San Floriano*).

GASTHOF OBEREGGEN
Owner: Pichler Family
39050 Obereggen (San Floriano)
Val d'Ega (BZ), Italy
tel: (0471) 61 57 22
12 rooms: Double Lire 120,000*
*Rate includes breakfast and dinner
Closed May and June
Credit cards: none accepted
Restaurant open daily
25 km SE of Bolzano, 3 km S of Nova Levante

The Stella d'Italia is located in San Mamete, a tiny, picturesque village nestled along the northern shore of Lake Lugano, just a few minutes' drive from the Swiss border. The hotel (which has been in the Ortelli family for three generations) makes an excellent choice for a moderately priced lakefront hotel. Mario Ortelli, an extremely cordial host, showed us throughout the hotel which has two adjoining wings, one quite old and the other a new addition. My choice for accommodation would be in the original part which has more "old-world" ambiance—the rooms I saw here were very pleasant with large French windows opening onto miniature balconies capturing views of the lake. The lounges and dining room have a few antique accents, but basically have a modern ambiance. The nicest feature of the hotel is the superb little lakefront garden—in summer this is where all the guests "live." Green lawn, fragrant flowers, lacy trees, and a romantic vine-covered trellised dining area make this an ideal spot for whiling away the hours. Steps lead down to a small pier from which guests can swim. The ferry dock for picking up and dropping off passengers is adjacent to the hotel. Another interesting feature for golf enthusiasts is that there are several golf courses within an easy drive from the hotel—one of these (near the town of Grandola) is one of the oldest in Italy.

STELLA D'ITALIA
Owner: Mario Ortelli
San Mamete
Lake Lugano 22010 Valsolda (CO), Italy
tel: (0344) 68 139 fax: (0344) 68 729
36 rooms: Double Lire 104,000–117,000
Open April to September
Credit cards: all major
Restaurant open daily
Lakefront hotel
8 km E of Lugano, 100 km N of Milan

The Pensione Accademia is enchanting—a fairytale villa with delightful gardens, romantic canal-side location, and cozy antique-filled interior. The hotel has a fabulous setting on an oasis of land almost looped by canals. In front is a beautiful, completely enclosed, "secret" garden whose walls are so heavily draped with vines that it is not until you discover black iron gates that you see steps leading down to the villa's own gondola landing. As you leave the garden and enter the wisteria-covered palazzo, the magic continues with family heirlooms adorning the spacious rooms where sunlight filters through large windows. A staircase leads upstairs where some of the guest rooms are located in the original villa and others, connected by a hallway, in a portion of the hotel borrowed from an adjacent building. No two of the guest rooms are alike, none are "decorator perfect"—they are like guest rooms in a private home. Some of those in the front have canal views but are noisier than those looking over the garden. The only hitch to this picture of perfection is that your chances are slim of snaring a room in this romantic hideaway—the hotel is so special that loyal guests reserve "their" own favorite room for the following year as they leave. Spring and fall are most heavily booked—your chances are better in July and August and the prices are even a little lower. Since we last visited the Pensione Accademia, it has come under new management. We will be eager to hear readers' comments.

PENSIONE ACCADEMIA
Owner:: Giovnna Salmaso
Dorsoduro 1058
3123 Venice, Italy
tel: (041) 52 37 84 6 fax: (041) 52 39 15 2
26 rooms: Double Lire 155,000–198,000
Double without private bath Lire 110,000–130,000
Open all year
Credit cards: all major
No restaurant, breakfast only
Near the Accademia boat stop

The Agli Alboretti Hotel is conveniently located just steps from the Accademia boat landing. Although only a two star hotel, it has more charm than many others charging much higher prices. But it is not price alone that makes the hotel appealing: there is a cozy ambiance from the moment you step into the intimate lobby, paneled with dark mellowed wood and decorated with some attractive prints on the walls and a perky ship model in the window. At the front desk will be either Dina Linguerri or her daughter Anna. I did not meet Anna, but her mother is most gracious and speaks excellent English. Beyond the reception area is a small lounge and then one of the very nicest features of the hotel—a tranquil garden sheltered by an overhanging trellis which in summer is completely covered by vines—a welcome, cool oasis after a day of sightseeing. White wrought iron tables and chairs are set for morning breakfast, afternoon tea, or summer evening dinner. The guest rooms vary in size, but all have a private bath or shower. Be sure to request a guest room with a bath tub because the showers are the type without a separate enclosure. Whichever room you have, however, it should be quiet since the hotel is tucked onto a peaceful square. NOTE: There is a restaurant which serves dinner every night except Wednesday.

AGLI ALBORETTI HOTEL
Owners: Dina and Anna Linguerri
Dorsoduro 882-884
30123 Venice, Italy
tel: (041) 52 30 05 8 fax: (041) 52 10 15 8
20 rooms: Double Lire 160,000–215,000
Open all year
Credit cards: all major
Restaurant closed Wednesdays
Near the Accademia boat stop

The Hotel Flora is reached down a tiny lane, just off one of the main walkways to St Mark's Square: a secluded hideaway, protected from the bustle of the city yet conveniently close to all the action. At the end of the tiny alley the doors open into a small lobby, beyond which is an enchanting small garden, an oasis of serenity with white wrought iron tables and chairs surrounding a gently tinkling fountain. Potted plants, small trees and lacy vines complete the idyllic scene. The hotel encloses the garden on three sides: doors open to the right to a dear little bar and the breakfast room. The lounges are Victorian in mood with dark furniture. The bedrooms vary in their size and decor, but all are fancy and have ornate, antique furnishings. Victorian-style wallpaper covers many of the walls. The ambiance is a bit fussy, but with a definite old world atmosphere. There is no restaurant at the hotel, which is absolutely no problem since Venice abounds with wonderful places to dine. Breakfast, of course, is served to guests. Signor Romanelli, who owns this small hotel, personally sees that his guests are well taken care of. The Hotel Flora is a favorite of many travellers to Venice. Although it is a relatively simple hotel and would not appeal to those looking for deluxe accommodations, it is a real find for those who want a relatively inexpensive place to stay in the heart of Venice.

HOTEL FLORA
Owner: Alex Romanelli
Calle larga 22 Marzo, 2283/a
30124 Venice, Italy
tel: (041) 52 05 844 fax: (041) 52 28 217
44 rooms: Double Lire 230,000
Open February to November 20
Credit cards: all major
No restaurant, breakfast only
3-minute walk from St Mark's Square

If you love opulent elegance, and if cost is of no consequence to you, the Gritti Palace is an excellent choice for your hotel in Venice. The location is marvelous—just a short walk from St Mark's Square yet far enough removed to miss the city's noise and summer mob of tourists. In fact, with careful planning, you can be entirely insulated in a private and very special world from the moment you arrive until you reluctantly depart. If you take a private motor launch from the airport or the Piazza Roma, you can descend stylishly at the deluxe little private pier in front of the hotel where porters will be waiting to whisk you to your room to be pampered and spoiled. All at a price, of course. The Gritti Palace is expensive, very expensive. But then what would you expect when staying in the 15th-century palace of the immensely wealthy Venetian Doge, Andrea Gritti. The Gritti Palace has a charming terrace on the bank of the Grand Canal where you dine in splendor and watch the constant stream of boat traffic. The lobby and lounge areas open off the terrace and are grandly decorated with antiques. The bedrooms are large and very fancy in decor, and those that face the canal are presented with a 24-hour show.

HOTEL GRITTI PALACE
Manager: Vincenzo Finizzola
Campo Santa Maria del Giglio, 2467
30124 Venice, Italy
tel: (041) 79 46 11 fax: (041) 52 00 942
99 rooms: Double Lire 660,000–749,000
Open all year
Credit cards: all major
Restaurant open daily
Near St Mark's Square
U.S. Rep: CIGA Hotels 800-221-2340

The Hotel La Fenice et Des Artistes, although not inexpensive, costs less than many other hotels which do not offer nearly its charm. The lobby is small, but seems spacious since there are two small garden patios which open from it. Here guests sit in the late afternoon for a cup of tea or an aperitif before dinner. Doors to the right lead to a club-like lounge and an intimate bar. The reception area is a triangle which connects the original building on the right with a newer wing on the left. Both sections are nice, although in summer only the newer wing offers the option of air conditioning, which can be very welcome on a hot day (there is an additional charge for air conditioned rooms.) The bedrooms are not large, but adequate, and color coordinated with a different wallpaper in each room setting the theme. Breakfast is the only meal served, but this is almost a blessing since within a few blocks there is a fabulous choice of appealing places to dine. The fascinating La Fenice Theater, one of the oldest and most beautiful theaters in Europe, is just around the corner—most conveniently located for music lovers. The "Taverna La Fenice", one of the oldest and most elegant restaurants in Venice, is incorporated into the "old Wing" of the hotel.

HOTEL LA FENICE ET DES ARTISTES
Manager: Dante Appollonio
Campiello de la Fenice, S. Marco 1936
30124 Venice, Italy
tel: (041) 52 32 333 fax: (041) 52 03 721
75 rooms: Double Lire 230,000
Open all year
Credit cards: EC, MC, VS
Restaurant open daily
Near La Fenice Theatre

Although La Residenza, with its arched windows, lacy detailing, and columned balcony, is a brilliant example of the finest 15th-century Venetian architecture, I was at first a bit half-hearted in my enthusiasm due to the somewhat dilapidated condition of the small plaza it faces. When I visited the hotel, the massive door was locked and I started to turn away until I discovered a discreetly camouflaged small button incorporated into a brass lion ornament to the left of the door. This I rang and the owner, Franco Tagliapietra, leaned out the window and instructed me in Italian to push open the door when he released the lock. How glad I was that I had persevered. After entering the door and climbing up a flight of stairs, I was magically surrounded by a beautiful, museum-quality room with walls and ceiling adorned with intricate plaster designs. The softly toned walls and the marble floor were enhanced by dark wooden furniture. All of the bedrooms have a private bath and are accented with fine antiques. You might have a problem booking this small hotel, since no one seems to speak English. However, perhaps use the Italian form letter in the back of this guide or get an Italian speaking friend to call for you. It is no wonder the palace is so splendid—it was the residence of the Gritti family, a most prestigious name in Venice. NOTE: Readers have written that their deposits were not returned when they had to cancel reservations.

LA RESIDENZA
Owner: Gian Franco Tagliapietra
Campo Bandiera e Moro
30122 Venice, Italy
tel: (041) 52 85 315 fax: (041) 52 38 859
15 rooms: Double Lire 140,000
Closed February 8-20
Credit cards: all major
Restaurant open daily, only for guests
Located 10-minute walk from St Mark's Square

At first glance the exterior of the Pensione Seguso appears quite bland: a rather boxy affair without much of the elaborate architectural enhancements so frequently evident in Venice. However, the inside of the pensione radiates warmth and charm with Oriental rugs setting off antique furniture and heirloom silver service. The hotel is located on the "left bank" of Venice—across the Grand Canal from the heart of the tourist area, about a 15-minute walk to St Mark's Square (or only a few minutes by ferry from the Accademia boat stop). For several generations the hotel has been in the Seguso family who provide a homelike ambiance for the guest who does not demand luxury. In front there is a miniature terrace harboring a few tables set under umbrellas. Several of the bedrooms have views of the canal (although these rooms are the noisiest due to the canal traffic). Remember this is a simple pension, most of the rooms share a bathroom: if you are looking for the amenities offered by a hotel, the Pensione Seguso would not be for you. But, the most pleasant surprise is that the value-conscious tourist can stay at the Pensione Seguso with breakfast and dinner included for what the price of a room alone would cost for most hotels in Venice. NOTE: Although a small pensione, the Seguso has an elevator—handy if you have a problem with stairs.

PENSIONE SEGUSO
Owner: Seguso Family
Grand Canal Zattere, 779
30123 Venice, Italy
tel: (041) 52 86 858 fax: (041) 5222340
36 rooms: Double Lire 179,000–211,500
Rates include breakfast and dinner
Credit cards: none accepted
Restaurant open daily, only for guests
10-minute walk from the Accademia boat stop

The Casa Frollo, located on Giudecca Island across from St Mark's Square, is a real gem: a moderately-priced oasis just minutes from the heart of Venice. There is constant ferry service to and from the island so the distance is not a problem (actually the boat ride is quite fun). Once you arrive at Giudecca (getting off at the Riva degli Schiavoni dock), walk to your right and you will see the Casa Frollo, an old villa across the street from the water. You enter through huge doors and then climb the stairs to your right to bring you into an enormous reception—all-purpose room. When I first visited the Casa Frollo, is was run by Flora Soldan, but now her son, Marino has taken over the management. My heart was won the moment I stepped into the room which is brimming with priceless antiques and was enveloped by its awesome size. The room runs the length of the building and the front windows (where tables are set for breakfast and drinks) open onto a sensational view of Venice. The bedrooms vary in decor but are spacious and many with antiques. The rear windows open onto a lazy, lush garden. For those on a tight budget, there are some rooms without baths. For splurges, request a bath and a view of Venice.

CASA FROLLO
Manager: Marino Soldan
Giudecca, 50
30133 Venice, Italy
tel: (041) 52 22 723 fax: (041) 52 06 203
26 rooms: Double Lire 100,000–140,000
Open March 18 to November 21
Credit cards: none accepted
No restaurant, breakfast only
17th-century palace
On Giudecca Island

The Hotel Cipriani was founded by the late Giuseppe Cipriani, who during his lifetime became almost a legend in Venice. This beloved man, who founded the internationally famous Harry's Bar in Venice, had a dream of building a fabulous hotel within easy reach of St Mark's Square and yet far enough away to guarantee seclusion and peace. He bought three acres on the island of Giudecca and with the financial assistance of some of his prestigious friends, such as Princess Briget of Prussia and the Earl of Iveagh (head of the Guinness brewing company in Dublin), he accomplished his dream—an elegant Venetian palace-style hotel. The Cipriani is the perfect hotel for those of you who must have a pool, for it is the only hotel with a pool in Venice. And what a pool—it is Olympic size and surrounded by beautiful gardens. The splendor continues inside where the lounges are tastefully decorated in whites and beiges and the bedrooms are large and elegant. You truly have the best of all worlds at the Cipriani—you are at a superior resort yet only minutes from the heart of Venice in the private launch which waits to whisk you, any time of the day or night, to St Mark's Square. NOTE: Since our last visit, 9 super deluxe apartments have opened in the renovated Palazzo Vendramin, adjacent to the hotel. We have not yet been able to inspect this new addition, but from the pictures look beautiful.

HOTEL CIPRIANI
Manager: Dr. Natale Rusconi
Isola della Giudecca, 10
30123 Venice, Italy
tel: (041) 52 07 74 4 fax: (041) 52 03 93 0
105 rooms: Double Lire 719,000–933,000
Palazzo Vendramin: Lire 870,000–1,700,000
Open March to November
Credit cards: all major
Restaurant open daily
On Giudecca Island

If the idea of being close to Venice and yet near a beach and casino appeals to you, then perhaps you should consider a hotel located on the Lido, a small island opposite St Mark's Square. A fifteen-minute boat ride and a short taxi trip brings you to the Albergo Quattro Fontane, a charming inn which reminds me more of a French country home than an Italian villa. It has a white stuccoed exterior with gabled roof, green shutters, and vines creeping both over the door and around some of the small balconies. To the left of the main building is a lovely courtyard whose privacy is established by another wing of the hotel giving the garden a cozy, "walled in" effect. Inside the hotel there is an ambiance of a country home with antiques cleverly used throughout the lounges. The beach is only a short distance away and the Albergo Quattro Fontane can make arrangements for you to reserve a private beach cabana when you arrive at the inn. The cost per day will vary, depending both upon the location and the comparative luxury of the cabana you choose. The beach is wide and the water inviting and clear, although the sand is not as fine and white as we have seen on some of the beaches in southern Italy. Still, it is quite an experience just to sample the interesting hierarchy of the Italian beach system.

ALBERGO QUATTRO FONTANE
Manager: Bente Bevilacqua
Via 4 Fontane
30126 Lido of Venice
Venice, Italy
tel: (041) 52 60 22 7 fax: (041) 52 60 72 6
68 rooms: Double Lire 260,000–300,000
Open end of April to October 1
Credit cards: all major
Restaurant open daily
On the Lido, across from Venice

The tiny island of Torcello is located about fifty minutes from Venice by boat. This lovely, sleepy little island is usually considered a short stop for the tour boats as they ply their way among the maze of little islands surrounding Venice. But, for those who want to linger on Torcello, where they can be close to Venice yet feel out in the country, there is a deluxe inn which is owned by the Cipriani family. This small inn, the Locanda Cipriani, is well known to knowledgeable gourmets as a fantastic restaurant. Many arrive every day from Venice just to dine, and depart never knowing that upstairs this restaurant also has guest rooms. The inn is very simple, much more like a small farmhouse than a deluxe hotel. Inside there is a rustic, cozy dining room and outside a beautiful dining terrace surrounded by gardens brilliant in summer with all varieties of flowers. There are only a few bedrooms which are all suites. Breakfast and dinner are included in the room rate. This is an expensive inn, but an elegant hideaway for relaxing and dining royally in a beautiful country setting. Many famous guests have already discovered this oasis—including Hemingway, who came here to write. I think you will share his belief that the Locanda Cipriani Torcello is a very special place.

LOCANDA CIPRIANI TORCELLO
Owner: Carla Cipriani
Manager: Bonifacio Brass (son)
30012 Isola Torcello
Venice, Italy
tel: (041) 73 01 50 fax: (041) 73 54 33
5 suites: Lire 520,000
Rate includes breakfast and dinner
Closed November 4 to March 15
Credit cards: all major
Restaurant closed Tuesdays
Island location
Reached by boat from Venice

The Hotel Gabbia d'Oro, superbly positioned in the heart of romantic Verona, is truly a gem. From the moment you step inside you are surrounded by an understated elegance. Although a very deluxe hotel, there is no feeling of stiff formality—your welcome is genuinely warm and friendly. Just off the spacious reception area, is a cozy lounge with massive beamed ceilings, ancient stone walls, fine antiques, and handsome old prints in gold frames. Beyond the lobby is an intimate bar with rich wood paneling set off to perfection by chairs upholstered in cheerful cherry red fabric. There is also a lovely, quiet, inner garden courtyard where on occasion intimate concerts are held. The guest rooms are individually decorated, reflecting exquisite taste: antiques abound and rich, color coordinating fabrics are used throughout. Nothing has been spared to make each room beautiful. The standard bedrooms are very pretty, but if you can afford to splurge, the junior suites are much more spacious. It is such a pleasure to see a new hotel emerge after renovation that reflects so beautifully the authentic rich heritage of the original building The Hotel Gabbia d'Oro truly captures the romance of Verona. Although excellent restaurants abound in Verona, the hotel offers a buffet and pre-theater restaurant, exclusively for guests. Also, in summer, private, elegant dinners can be arranged with advance notice.

HOTEL GABBIA D'ORO
Manager: Miss Camilla Balzarro
Corso Portani Borsari 4/A
37121 Verona, Italy
tel: (045) 80 03 060 fax: (045) 59 02 93
27 rooms, Double: from Lire 385,000
Suites to Lire 600,000
Open all year
Credit cards: all major
Restaurant open daily, only for guests
Located in heart of Verona

The entrance to the Hotel Victoria is starkly modern—almost with a museum-like quality. The white walls, white ceiling, white floors, and an enormous skylight are softened by the green plants. At first glance I was disappointed since I had heard so many glowing reports of the merits of this small hotel. However, the mood begins to change as you enter the reception area with its Oriental carpets and, by the time you arrive in the lounge area, the feeling is definitely moving toward an antique ambiance with the original heavy ancient wooden beams and one of the original stone walls exposed, leather chairs, and some lovely antique tables. The bedrooms are extremely modern and beautifully functional with good reading lights, comfortable chairs, and excellent bathrooms. The Victoria actually dates back centuries and the new hotel is built within the shell of an ancient building. The architect even incorporated some of the archaeologically interesting finds of the site into a museum in the basement level. When the hotel is not full and all of the dining room tables are not needed, special "windows" open up on the floor of the restaurant and the museum below is lit so that you can study the artifacts as you dine.

HOTEL VICTORIA
Manager: Andrea Tamburini
Via Adua, 8
37121 Verona, Italy
tel: (045) 59 05 66 fax: (045) 59 01 55
46 rooms: Double Lire 275,000
Open all year
Credit cards: all major
No restaurant, breakfast only
In the heart of Verona
U.S. Rep: Harry Jarvinen & Ass 800-876-5278

The Hotel Turm belongs to the Romantik Hotel Chain. Just being a member of this exclusive "club" indicates the hotel is pretty special because to belong the inn must have the owner personally involved in the management and the interior must have an antique ambiance. The Hotel Turm is no exception. There is an especially attractive little dining room with vaulted whitewashed ceilings and chalet-style rustic wooden furniture. There are a few antiques in the hallways and lounges. The bedrooms are simple, but very pleasant, with light pine furniture and fluffy down comforters on the beds. There is a swimming pool on the terrace where one can swim or lounge while gazing out to the little town and the mountains beyond. There is even a small indoor pool. The Hotel Turm dates back to the 13th Century and Mr. Pramstrahler takes great care to maintain touches of the "old-world" charm by interspersing antique chests, cradles, chairs and ancient artifacts. NOTE: Völs is called Fié on some maps.

ROMANTIK HOTEL TURM
Owner: Pramstrahler Family
Fié Allo Schiliar
1-39050 Völs am Schlern
Sudtirol (BZ), Italy
tel: (0471) 72 50 14 fax: (0471) 72 54 74
24 rooms: Double Lire 315,000*
*Rate includes breakfast and dinner
Closed November 15 to December 20
Credit cards: EC, MC, VS
Restaurant open daily
16 km E of Bolzano, 7 km S of Siusi (Seis)
U.S. Rep: Euro-Connection 800-645-3876

The Hotel Völser Heubad is located in one of the most idyllic regions of Italy—the spectacularly beautiful Dolomites. In this mountain paradise, the meadows and mountains surrounding Völs (also called Fié) provide many miles of memorable trails for walking. The Hotel Völser-Heubad is located just a short walk from the center of the medieval village. The hotel is in two buildings which face each other across a central courtyard. From the outside, the inn does not exude much character, but the interior holds much more promise—two of the dining rooms are rustic masterpieces their walls and ceilings richly paneled in wood that has the mellow glow of age, Tyrolian-style carved tables and chairs, and hanging brass lamps. Guest rooms are located in both sections of the hotel. Those in the wing on the right (where the reception area is located) are pleasantly furnished in light woods. The guest rooms in the building on the left (the same part that houses the restaurants) have a more antique ambiance. Most of the bedrooms were occupied at the time of our visit, but all that we saw were most attractive. Room 18, although not large, was especially appealing with pretty antique furniture and a view out over the back garden and the swimming pool. The Völser Heubad is also famous as a spa, where guests have the questionably exciting option of being packed in hay—a very old village custom guaranteed to relieve what ails you!

HOTEL VÖLSER HEUBAD
Family Kompatscher
39050 Völs am Schlern (BZ), Italy
tel: (0471) 72 50 20 fax: (0471) 72 54 25
37 rooms, Double: Lire 140,000–156,000*
*Rate includes breakfast and dinner
Closed November to Christmas
Credit cards: EC, MC, VS
Restaurant open daily
16 km E of Bolzano, 7 km S of Siusi (Seis)

Discoveries
from
Our Readers

Some of the new hotels featured in this edition of "Italian Country Inns & Itineraries" are those that travellers have recommended to us. We inspected them and agreed wholeheartedly with our readers' appraisals. However, on our research trip to Italy we did not have time to visit every place suggested to us. Since many of these "tips" sound too good to pass up, we're passing them on to you in this "Discoveries from Our Readers" section. Thank you for sharing your discoveries. Please keep them coming.

MARATEA-ACQUAFREDDA   HOTEL VILLA CHETA ELITE

Hotel Villa Cheta Elite, Strada Statale, Maratea-Acquafredda, 85041 Potenza, Italy; Owners: Marisa and Lamberto Aquadro; tel: (0973) 878134, fax: (0973) 878134; Open April to September; 18 rooms: Double Lire 105,000–145,000.

We had targeted the Hotel Villa Cheta Elite as a potential "to see" for this edition, but our research did not take us to the south of Italy. We have seen pictures and received rave reviews of this small hotel located in one of our favorite coastal regions on the western coast of southern Italy and it sounds like a real winner. The hotel overlooks the sea and meals are served on the terrace when the weather is balmy outside. The food is supposed to be good, featuring fish specialties. One reader (of Italian heritage) who stayed at the Hotel Villa Cheta Elite wrote: "From an Italian's point of view, the hotel is absolutely delightful. The handsome owners are warm and gracious, and, although they speak no English, are excellent hosts to all their guests." We are eager to try out the hotel ourselves—we definitely will on our next trip to Italy.

LUCCA VILLA RINASCIMENTO

Villa Rinascimento, Carla and Vincenzo Zaffora, 55058 Maria del Giudice, Lucca, Italy; tel: (0583) 370238 or (0583) 378201; 15 rooms: Double Lire 90,000; Recommended by Marilyn and Charles Coffaro, Harrison, Ohio.

Situated only 9 kilometers from Lucca, a marvelous city completely enclosed by walls, is a new recommendation: "While on a trip to Italy last month we discovered the Villa Rinascimento which we believe meets your standards. We stayed two nights and it was wonderful. Carla (she's Dutch) and Vincenzo have spent 7 years restoring the building. Carla speaks English, German and French along with Italian. There is a swimming pool and lovely garden. It is very peaceful and a great spot to visit Lucca and Pisa from. They are constantly improving the surrounding green area around the Villa. It is truly a great bargain." NOTE: We have received some further comments from readers who say that they like the Villa Rinascimento, but it that it doesn't seem completely finished yet.

MASSA COZZILE VILLA PASQUINI

Villa Pasquini, Family Innocenti, Via Vacchereccia, 56, Montecatini-Massa Cozzile (PT), Italy; tel: (0572) 72205; Double Lire 96,000; Recommended by Anna La Porta-Balsamo, Brooklyn, New York.

"We found the fantastic Villa Pasquini (remodeled in 1990) near Montecatini, 20 minutes from Florence. You are greeted by Mr. Innocenti and his family who are dedicated to making your stay a happy one. The dining room overlooks the gorgeous mountains and farms and groves. The bedrooms are really too beautiful to be real. I could go on and on, but I must end by telling you about the gourmet meals of classic Tuscan food served nightly in an elegant atmosphere in the main dining room with classical music accenting the already perfect evening. We loved the Villa Pasquini so much that we ended up staying a week and going each day by bus to Florence."

MILAN	HOTEL VILLA MALPENSA

Hotel Villa Malpensa, Manager Patrizio Strino, Via don Andrea Sacconago, 1/3, 21010 Vizzola Ticino (VA) Italy, tel: (0331) 23 09 44 fax: (0331) 23 09 50, 43 rooms: Double: Lire 230,000; Open all year, Credit cards: all major. Recommended by Anonymous, Hillsborough, California.

We are absolutely delighted to be able to share an enthusiastic recommendation for a recently opened hotel near Milan's large international airport, Malpensa. For years we have been looking for an airport close to the airport for the convenience of travellers leaving on an early morning flight, or as an alternative to staying in the center of Milan. The manager of the hotel sent us a brochure: the stately, formal looking hotel does indeed look most inviting. It was once the summer residence of the Counts of Caproni (one of the wealthiest families of northern Italy). It is located in the middle of the Ticino National Park and is only two kilometers from the Malpensa International Airport.

SORRENTO	IMPERIAL TRAMONTANO HOTEL

Imperial Tramontano Hotel, via Vittorio Veneto, 80067 Sorrento, Italy; tel: (081) 878 1940, fax: (091) 8072344; 109 rooms: Double Lire 275,000; Open April to October; Recommended by Debby Lumkes.

Sorrento makes a good base for an overnight before an excursion to the Isle of Capri, so it is always fun to share another suggestion: "You may want to check out the Imperial Tramontano Hotel in Sorrento. We had a room that had a sitting room, bedroom and huge bathroom; with two balconies, one in the sitting room and one in the bedroom, overlooking the harbor, Capri and Vesuvius. The facilities are wonderful, the lobby is beautiful and there is greenery surrounding the entrance to the establishment."

Hotel Pausania, Dorso Duro, 2824, Venice 30100, Italy; tel: (041) 5222083; 26 rooms: Double Lire 240,000; Recomended by Anonymous, California.

"I have a hotel for you in Venice, an absolutely perfect one, Hotel Pausania. One takes the #11 Ca'Rezzonica ferry stop (the one before the Accademia), walks along the passageway to the small square where one can go left through portals and toward Accademia, then along that small canal to about the eighth doorway. There are about 26 rooms, all up a tall narrow courtyard staircase. The help took care of all bookings, all stamps, etc. There is a fine breakfast room and a garden in the rear is being rebuilt—for dining I think. Our rooms were on the canal itself. The best thing is that we felt like residents—no tourists in sight."

HOTEL RESERVATION REQUEST LETTER IN ITALIAN

HOTEL NAME & ADDRESS – clearly printed or typed

Vi prego di voler riservare:
I would like to request:

_____ Numero delle camere con bagno o doccia privata
Number of rooms with private bath or shower

_____ Numero delle camere senza bagno o doccia
Number of rooms without private bath or shower

_____ Data di arrivo_____ Data di Partenza
Date of arrival *Date of departure*

Vi prego inoltre de fornirmi le seguenti informazioni:
Please let me know as soon as possible the following:

Potete riservare le camere richieste?	SI	NO
Can you reserve the space requested?	*Yes*	*No*
I pasti sono compresi nel prezzo?	SI	NO
Are meals included in your rate?	*Yes*	*No*
E necessario un deposito?	SI	NO
Do you need a deposit?	*Yes*	*No*

Prezzo giornaliero _____
Price per night

Quanto e necessario come deposito? _____
How much deposit do you need?

Ringraziando anticipatamente, porgo distinti saluti,
Thanking you in advance, I send my best regards,

YOUR NAME & ADDRESS – clearly printed or typed

Reservation Request Letter

242

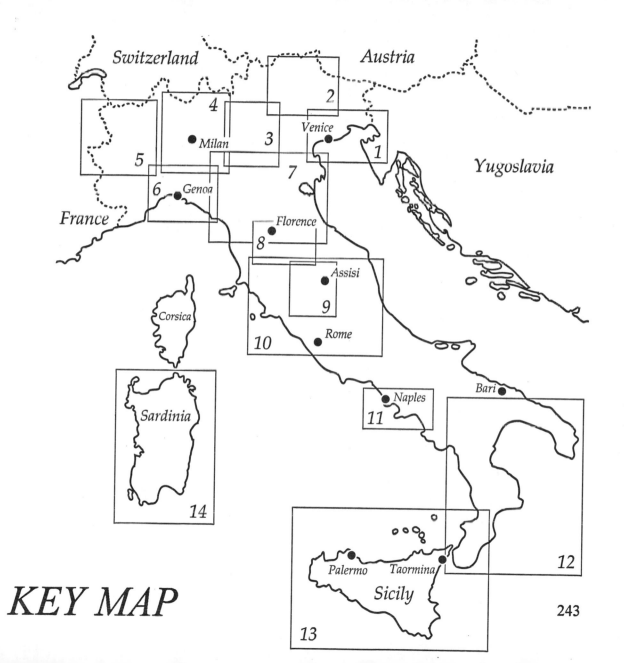

KEY MAP

243

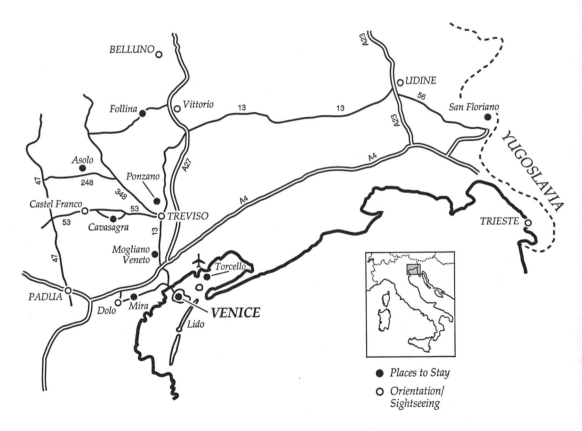

Places to Stay

Orientation/
Sightseeing

Map 1

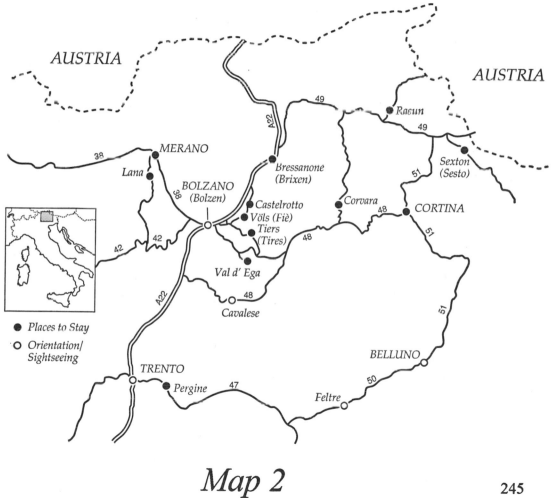

AUSTRIA

AUSTRIA

38

MERANO

Lana

Rasun

49

49

BOLZANO
(Bolzen)

38

Bressanone
(Brixen)

A22

Sexton
(Sesto)

51

Castelrotto

Corvara

48

CORTINA

Völs (Fiè)

Tiers
(Tires)

48

51

42

42

Val d' Ega

48

Cavalese

● *Places to Stay*

○ *Orientation/*
  Sightseeing

A22

BELLUNO

51

TRENTO

Pergine

47

Feltre

50

Map 2

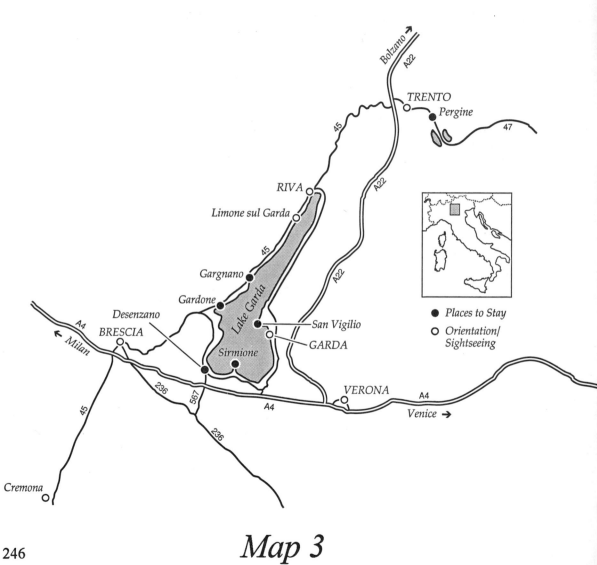

Places to Stay

Orientation/
Sightseeing

246

Map 3

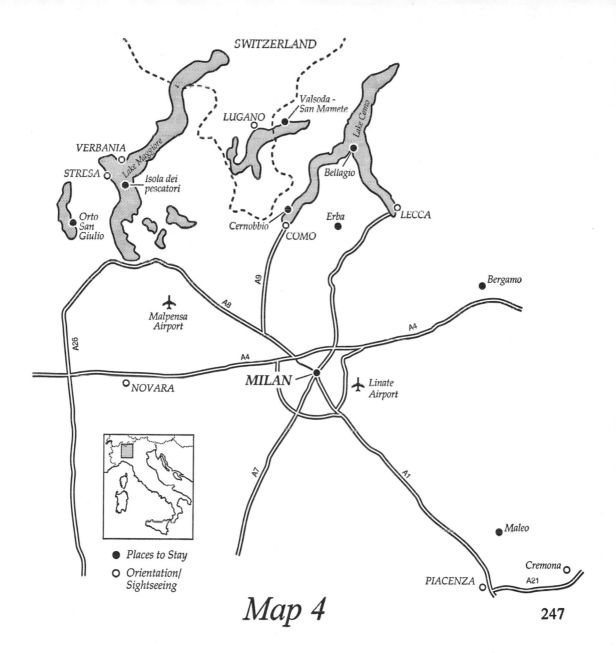

SWITZERLAND

Valsoda –
San Mamete

LUGANO

Lake Como

VERBANIA

Lake Maggiore

STRESA

Isola dei
pescatori

Bellagio

Orto
San
Giulio

Cernobbio

LECCA

COMO

Erba

A9

Bergamo

Malpensa
Airport

A8

A4

A26

A4

Linate
Airport

MILAN

NOVARA

A7

A1

● *Places to Stay*

○ *Orientation/*
Sightseeing

Maleo

Cremona

PIACENZA   A21

Map 4

247

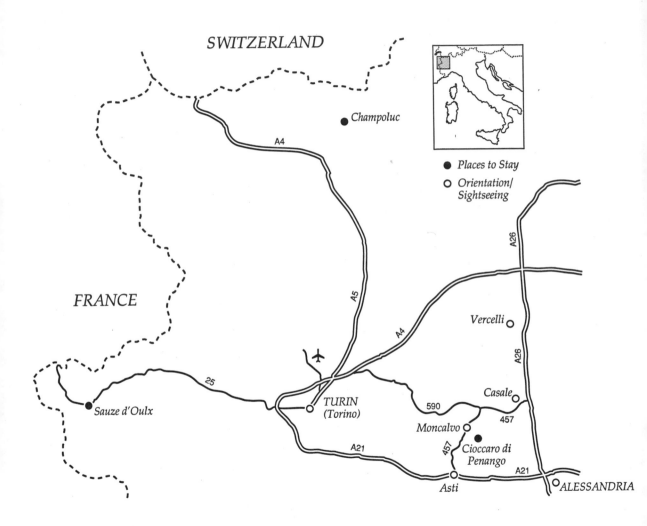

SWITZERLAND

● Champoluc

A4

● Places to Stay
○ Orientation/
Sightseeing

A5

FRANCE

A4

A26

Vercelli ○

A26

25

✈

TURIN
(Torino)

590

Casale ○

● Sauze d'Oulx

457

Moncalvo ○

457

● Cioccaro di
Penango

A21

457

A21

○ Asti

○ ALESSANDRIA

248

Map 5

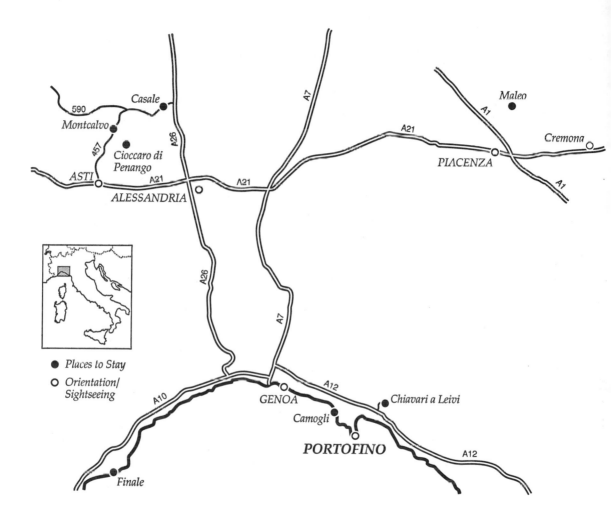

Map 6

249

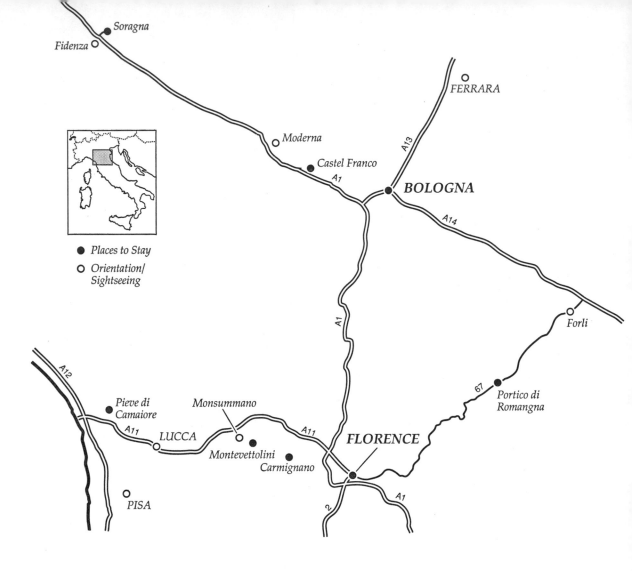

Soragna

Fidenza

Moderna

Castel Franco

A1

A13

FERRARA

BOLOGNA

A14

● *Places to Stay*

○ *Orientation/
Sightseeing*

Forli

A1

A12

Pieve di
Camaiore

Monsummano

A11

LUCCA

Montevettolini

Carmignano

A11

67

Portico di
Romangna

FLORENCE

PISA

2

A1

250   *Map 7*

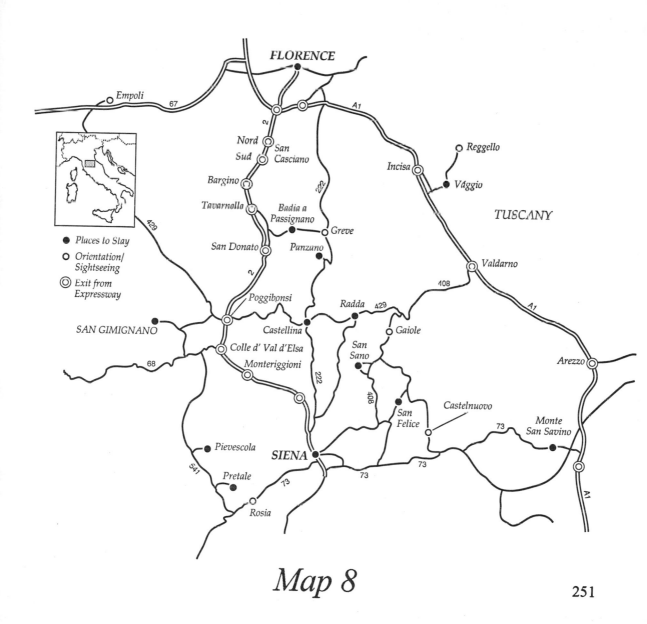

Map 8

251

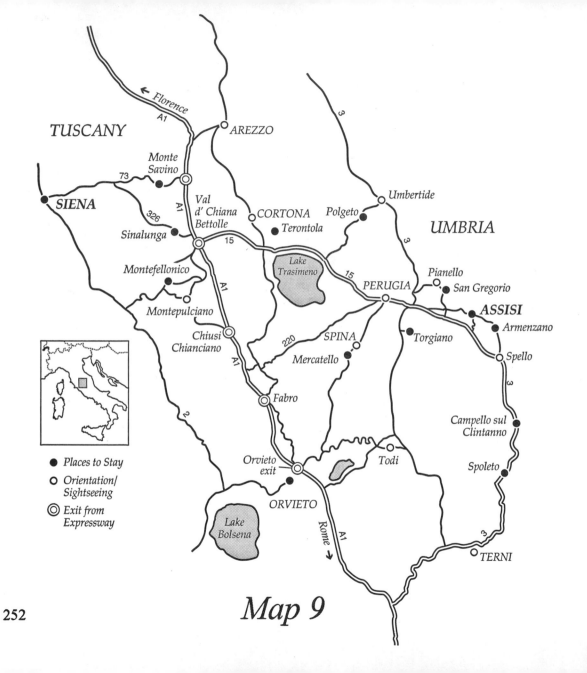

TUSCANY

Florence
A1

AREZZO

Monte
Savino

73

A1

SIENA

326

Val
d' Chiana
Bettolle

CORTONA

Polgeto

Umbertide

UMBRIA

Sinalunga

15

Terontola

Montefellonico

Lake
Trasimeno

15

PERUGIA

Pianello

San Gregorio

Montepulciano

A1

ASSISI

Chiusi
Chianciano

220

SPINA

Torgiano

Armenzano

A1

Mercatello

Spello

3

Fabro

Campello sul
Clintanno

2

Todi

Spoleto

Orvieto
exit

ORVIETO

Rome

A1

3

Lake
Bolsena

TERNI

● Places to Stay

○ Orientation/
   Sightseeing

◎ Exit from
   Expressway

Map 9

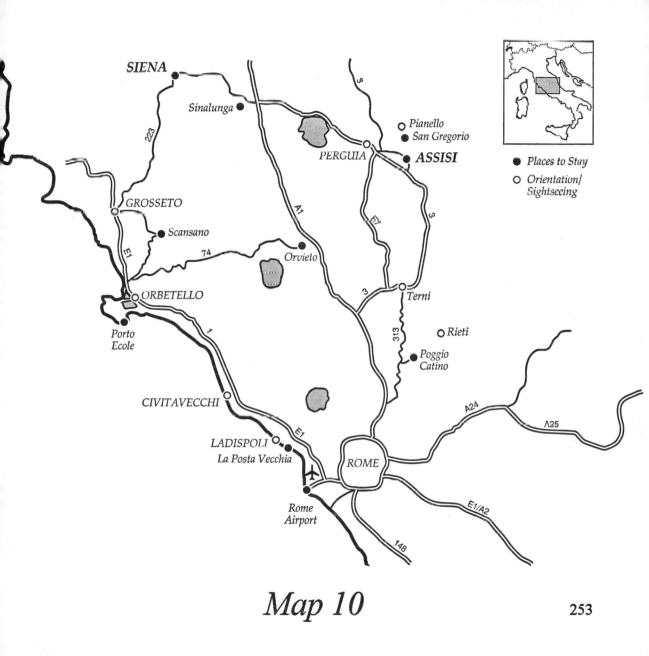

Map 10

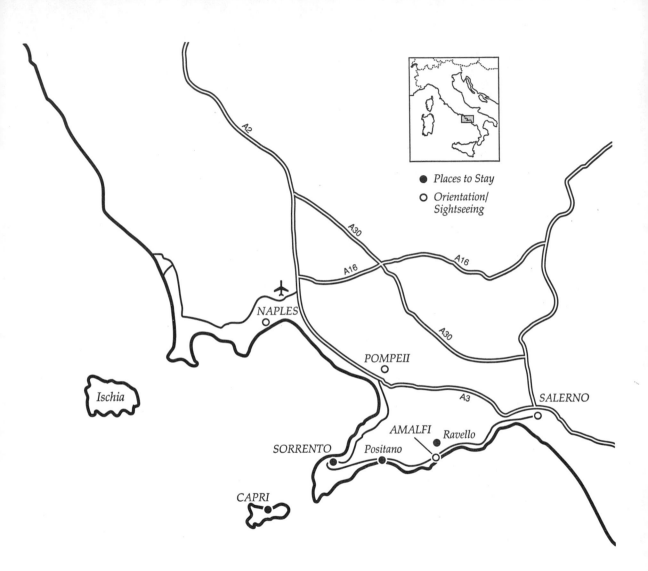

Map 11

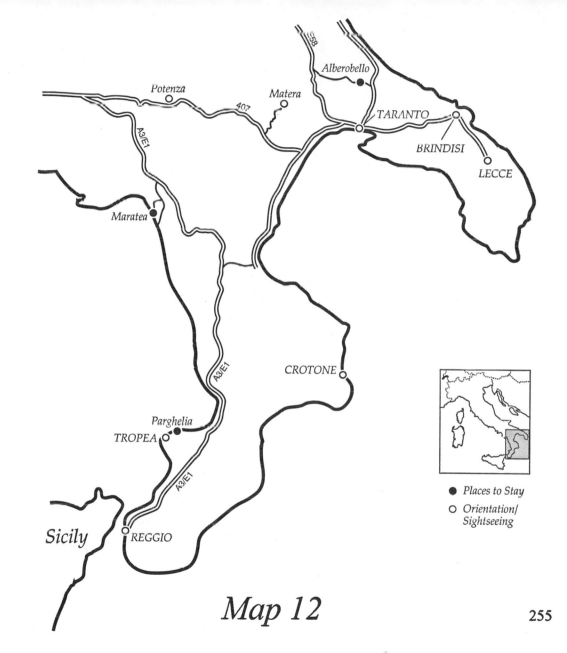

Potenza

Matera

Alberobello

TARANTO

BRINDISI

LECCE

A3/E1

407

S58

Maratea

CROTONE

Parghelia

TROPEA

A3/E1

A3/E1

Sicily

REGGIO

● *Places to Stay*

○ *Orientation/*
   Sightseeing

Map 12

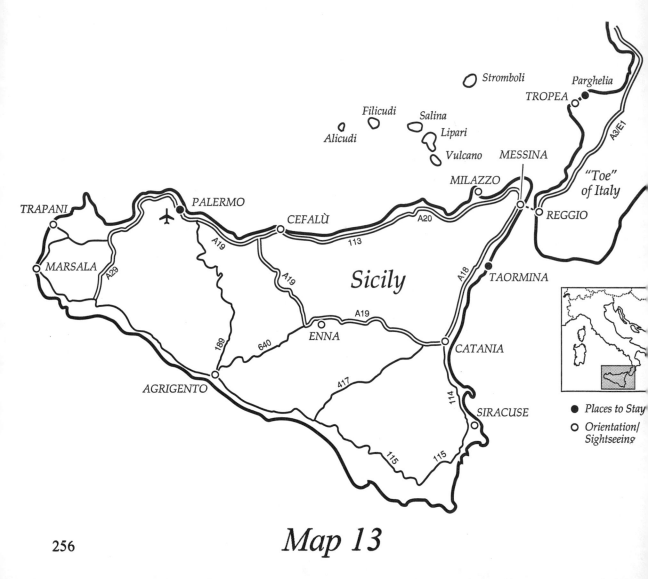

Stromboli

Parghelia

TROPEA

Filicudi

Salina

Alicudi

Lipari

Vulcano

MESSINA

A3/E1

"Toe"
of Italy

MILAZZO

TRAPANI

PALERMO

REGGIO

CEFALÙ

A20

113

MARSALA

A19

Sicily

A18

TAORMINA

A29

A19

ENNA

A19

189

640

417

CATANIA

AGRIGENTO

114

SIRACUSE

115

115

● Places to Stay

○ Orientation/
Sightseeing

Map 13

PORTO
CERVO

OLBIA

SASSARI

597

ALGHERO

131

131

NUORO

537

ORISTANO

SARDINIA

131

● Places to Stay
○ Orientation/
Sightseeing

CARBONIA

CAGLIAR

Map 14

Index

A

Abbazia, Romantik Hotel, Follina, 137
Abbey of Monte Cassino, 76
Abbey of Monte Oliveto Maggiore, 41
Accademia, Pensione, Venice, 222
Agli Alboretti Hotel, Venice, 223
Albergo al Vecchio Convento, Portico di Romagna, 169
Albergo Casa Albertina, Positano, 173
Albergo del Sole, Maleo, 146
Albergo del Sole, Rome, 186
Albergo Quattro Fontane, Venice, 231
Albergo Vecchio Molino, Campello sul Clitunno, 104
Alberobello, 81, 83
    Hotel dei Trulli, 92
Amalfi, 79
Amalfi Drive, 75, 77
Anna Maria, Villa, Champoluc, 117
Ansitz Heufler Hotel, Rasun di Sopra, 179
Antichita "Three Esse" Country House, Assisi, 96
Antico Casale di Scansano, Scansano, 203
Antico Pozzo, Hotel L', San Gimignano, 197
Anzio, 76
Apuan Alps, 67
Arezzo, 37
Argrigento, Sicily, 90

Armenzano
    Romantik Hotel "Le Silve di Armenzano", 93
Artimino
    Paggeria Medicea, 109
Asolo, 48, 94
    Hotel Duse, 95
    Hotel Villa Cipriani, 94
Assisi, 38
    Antichita "Three Esse" Country House, 96
    Hotel Subasio, 97
    Hotel Umbra, 98

B

Badia a Passignano
    La Scuderia, 163
Badia, La, Orvieto, 160
Baia d'Oro, Gargnano-Villa, 141
Baia Paraelios, Tropea-Parghelia, 84, 218
Barone, Villa Le, Panzano in Chianti, 162
Bassano del Grappa, 49
Bed & Breakfast of Tuscany, Montevettolini, 158
Bellagio, 58
    Grand Hotel Villa Serbelloni, 100
    Hotel Florence, 99
Bencista, Pensione, Fiesole-Florence, 135
Bergamo, 57

Berghotel Tirol, Sexten, 204
Blue Grotto, Capri, 34, 74
Boats, 16
Bologna
    Hotel Corona d'Oro, 101
Bolzano, 53
Borgo Paraelios, Hotel, Poggio Mirteto, 167
Borgo Pretale, Sovicille, 211
Borgo San Felice, Hotel Relais, San Felice, 195
Brenner Pass, 53
Bressanone, 53
    Hotel Elefant, 53, 102
Brindisi, 75, 83
Browning, Robert, 48
Brunella, Villa, Capri, 108
Burano, 27

C

Ca'Peo, Chiavari a Leivi, 69, 120
Camogli
    Hotel Cenobio dei Dogi, 103
Candeli-Hotel Villa La Massa, 134
Capri, 31, 33
    Grand Hotel Quisisana, 106
    Hotel Flora, 105
    Hotel Luna, 107
    Villa Brunella, 108
Capricorno, Il, Sauze d'Oulx, 202
Carrara, 67

Carriage, Hotel, Rome, 187
Carrobbio, Hotel, Milan, 152
Carthusian Monastery, 70
Caruso Belvedere, Hotel, Ravello, 180
Casa Frollo, Venice, 229
Cassino, 76
Castel Freiberg, Merano, 54
Castel Labers, Hotel, Merano, 149
Castel Pergine, Pergine, 164
Castel San Gregorio, San Gregorio, 199
Castelfranco Emilia
    Villa Gaidello Club, 110
Castellana Caves, 82
Castellina in Chianti
    Hotel Il Colombaio, 112
    Pensione Salivolpi, 113
    Tenuta di Ricavo, 114
Castello di Gargonza, Monte San Savino, 156
Castello di Polgeto, Umbertide, 219
Castello di Pomerio, Hotel, Erba, 123
Castelrotto
    Hotel Cavallino, 111
Castelvetrano, Sicily, 89
Catania, Sicily, 88
Cavallino d'Oro, Hotel, Castelrotto, 111
Cavasagra
    Villa della Regina Cavasagra, 115
Cefalu, Sicily, 90

Cenobio dei Dogi, Hotel, Camogli, 103
Cernobbio
    Villa d'Este, 116
Certosa di Maggiano, Siena, 205
Certosa di Pavia, 70
Champoluc, 61
    Villa Anna Maria, 117
Chiavari, 68
Chiavari a Leivi, 69
    Ca'Peo, 120
Cimbrone, Villa, Ravello, 183
Cinque Terre, 67
Cioccaro di Penango
    Locanda del Sant'Uffizio, 118, 119
Cisterna, La, San Gimignano, 198
Claretta, 57
Clothing, 17
Colombaio, Hotel Il, Castellina in Chianti, 112
Colonnata, 67
Colosseum, Rome, 65
Corona d'Oro, Hotel, Bologna, 101
Cortina, 50
Cortina d'Ampezzo, 51
    Hotel Menardi, 121
Cortine Palace Hotel, Villa, Sirmione, 208
Cortona, 37
Corvara
    La Perla, 122

Courmayeur, 62
Credit Cards, 7
Current (Electrical power), 3

D

D'Annunzio, 56
David, Michelangelo's, 29
Dei Trulli, Hotel, Alberobello, 82, 92
Della Robbia, 43
Desenzano, 22
Dolomites, 50
Driver's License, 3
Driving, 3

E

Eleanora Duse, 56
Electrical power, 3
Elefant, Hotel, Bressanone, 53, 102
Emerald Grotto, Amalfi Coast, 74, 79
Emperor Tiberius's Palace, 34
Enna, Sicily, 88
Erba
    Hotel Castello di Pomerio, 123
Erice, Sicily, 89
Eurailpass, 15
Excelsior Vittoria, Grand Hotel, Sorrento, 210

F

Fasano di Gardone Riviera
    Villa del Sogno, 138

Fax, 11
Ferries, 17
Fiesole-Florence
    Pensione Bencista, 135
    Villa San Michele, 136
Finale Ligure
    Hotel Punta Est, 124
Fiordaliso, Villa, Gardone Riviera, 139
Flora, Hotel, Capri, 105
Flora, Hotel, Venice, 224
Florence, 27, 37
    Grand Hotel Villa Cora, 125
    Hotel Helvetia & Bristol, 126
    Hotel Monna Lisa, 130
    Hotel Regency, 131
    Hotel Tornabuoni, 132
    Loggiato dei Serviti,, 127
    Lungarno Hotel, 128
    Mario's, 129
    Torre di Bellosguardo, 133
Florence Hotel, Bellagio, 99
Florence-Candeli
    Villa La Massa, 134
Florence-Fiesole
    Pensione Bencista, 135
    Villa San Michele, 136
Follina
    Romantik Hotel Abbazia, 137

Food, 4
Freiberg, Hotel Castel, Merano, 148

G

Gabbia d'Oro Hotel, Milan, 24
Gardone Riviera
    Villa Fiordaliso, 139
Gargnano
    Hotel Villa Giulia, 140
Gargnano-Villa
    Baia d'Oro, 141
Gargonza, Castello di, Monte San Savino, 156
Gasoline, 3
Gasthof Obereggen, Obereggen, 220
Gattapone, Hotel, Spoleto, 212
Giulia, Hotel Villa, Gargnano, 140
Golf Hotel, Romantik, San Floriano del Collio, 196
Gondolas, 47, 48
Grand Canal, Venice, 27
Grand Hotel Excelsior Vittoria, Sorrento, 32, 210
Grand Hotel Plaza, Rome, 188
Grand Hotel Quisisana, Capri, 33, 106
Grand Hotel Villa Cora, Florence, 125
Grand Hotel Villa Serbelloni, Bellagio, 57, 100
Gregoriana, Hotel, Rome, 189
Gritti Palace, Milan, 26
Gritti Palace, Venice, 225

H

Hallwag maps, 13

Hassler, Hotel, Rome, 190

Helvetia & Bristol, Hotel, Florence, 126

Highlights of Southern Italy & Sicily, 74

Hotel Borgo Paraelios, Poggio Mirteto, 167

Hotel Carriage, Rome, 187

Hotel Carrobbio, Milan, 152

Hotel Caruso Belvedere, Ravello, 180

Hotel Castel Freiberg, Merano, 148

Hotel Castel Labers, Merano, 149

Hotel Castello di Pomerio, Erba, 123

Hotel Cavallino d'Oro, Castelrotto, 111

Hotel Cenobio dei Dogi, Camogli, 103

Hotel Cipriani, Venice-Giudecca, 230

Hotel Corona d'Oro, Bologna, 101

Hotel d'Inghilterra, Rome, 29, 191

Hotel dei Trulli, Alberobello, 82, 92

Hotel Elefant, Bressanone, 53, 102

Hotel Flora, Capri, 105

Hotel Flora, Venice, 224

Hotel Florence, Bellagio, 58, 99

Hotel Gabbia d'Oro, Milan, 24

Hotel Gattapone, Spoleto, 212

Hotel Gregoriana, Rome, 189

Hotel Hassler, Rome, 190

Hotel Helvetia & Bristol, Florence, 126

Hotel Il Colombaio, Castellina in Chianti, 112

Hotel L'Antico Pozzo, San Gimignano, 43, 197

Hotel la Fenice e des Artistes, Venice, 226

Hotel Le Palme, Limone sul Garda, 144

Hotel Lord Byron, Rome, 192

Hotel Luna, Capri, 107

Hotel Majestic Roma, Rome, 193

Hotel Menardi, Cortina d'Ampezzo, 121

Hotel Monna Lisa, Florence, 130

Hotel Palazzo Murat, Positano., 174

Hotel Palumbo, Ravello, 78, 182

Hotel Pierre Milan, Milan, 71, 153

Hotel Pitrizza, Porto Cervo, 170

Hotel Punta Est, Finale Ligure, 124

Hotel Regency, Florence, 131

Hotel Relais Borgo San Felice, San Felice, 195

Hotel Representatives, 11

Hotel Residence San Sano, San Sano, 200

Hotel Santavenere, Maratea, 147

Hotel Splendido, Portofino, 68, 172

Hotel Subasio, Assisi, 38, 97

Hotel Tornabuoni Beacci, Florence, 132

Hotel Umbra, Assisi, 98

Hotel Verbano, Isola dei Pescatori, 60, 165

Hotel Vigiljoch, Lana bei Merano, 150

Hotel Villa Cheta Elite, Maratea-Acquafredda, 237

Hotel Villa Cipriani, Asolo, 49, 94

Hotel Villa Franca, Positano, 177

Hotel Villa Giulia, Gargnano, 140

Hotel Villa La Massa, Florence-Candeli, 134
Hotel Villa La Principessa, Lucca, 145
Hotel Villa Margherita, Mira, 154
Hotel Villa Rigacci, Vaggio-Reggello, 185
Hotels
    Basis for Selection, 6
    Costs, 6
    Decor, 7
    How to Economize, 8
    How to Interpret the Rate, 8

I

Igiea Grand Hotel, Villa, Palermo, 88
Il Capricorno, Sauze d'Oulx, 202
Il Pellicano, Porto Ercole, 171
Il San Pietro di Positano, Positano, 175
Information-General, 12
Inghilterra, Hotel d', Rome, 191
Isola Bella, 60
Isola dei Pescatori, 60
    Hotel Verbano, 165
Isola Madre, 60
Italian Government Travel Offices, 12
Italian Highlights by Train & Boat, 20
Italian Rail Passes, 15
Itineraries
    Highlights of Southern Italy & Sicily, 74
    Italian Highlights by Train & Boat, 20
    Mountain & Lake Adventures, 46

Itineraries
    Romantic Hilltowns of Tuscany & Umbria, 36
    Rome to Milan via the Italian Riviera, 64

K

Kastelruth
    Hotel Cavallino, 111

L

L'Antico Pozzo, San Gimignano, 42
La Badia, Orvieto, 160
La Chiusa, Montefollonico, 157
La Cisterna, San Gimignano, 42, 198
La Mangiatoia, 42
La Perla, Corvara, 122
La Posta Vecchia, Ladispoli, 143
La Residenza, Rome, 194
La Residenza, Venice, 227
La Scala, Milan, 21
La Scuderia, Badia a Passignano, 163
La Spezia, 67
La Suvera, Pievescola di Casole d'Elsa, 166
Labers, Hotel Castel, Merano, 149
Ladispoli
    La Posta Vecchia, 143
Lake Como, 57
    Villa d'Este, 116
Lake Garda, 22, 24, 56
Lake Maggiore, 59

Lake Toblino, 55
Lake Trasimeno, 37
Lana bei Merano
    Hotel Vigiljoch, 150
Le Silve di Armenzano, Romantik Hotel, Armenzano, 93
Le Sirenuse Hotel, Positano, 176
Le Tre Vaselle, Torgiano, 39, 217
Leaning Tower of Pisa, 65
Leon d'Oro, Orta San Giulio, 159
Levanto, 67
Limone sul Garda
    Hotel Le Palme, 144
Locanda del Lupo, Soragna, 209
Locanda del Sant'Uffizio, Cioccaro di Penango, 119
Locanda dell'Amorosa, Sinalunga, 40, 207
Locanda San Vigilio, San Vigilio, 55, 201
Loggiato dei Serviti, Florence, 127
Lord Byron, 67
Lord Byron, Hotel, Rome, 192
Lucca, 66
    Hotel Villa La Principessa, 145
Luna, Hotel, Capri, 107
Lungarno Hotel, Florence, 28, 128

M

Majestic Roma, Hotel, Rome, 193
Maleo
    Albergo del Sole, 146
Manorola., 67

Map Section-Showing Hotel Locations, 243-257
Maps-What maps you need to buy, 13
Maratea
    Hotel Santavenere, 147
Maratea-Acquafredda
    Hotel Villa Cheta Elite, 237
Mario's, Hotel, Florence, 129
Marmorata Hotel, Ravello, 181
Marostica, 49
Marsala, Sicily, 89
Maser, 48
Matera, 81
Menardi Hotel, Cortina d'Ampezzo, 51
Merano, 54
    Hotel Castel Freiberg, 148
    Hotel Castel Labers, 149
Merano-Lana
    Hotel Vigiljoch, 150
Mercatello
    Villa di Monte Vibiano, 151
Messina, Sicily, 86, 87
Michelangelo, 67
Michelangelo's David, 29
Milan, 21
    Hotel Carrobbio, 152
    Hotel Pierre Milan, 71, 153
Mira
    Hotel Villa Margherita, 154

Mogliano Veneto
  Villa Condulmer, 155
Monna Lisa, Hotel, Florence, 130
Monreale, Sicily, 90
Monte Pellegrino, 90
Monte San Savino
  Castello di Gargonza, 156
Montefollonico
  La Chiusa, 157
Monteluco, 40
Montevettolini
  Bed & Breakfast of Tuscany, 158
Motoscafi, 47
Mountain & Lake Adventures, 46
Murano, 27
Mussolini, 57

N
Naples, 31, 77
National Archaeological Museum, Naples, 77
Nettuno, 76

O
Obereggen
  Gasthof Obereggen, 220
Old Dolomite Road, 51
Orta San Giulio
  Leon d'Oro, 159

Orvieto, 40
  La Badia, 160

P
Paestum, 80
Palazzo Murat, Hotel, Positano, 174
Palazzo Ravizza, Pensione, Siena, 206
Palermo, Sicily, 88
Palermo-Sicily
  Villa Igiea Grand Hotel, 161
Palio delle Contrade, Siena, 42
Palladio, 48
Palme, Hotel Le, Limone sul Garda, 144
Palumbo, Hotel, Ravello, 78, 182
Panzano in Chianti, 42
  Villa Le Barone, 44, 162
Paolo Veronese, 48
Parghelia, 84
Passignano, Badia a
  La Scuderia, 163
Pellicano, Il, Porto Ercole, 171
Pension Panorama, Tiers-St Zyprian, 215
Pensione Accademia, Venice, 222
Pensione Bencista, Fiesole-Florence, 135
Pensione Palazzo Ravizza, Siena, 206
Pensione Salivolpi, Castellina in Chianti, 113
Pensione Seguso, Venice, 228
Pensione Stefaner, Tiers-St Zyprian, 52

Pergine
  Castel Pergine, 164
Pescatori, Isola dei
  Hotel Verbano, 165
Petrol, 3
Piazza Armerina, Sicily, 88
Piazzale Roma, Venice, 47
Pienza, 41
Pierre Milan, Hotel, Milan, 71, 153
Pievescola di Casole d'Elsa
  La Suvera, 166
Pisa, 65
Pitrizza, Hotel, Porto Cervo, 170
Poggio Mirteto
  Hotel Borgo Paraelios, 167
Polgeto, Castello di, Umbertide, 219
Pompeii, 31, 74, 77
Ponte Vecchio, 28
Ponzano
  Relais El Toula, 168
Portico di Romagna
  Albergo al Vecchio Convento, 169
Porto Cervo-Sardinia
  Hotel Pitrizza, 170
Porto Ercole
  Il Pellicano, 171
Portofino, 68
  Hotel Splendido, 172

Portoverere, 67
Positano, 79
  Albergo Casa Albertina, 173
  Hotel Palazzo Murat, 174
  Hotel Villa Franca, 177
  Il San Pietro di Positano, 175
  Le Sirenuse Hotel, 176
Posta Vecchia, La, Ladispoli, 143
Potenza, 80
Prices of Hotels, 8
Princess Carlotta, 59
Principessa, Villa La, Lucca, 66
Punta Est, Hotel, Finale Ligure, 124

Q
Quisisana, Grand Hotel, Capri, 106

R
Radda in Chianti
  Relais Fattoria Vignale, 178
Rail Passes, 15
Rand McNally Maps, 13
Rasun di Sopra
  Ansitz Heufler Hotel, 179
Rates of Hotels, 8
Ravello, 78, 80
  Hotel Caruso Belvedere, 180
  Hotel Palumbo, 182
  Marmorata Hotel, 181

Ravello
    Villa Cimbrone, 183
    Villa Maria, 184
Regency, Hotel, Florence, 131
Relais El Toula, Ponzano, 168
Relais Fattoria Vignale, Radda in Chianti, 178
Reservations
    by Fax, 11
    by Hotel Representative, 11
    by letter, 10
    by Telephone, 10
    by Travel Agent, 10
Residenza, La, Rome, 194
Restaurants, 4
Riomaggiore, 67
Riva, 24
Road Signs, 4
Roads, 3
Robert Browning, 48
Roman Amphitheater, Verona, 24
Roman Forum, The, 65
Romantic Hilltowns of Tuscany & Umbria, 36
Romantik Golf Hotel, San Floriano del Collio, 196
Romantik Hotel "Le Silve di Armenzano", Armenzano, 93
Romantik Hotel Abbazia, Follina, 137
Rome, 29, 65, 75
    Albergo del Sole, 186
    Grand Hotel Plaza, 188

Rome, 29, 65, 75
    Hotel Carriage, 187
    Hotel d'Inghilterra, 191
    Hotel Gregoriana, 189
    Hotel Hassler, 190
    Hotel Lord Byron, 192
    Hotel Majestic Roma, 193
    La Residenza, 194
Rome to Milan via the Italian Riviera, 64

S

Salerno, 80
Salivolpi, Pensione, Castellina in Chianti, 113
San Bernardino tunnel, 62
San Domenico Palace, Taormina-Sicily, 87, 213
San Felice
    Hotel Relais Borgo San Felice, 195
San Floriano
    Gasthof Obereggen, 220
San Floriano del Collio
    Romantik Golf Hotel, 196
San Gimignano, 42
    Hotel L'Antico Pozzo, 197
    La Cisterna, 198
San Gregorio
    Castel San Gregorio, 199
San Margherita, 68
San Michele, Villa, Fiesole-Florence, 136
San Pietro di Positano, Il, Positano, 175

San Sano
    Hotel Residence San Sano, 200
San Terenzo, 67
San Vigilio, 55
    Locanda San Vigilio, 201
Santavenere, Hotel, Maratea, 147
Sardinia-Porto Cervo, Hotel Pitrizza, 170
Sauze d'Oulx
    Il Capricorno, 202
Scansano
    Antico Casale di Scansano, 203
Security while Travelling, 14
Selinunte, Sicily, 89
Sesto
    Berghotel Tirol, 204
Sestri Levante, 68
Sexten
    Berghotel Tirol, 204
Shopping, 14
Sicily, 86
Sicily-Palermo
    Villa Igiea Grand Hotel, 161
Sicily-Taormina
    San Domenico Palace, 213
    Villa Sant'Andrea, 214
Siena, 42
    Certosa di Maggiano, 205
    Pensione Palazzo Ravizza, 206

Simplon Tunnel, 61
Sinalunga, 41
    Locanda dell'Amorosa, 207
Sirenuse Hotel, Le, Positano, 176
Sirmione, 22, 56
    Villa Cortine Palace Hotel, 208
Sogno, Villa del, Fasano di Gardone Riviera, 138
Sole, Albergo del, Maleo, 146
Sole, Albergo del, Rome, 186
Soragna
    Locanda del Lupo, 209
Sorrento, 31, 32
    Grand Hotel Excelsior Vittoria, 210
Sovicille
    Borgo Pretale, 211
Spanish Steps, Rome, 65
Splendido, Hotel, Portofino, 68, 172
Spoleto, 39
    Hotel Gattapone, 212
St Francis, 38, 40
St Mark's Square, Venice, 26
St Patrick's Well, Orvieto, 41
St Zyprian-Tiers, 52
    Pensione Stefaner, 216
Stefaner, Pensione, Tiers-St Zyprian, 216
Stella d'Italia, Valsolda, 221
Stresa, 60
Subasio, Hotel, Assisi, 97

Syracuse, Sicily, 88

T

Taormina-Sicily, 87
    San Domenico Palace, 213
    Villa Sant'Andrea, 214
Taranto, 83
Telephones, 10
Tenuta di Ricavo, Castellina in Chianti, 114
The Pantheon, Rome, 65
Tiers-St Zyprian, 52
    Pension Panorama, 215
    Pensione Stefaner, 216
Tires, 52
Todi, 40
Toll Roads, 3
Torcello, 27
Torgiano, 39
    Le Tre Vaselle, 217
Tornabuoni Beacci, Hotel, Florence, 132
Torre di Bellosguardo, Florence, 133
Tourist Offices, 12
Tower of Apponale, 56
Trains, 15
Trapani, Sicily, 89
Treviso, 48
Tropea, 84
    Baia Paraelios, 218
Trulli Houses, 81

Tuscany, 29

U

Umbertide
    Castello di Polgeto, 219
Umbra, Hotel, Assisi, 98

V

Vaggio-Reggello
    Hotel Villa Rigacci, 185
Valley of the Temples, Sicily, 90
Vaporetti, 47
Vatican, Rome, 65
Vecchio Molino, Albergo, Campello sul Clintunno, 104
Venice, 25, 47
    Agli Alboretti Hotel, 223
    Gritti Palace, 26, 225
    Hotel Flora, 224
    Hotel Gritti Palace, 225
    Hotel la Fenice et des Artistes, 226
    La Residenza, 227
    Pensione Accademia, 222
    Pensione Seguso, 228
Venice-Giudecca
    Casa Frollo, 229
    Hotel Cipriani, 230
Venice-Lido
    Albergo Quattro Fontane, 231

Verbano, Hotel, Isola dei Pescatori, 60, 165
Verona, 24
Vesuvius, 31
Vigiljoch, Hotel, Lana bei Merano, 150
Villa Anna Maria, Champoluc, 61, 117
Villa Bararo, 48
Villa Brunella, Capri, 108
Villa Carlotta, 59
Villa Cheta Elite, Hotel, Maratea-Acquafredda, 237
Villa Cimbrone, Ravello, 183
Villa Cipriani, Hotel, Asolo, 94
Villa Condulmer, Mogliano Veneto, 155
Villa Cora, Grand Hotel, Florence, 125
Villa Corner della Regina, Cavasagra, 115
Villa Cortine Palace Hotel, Sirmione, 22, 208
Villa d'Este, Cernobbio, 116
Villa del Sogno, Fasano di Gardone, 138
Villa di Maser, 48
Villa di Monte Vibiano, Mercatello, 151
Villa Fiordaliso, Gardone Riviera, 56, 139
Villa Franca, Hotel, Positano, 177

Villa Gaidello Club, Castelfranco Emilia, 110
Villa Igiea Grand Hotel, Palermo, 88
Villa Igiea Grand Hotel, Palermo-Sicily, 161
Villa La Massa, Hotel, Florence-Candeli, 134
Villa La Principessa, Hotel, Lucca, 145
Villa La Principessa, Hotel, Lucca,, 66
Villa Le Barone, Panzano in Chianti, 44, 162
Villa Margherita, Hotel, Mira, 154
Villa Maria, Ravello, 184
Villa of Casale, Sicily, 88
Villa Rigacci, Hotel, Vaggio-Reggello, 185
Villa San Giovanni, Sicily, 86
Villa San Michele, Fiesole-Florence, 136
Villa Sant'Andrea, Taormina-Sicily, 214
Villa Serbelloni, Grand Hotel, Bellagio, 100

W
Weather, 17
What to Wear, 17
Wines, 5

Discoveries from Our Readers

If you have a favorite hideaway that you would be willing to share with other readers, we would love to hear from you. The type of accommodations we feature are those with old world ambiance, special charm, historical interest, attractive setting, and, above all, warmth of welcome. Please send the following information:

1. Your name, address and telephone number.
2. Name, address and telephone number of your discovery.
3. Rate for a double room including tax, service and breakfast
4. Brochure or picture (we cannot return material).
5. Permission to use an edited version of your description.
6. Would you want your name, city, and state included in the book?

Please send information to:

KAREN BROWN'S GUIDES
Post Office Box 70, San Mateo, CA 94401, U.S.A.
Telephone (415) 342-5591   Fax (415) 342-9153

Karen Brown's Guides

For Europe And California

The Most Reliable & Informative Series On Charming Places To Stay

U.S.A. Order Form

Please ask in your local bookstore for KAREN BROWN'S GUIDES. If the books you want are unavailable, you may order directly from the publisher.

California Country Inns & Itineraries $14.95

English Country Bed & Breakfasts $13.95

English, Welsh & Scottish Country Hotels & Itineraries $14.95

French Country Bed & Breakfasts $13.95

French Country Inns & Itineraries $14.95

German Country Inns & Itineraries $14.95

Irish Country Inns & Itineraries $14.95

Italian Country Bed & Breakfasts $13.95

Italian Country Inns & Itineraries $14.95

Portuguese Country Inns & Pousadas (1990 edition) $6.00

Spanish Country Inns & Paradors (1989 edition) $6.00

Swiss Country Inns & Itineraries $14.95

Name _____ Street _____

City _____ State ___ Zip _____ tel. _____

Credit Card (MasterCard or Visa) _____ Exp: _____

Add $3.50 for the first book and .50 cents for each additional book for postage & packing. California residents add 8.25% sales tax. Order form only for shipments within the U.S.A. Indicate number of copies of each title; send form with check or credit card information to:

KAREN BROWN'S GUIDES
Post Office Box 70, San Mateo, California, 94401, U.S.A.
Tel: (415) 342-9117   Fax: (415) 342-9153

KAREN BROWN wrote her first travel guide, French Country Inns & Chateaux, in 1979. This original guide is now in its 6th edition plus 13 books have been added to the series which has become known as the most personalized, reliable reference library for the discriminating traveller. Although Karen's staff has expanded, she is still involved in the publication of her guide books. Karen, her husband, Rick, their daughter, Alexandra, and son, Richard, live on the coast south of San Francisco at their own country inn, Seal Cove Inn, in Moss Beach, California.

CLARE BROWN, CTC, has many years of experience in the field of travel and has earned the designation of Certified Travel Consultant. Since 1969 she has specialized in planning itineraries to Europe using charming small hotels in the countryside for her clients. The focus of her job remains unchanged, but now her expertise is available to a larger audience—the readers of her daughter's Country Inn guides. Clare lives in the San Francisco Bay area with her husband, Bill.

BARBARA TAPP, the talented artist responsible for all of the hotel sketches and delightful illustrations in this guide, was raised in Australia where she studied in Sydney at the School of Interior Design. Although Barbara continues with freelance projects, she devotes much of her time to illustrating Karen's Country Inn guides. Barbara live s in the San Francisco Bay area with her husband, Richard, their two sons, Jonothan and Alexander, and young daughter, Georgia.

JANN POLLARD, the artist responsible for the beautiful painting on the cover of this guide and others in the Karen Brown series, has studied art since childhood, and is well-known for her outstanding impressionistic-style water colors which she has exhibited in numerous juried shows, winning many awards. Jann travels frequently to Europe (using Karen Brown's guides) where she loves to paint old world architecture. Jann lives in the San Francisco Bay area with her husband, Gene, and two daughters.

Karen Brown's
Italian Country Bed & Breakfasts

Bed & Breakfast Travel in Italy

The Latest and Delightfully Inexpensive Way
To Experience the Italian Countryside

Italian Country Bed & Breakfasts was written as a companion guide to Karen Brown's *Italian Country Inns & Itineraries*. Bed & Breakfast accommodation is a relatively new trend in Italy and this is the first guide ever written that has "hand-picked" the very best of the places to stay. All the pertinent information is given: description of the accommodation, sketch, price, driving directions, level of English spoken, what meals are served, name of the owner, telephone number, dates open, etc.

Italian Country Bed & Breakfast does not replace *Italian Country Inns & Itineraries*, but together they make the perfect pair for the traveller who wants to explore the countryside of Italy. Both feature places to stay with charm, warmth of welcome and old world ambiance: *Italian Country Inns & Itineraries* includes hotels and small inns, *Italian Country Bed & Breakfasts* has places to stay in private homes. The Bed & Breakfasts are located throughout Italy and offer an intriguing selection of accommodation from rustic Tuscan farmhouses and enchanting stone cottages to gracious country villas. This is an opportunity to meet Italians in their homes - almost like being a guest where you are welcomed like a friend of the family.

SEAL COVE INN - LOCATED IN THE SAN FRANCISCO AREA

Karen Brown Herbert (best known as author of the Karen Brown's Guides) and her husband, Rick, have put sixteen years of experience into reality and opened their own superb hideaway, Seal Cove Inn. Spectacularly set amongst wild flowers and bordered by towering cypress trees, Seal Cove Inn looks out to the ocean over acres of county park: an oasis where you can enjoy secluded beaches, explore tide-pools, watch frolicking seals, and follow the tree-lined path that traces the windswept ocean bluffs. Country antiques, original-watercolors, flower-laden cradles, rich fabrics, and the gentle ticking of grandfather clocks create the perfect ambiance for a foggy day in front of the crackling log fire. Each bedroom is its own haven with a cozy sitting area before a wood-burning fireplace and doors opening onto a private balcony or patio with views to the distant ocean. Moss Beach is a 35-minute drive south of San Francisco, 6 miles north of the picturesque town of Half Moon Bay, and a few minutes from Princeton harbor with its colorful fishing boats and restaurants. Seal Cove Inn makes a perfect base for whale-watching expeditions, salmon-fishing excursions, day trips to San Francisco, exploring the coast, or, best of all, just a romantic interlude by the sea, time to relax and be pampered. Karen and Rick look forward to the pleasure of welcoming you to their hide-away by the sea.

Seal Cove Inn, 221 Cypress Avenue, Moss Beach, California, 94038, U.S.A.
telephone: (415) 728-7325   fax: (415) 728-4116